The Mack Marsden Murder Mystery

Vigilantism or Justice?

by Joe Johnston

Missouri History Museum
St. Louis
Distributed by University of Missouri Press

To Jan Kizziar, teacher

Unless otherwise noted, the photos in this book are from a variety of public domain sources, such as the Jefferson County Missouri Historical Society, DeSoto Public Library, the author's private collection, and descendants of Mack Marsden and other figures in the book.

 15 14 13 12 11 • 1 2 3 4 5

Library of Congress Cataloging-in-Publication Data

Johnston, Joe, 1948-
The Mack Marsden murder mystery : vigilantism or justice? / Joe Johnston.
p. cm.
Includes bibliographical references and index.
Summary: "For over three years Mack Marsden was suspected of every major crime in Jefferson County, Missouri, but he was never convicted of any wrongdoing. All of the available resources, including oral histories, are mined for clues that explain who ambushed and killed Marsden"--Provided by publisher.
ISBN 978-1-883982-69-0 (pbk. : alk. paper)
1. Marsden, Mack, 1849-1883. 2. Criminals--Missouri--Jefferson County--Biography. 3. Murder--Missouri--Jefferson County--Case studies. 4. Jefferson County (Mo.)--History--19th century. I. Title.
HV6248.M256J64 2011
364.152'3092--dc23

2011018071

Cover art by Joe Johnston
Distributed by University of Missouri Press
Printed and bound in the United States by Sheridan Books

Table of Contents

Table of Contents

Table of Contents

About the Author

Joe Johnston is a writer, artist, and songwriter based in Nashville. He's a native of Missouri and a lifelong outdoorsman. Besides publishing How to Fail in the Music Business *and* Jesus Would Recycle, *he is the inventor of the now-famous McDonald's Happy Meal.*

Foreword

Heading north, Lemay Ferry Road crosses the River des Peres in south St. Louis and becomes Ivory Avenue … or perhaps Ivory becomes Lemay Ferry. In any case, it's the other direction and another river fording that gave the road its name. Heading south, Lemay Ferry Road crosses the Meramec River into Jefferson County and becomes Jeffco Boulevard, then gets lost amid a tangle of roads and highways until it becomes itself again beyond the town of Arnold. It seems to end for good outside the village of Goldman, once called Sandy, where it meets up with Old Missouri 21 and gently disappears.

Jefferson County surrounds St. Louis and is considered part of the greater St. Louis metropolitan area. The county is one of the fastest-growing regions in Missouri, perhaps in the Midwest.

If you went from metropolitan St. Louis down to the town of Sandy in the 1880s, you had a wagon journey of perhaps two days ahead of you on a rough and rutted road. Now you can get to Goldman in well under an hour. That's not the only thing that has changed in Jefferson County in 130 years. The county now has almost 220,000 residents, which is 200,000 more than it had in 1880. The county courthouse of 1863 still stands, but the 1990s addition on the south side more than doubled its size. Other historic structures remain, but modern housing and commercial buildings are all over the area.

Yet what is truly important, persistent, and inherently valuable has not changed. In Joe Johnston's story of his ancestors, we find friendship and family, beauty and tragedy, loyalty and remembrance. Here in Mack Marsden's lifetime are the kinds of feelings and virtues—and vices, too—that are all recognizable in twenty-first-century humans. Here is a memory told and retold and now finally shared beyond family and close friends.

The Mack Marsden Murder Mystery is a mystery story, but unlike Agatha Christie or Arthur Conan Doyle, Joe Johnston cannot tie up everything neatly and give us a definitive finale. That is because it is also a true story, or as true as the author can make it from his work and research. We cannot always have a neatly packaged ending; we can merely keep telling the story and pass along what we know as best we can. Here is a tale that all of us can contemplate and find familiar, making yet another bond with the past and another step toward understanding ourselves and one another.

—Robert R. Archibald, Ph.D.
President, Missouri History Museum

Introduction

Home sweet home, Jefferson County, a true slice of all-American pie. But it hasn't always been so sweet.

Like most of America, it came to be a warm, welcoming place by the faithful efforts of one generation, then another. Each making it a little safer. A little richer with life. Trying to change what needed changing, while praying for the wisdom to keep the good things.

In the 1880s, there were three train stations and many more "milk stops" in the county. Today there are none. Back then, the main thoroughfare through the county seat of Hillsboro was a winding, rutted, two-lane gravel road. Today this little corner of Missouri is the suburban home of more than 200,000 people, many of whom take the interstate on their daily commute north to work in St. Louis. Well into the 1930s, teachers arrived long before the students on winter mornings to start fires in potbellied stoves and warm their one-room schools, where they mentored all grades together. Now there are computers in every classroom and students swarm around the community college day and night.

Yet one thing that has hardly changed in 150 years is the courthouse, built in the 1860s with local stone and with bricks baked right there on the site. Rumpled lawyers still shuffle back and forth from cluttered offices, carrying on the grinding work of government. The jail is still "out back," with the sheriff standing guard over a county almost unique in America; while 80 percent of Americans live in urban areas, Jefferson County is 70 percent rural. Much has changed—and much remains—in this place where vigilante justice once held sway, but those days are gone forever, vanished in the dust of frontier Missouri.

Let's set the time of this mystery. Sitting Bull surrendered in 1881, the same year President James Garfield was shot. Edison's light bulbs were just coming on the market. Deodorant and zippers were yet to be invented. Men buttoned starched collars onto their shirts for Sunday dress-up. The great cattle drives were in full force from Texas to the Kansas railroads. And in St. Louis, the baseball team that was forerunner to the Cardinals was playing at the just-opened Sportsman's Park

Though our action takes place in the era that we associate with classic Western movies, the people in Mack Marsden's story didn't have the rough riding, gun slinging, big hat and high-heeled boots style that we see in films. These people liked to dress simply, they worked hard, and they gave a lot of thought to progress for their fledgling community. Theirs was the mindset that built America: peace, home, shared good fortune, invention, modernization, organization, and authority.

Some who went before us were community builders, while others let the community pay the price for their lawless selfishness. It's been that way since the beginning of time. And so the march of humanity is more of a dance, two steps forward and one step back, the contributors always hoping they can outdistance the detractors.

It wasn't easy, the dust settling, the foundation building, the home making. Though nineteenth-century metropolitan centers bustled with commerce, technology, and culture, from New York to St. Louis, to New Orleans and San Francisco, one step over the city limits could put a person in jeopardy. There were threats from wild animals and wild weather. There were bold outlaws and furtive bandits who needed only an opportunity, the slightest opening, to do their worst. And in the absence of modern crime-solving techniques, most crimes went unsolved, remaining unanswered to this day. America's frontier history is a collection of clues, waiting for us to explain the mysteries they hide. Mack Marsden's story is one of those mysteries.

Most Jefferson County families of the 1800s lived in isolated farmhouses, separated by hills, fields, woods, and creeks. They had to be on guard against the occasional petty thieves, grifters, and career criminals who passed through on their way to the big pickings of St. Louis or sought refuge from big city lawmen in the Jefferson County forests, hollows, and caves. There was William Larkin, who walked across his farm, emerged from the trees into a field, and was shot dead. No one was ever arrested for his murder. There was the case of young Julie LeBlanc, who left a party in the town of Kimmswick and never made it home. Her skeleton and that of her boyfriend were found in a boat that came ashore some time later. The law decided it was a case of double murder by a jealous drifter who was never identified. Then there was the unsolved axe murder of the Bonaker couple in their bed.

In frontier Missouri, just as in towns like Tombstone and Dodge City, liquor too often provided the spark for trouble. In 1874 Frank Spaulding got into a fight over a bottle of whiskey and stabbed a man who would have died, had not his breastbone stopped the knife from penetrating farther. The court dropped the charges because Spaulding was drunk at the time, which was considered a pretty good defense in those days. In fact, criminals usually got away with their business because lawmen had little evidence with which to work. If there were no witnesses, then nobody was convicted, and that was as true in Hillsboro and St. Louis as it was in Abilene and Tucson. When the West was wild, it was wild all the way back to the Mississippi.

This is a true story. Mack Marsden was born two years after fellow Missourian Jesse James and died less than a year later than Jesse, but that's not where the similarities end. The more we know of one, the better we understand the other. Both were husbands and fathers, accused of multiple crimes of which they may or may not have been guilty. Both men were as loved as they were feared. Both men were surrounded by relatives and people who claimed to be relatives, some who could be trusted, and some who could not. Missouri governor Thomas Crittenden played a role in the lives of Jesse and Mack, two lives that ended in violence.

In some respects, there was no other way out for Mack and Jesse. Technology, the march of civilization, and people's desire for order all demand that such men sooner or later get blasted out of the way. Crime will win its brief victories, but cannot long hold sway over the great heart of people yearning to live in the freedom of peaceful society. Helping. Encouraging. Raising families. Laughing. Achieving. And preserving pleasant memories. These are the things of life and love, and these will prevail.

The history of Mack and the others in these pages has survived in newspaper and court archives, as well as in family legend. When such a tale is passed down, told and retold, often with years between the retellings, it changes. Details are lost, confused, transposed, and sometimes even added. But there's a clarion ring of truth to a family legend well told. It makes some of us want to dig and get to the heart of it. If this happened, why did it happen? If these feelings persist through the generations, what started those feelings? If this is true, then what else is true? Even the untruths may be well intentioned, innocent twists on the story to explain or make a point. Once unwound, they may lead to the facts of the matter. Now, after years of research, this is one family legend that turned out to be true. In fact, the traditional family oral history of Mack Marsden turns out to be more accurate than the newspaper accounts of his own day.

Although I knew I was distantly related to Mack before starting this book, my research revealed that I'm related to many characters in this story several different ways. Mack's parents were my great, great, great aunt and uncle. His son, Sammy, married my dad's second cousin, Stella. His grandson Ware married my mother's sister. Judith Thomas Moss was my great, great, great aunt, which makes her entire line of Moss descendants my distant cousins. And there are more connections through the Hensley, King, and Williams families.

I grew up enchanted by Mack's pistol, which hung in a frame in my uncle's study. I was intrigued by his story, but couldn't understand how it could be true. We're just not that kind of family. The fruit of our tree isn't crime. It was honestly as if Mack himself kept pushing me, wouldn't let me rest, until I dug to the bottom of it and his story was told.

Our task is not to whitewash or candy-coat our ancestors. We're to keep their stories alive, honestly, so we'll know who we are, how we got here, and what direction we're headed. All those who came before us did the best they could with the lives they had. However they walked, they cut a path to where we could begin our journey. We owe them our deepest gratitude for giving us life. Just like them, each of us has the opportunity to make it better for those who follow after us. Our children's children's children are looking to us now.

A note on historical accuracy

In a very real and tangible way, this is the story of more than one crime or another. It's more than a mystery, and far more than a recitation of cold facts and statistics. This is flesh on the bones. Blood in the veins. The actions, thoughts, and words of real people.

This is a tale of people in a particular place at a particular time. Since the 1880s, the land has changed, but not much. The buildings have changed, but some remain. Throughout my life I've visited Jefferson County, and in researching this story I found that the place still tells us a lot about who lived there, and how and why they did what they did in Mack's time. The story is written in roads, houses, barns, woods, rocks, trails, fences, creek banks, and crumbling foundations. Hearing that part of the story requires hiking, comparing maps, listening to farmers, poring through dusty old books, holding antique skillets, using homemade tools, and lingering in cemeteries. The truest revelation of history is equal parts physical evidence, logic, emotion, and spirit.

Every effort has been made to locate and accurately assemble the widely scattered tidbits of information on Mack and the other characters in his life. Arrest records, journals, and logs kept by lawmen are gone. Some newspapers of the period exist, but not all. Court dockets can be seen, but the transcripts are gone. Other resources that contributed to solving Mack's mystery include family Bibles, census records, photo albums, and brittle notes from dusty attics.

Included here is almost every quote that has survived in letters, newspapers, court records, and oral history. To the extent that it was reasonable I resisted inventing new quotes for the main characters. However, it was neither possible nor desirable to completely avoid re-creating the conversations that moved the story along. Likewise, scene-setting details and character descriptions are a blend of historic record, photo evidence, family legend, and creativity.

If the events of this story were simply listed in chronological order, they'd seem unbelievable. The criminal minds were so twisted, their thinking so convoluted, their actions so complex, and their crimes so heinous, it just wouldn't make sense. I had to write their conversations so the reader could understand their thinking, and how one thing followed another. It all makes sense. It just takes a little explaining to make sense to normal, morally upright people.

The nickname "Allie" was adopted for Allen Hensley to prevent any confusion with Allen Marsden. Marsdens were fond of nicknames, and all of Mack's siblings were called by such names. So this literary device is perfectly in character. A lot of people in this story have very similar names. Therefore, I call people by their first name or last name, whichever makes it most clear whom we're talking about.

After years of research, I filled in the blanks of who, what, when, where, and why things happened. I didn't invent anything that would change the story. But from a basket full of colorful scraps I stitched together the quilt of these people.

The strongest contribution to our detective work may be the legends that have been passed down. Before the research, our legends made one kind of sense. After the research, they make another kind of sense. Maybe the best teller of the story was Mack's granddaughter, Lelia Marsden Jacobs. Her version, including her notes, once seemed almost incoherent. But now we know that's how incredible this story is. The way she told it is almost exactly the way it happened.

As to the guilt or innocence of the people who lived this tale, I didn't know myself until the very end. Not until the last piece was in place. Then the puzzle suddenly became a picture.

From this time on, armed with the facts, we'll tell the story anew.

—Joe Johnston, Jefferson County, Missouri, 2011

Who's Who

Matthew & Mary Marsden

George Marsden
m Eliza Peppers
m Louisa Owens
Bessie
John, m Millie
Allen
Samuel Marsden
Priscilla
Buzz
Mack
Sammy
Samuel J.
Clarence
Isabella
Richard C. Marsden
m Eliz. Shelton
Cornelius

Fleming Hensley

Leander Hensley
m Cynthia Ann Williams
Emma Jean
Allen (Allie)
Lydia
Wm. H. Hensley
m Pauline
Bertha
Alex. Benj. Hensley
Lillie

Benj. & Eliz.Thomas Johnston

Louisa
m Jms. Smirl
Eliza
Judge Gabriel
Mary
Jesse
Julia
Johnny
James Lester
Gabe
Lizzie

Billy & Judith Thomas Moss

Mark R.
m Jane Beale
"Devil" Mark
Claibourn T.
m Emily Meggits Cox
Tommy
Jimmy, m Jane
Thomas
James Thomas (J. T.)
Fannie, m R. G. Hoeken
Melissa, m Sam Byrnes
Richard
George W.
Bent
Clay J.
Mary Eliz., m Jms. A. Williams
Phillip
Frank
Virginia Lillie
Amanda Ellen
Lewis Adams (Doc)

Eliz. Gillman, sister of John Gillman, m Eliz. Rogers, sister of Delo Rogers

Jasper Hamrick
Stella

This "family tree" helps illustrate the relationships between some of the main characters in this book. It does not show complete families. Because most of the characters are men, this tree is organized by patriarchs. (If mother and father are in two different columns, the child is listed under the father.) The first generation is in bold italics; the next generation is in bold. Siblings are not necessarily in order.

——— = *Marriage*

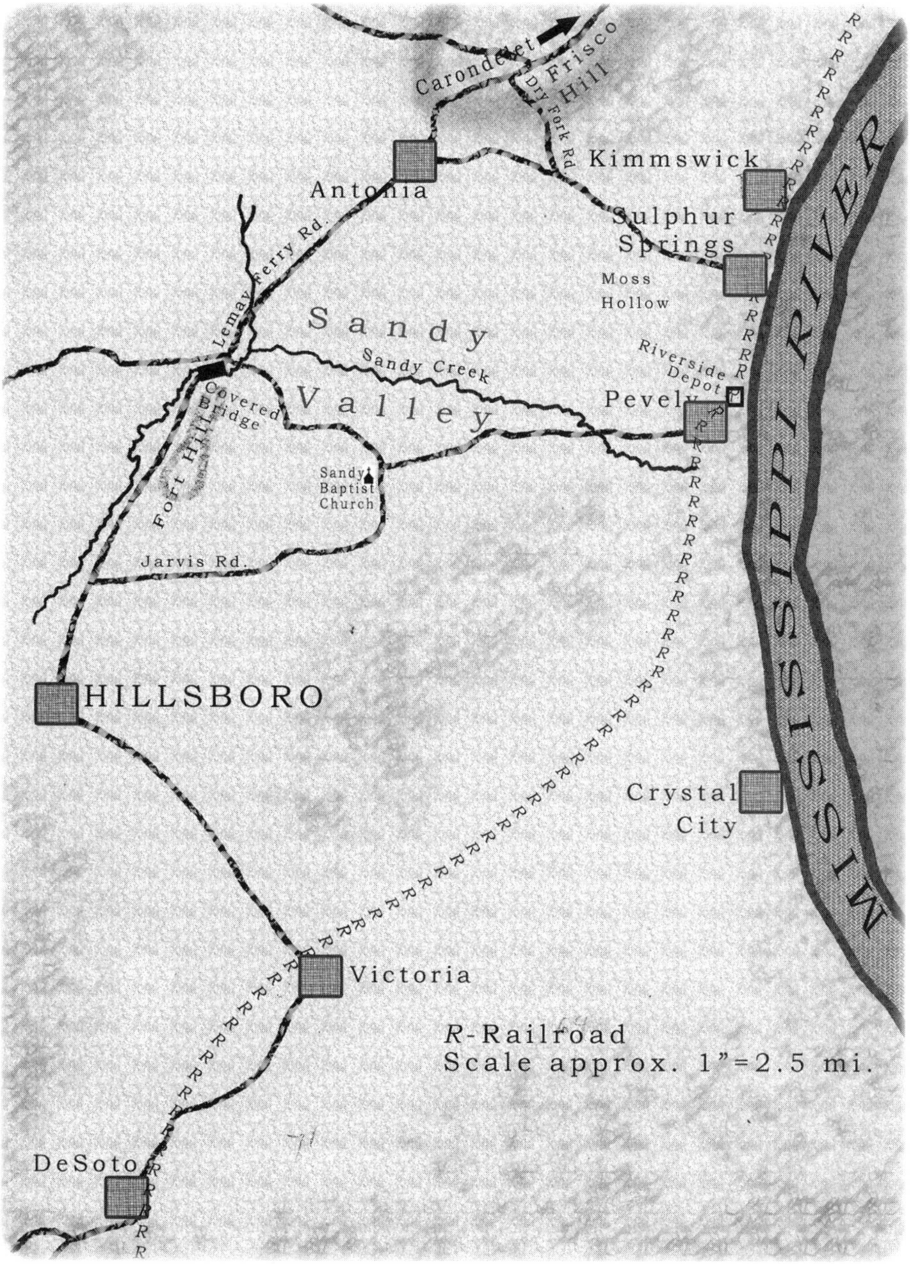

Partial map of Jefferson County, where the Marsdens settled.

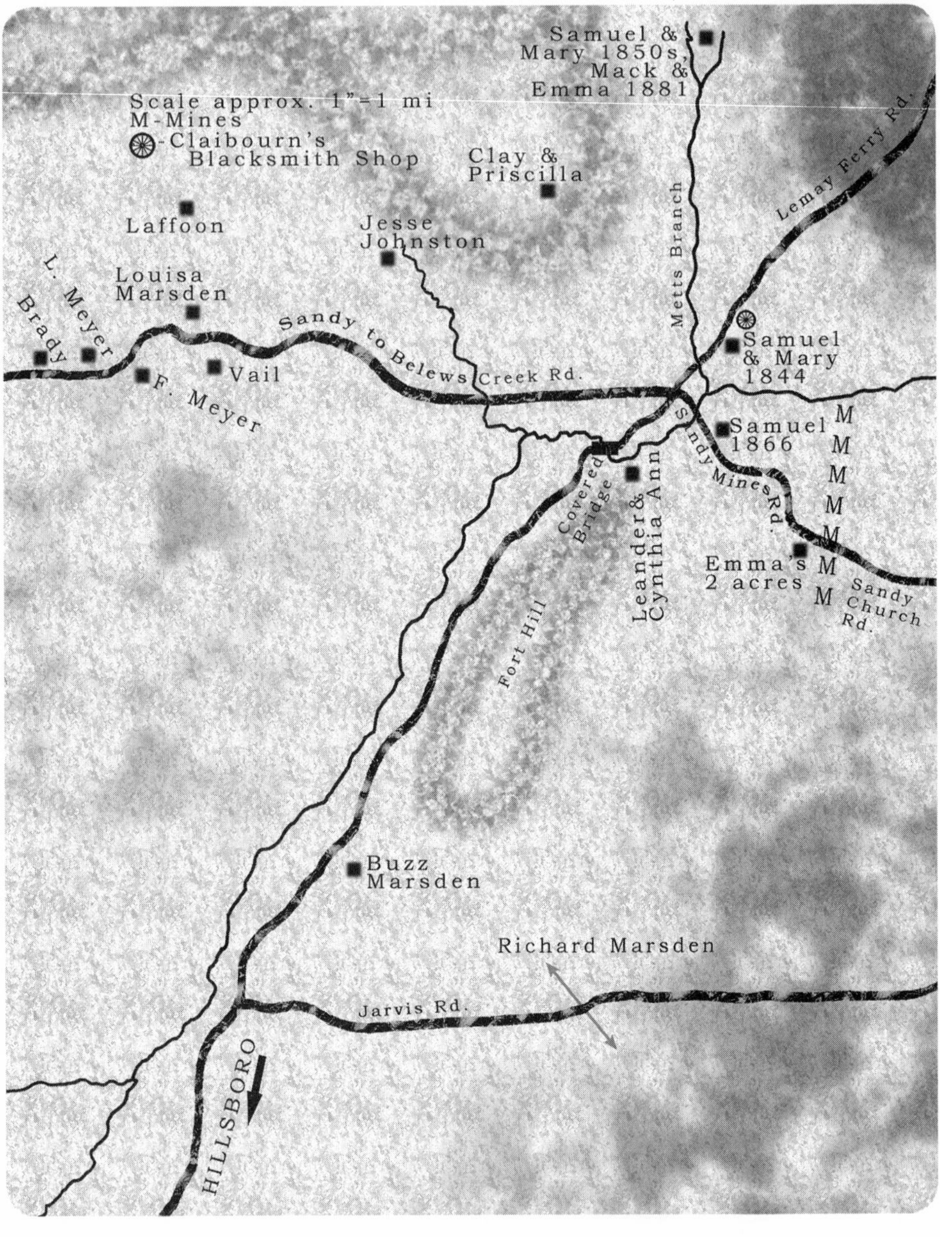

Map of the Sandy Valley, showing spots important to Mack Marsden.

Chapter One

Death in the Dust

It was almost noon and the August sun was stifling. Leaves hung limp, birds sought relief in the shade, and the only sound was the buzzing cicadas. A lightweight green wagon carrying two passengers came rolling easily along the gravel road that clung to the brow of Frisco Hill. As the wheels droned their song against the stones, the black horse's head bobbed wearily up and down.

Suddenly the animal braced. There was movement in the bushes, a rush of figures stepping into the wagon's path, and the driver's startled, "For God's sake, don't shoot, boys!" The words were scarcely out of his mouth before a shotgun's "blam!" shattered the stillness, rolling and rebounding down the slope, and fading into the wooded hollow below. The force of the blast at such close range blew Mack Marsden off the wagon and into the gravel road. With the second shot, Big Allie Hensley flopped backward, his limp body dangling awkwardly over the seat back. The horse reared and jerked its head with the first shot, and at the second one bolted ahead, brushing the assailants aside and cantering down the hill with its wounded passenger bouncing like a bloody rag doll. The men leaped off the edge of the road and into the brush, stumbled in the thickets, then regained their footing, scrambled down the incline, and emerged through a little hollow to the Sandy Valley. There they slowed to a brisk walk, but still kept to the forest shadows. They spoke not a word, nor did their eyes meet.

The assassins waited around this curve on the brow of Frisco Hill.

The violent scene on Frisco Hill was over, and the heavy air pressed in just like before. The only change was that now a thirty-five-year-old man lay motionless with his pistol still in his pocket, at least five buckshot in his head, thirty more in his body, and his blood disappearing into the parched Missouri dust.

William C. Fine, carrying the Hillsboro mail in a heavy satchel slung behind his saddle, had left south St. Louis only a few minutes after Marsden and Hensley. Though he wasn't far behind them, they were beyond the curve of the hill. With the squeak of his saddle and clatter of his horse's hooves on gravel, he didn't hear the shots. Besides, he was thinking about the heat, wiping the sweat from his forehead with his kerchief, fanning himself with his hat, and worrying about the blister his new shoes made on his heel. Every time he relaxed he had to shoo another black fly. Or green fly. Or horsefly. Or those awful gnats. The horse knew the way, and Fine's reins hung lazily across the gray's neck. He was guessing he had a little over two miles to go before he could stop and rest in the shade beside the town pump in the village of Antonia. That's when he saw the body near the edge of the road.

Thinking it might be some pitiful drunk sleeping off his indiscretions, Fine intended to ride on past. After all, he had a mail schedule to keep. But his horse knew better, snorted, ducked his head, and sidestepped, refusing to pass. Looking closer, Fine saw blood on the man's white shirt collar and dismounted immediately.

Gingerly, he rolled the poor soul over, revealing a face so horribly ravaged by a hail of lead that it rendered the poor victim almost unrecognizable. Almost. Fine knew who it was, and he couldn't stop a shiver from running down his back. But he gathered himself, quickly stood and grabbed at the saddle, which made the horse circle away from him, and the harder he pulled on the reins, the farther the tail swung away from him. At last he stopped, sighed, and the old gray let him climb aboard in his usual awkward manner. He had to admit he was no good at emergencies, but if he'd just stay calm he'd be okay. He looked around, deciding where to go, then kicked up his mount as fast as the docile mail horse would go, three hundred yards to the closest house, the home of farmer Lena Meng, who opened the door to Fine's excited knocking. Fine blurted out what he'd seen, and as the two men ran back to the road, Meng exclaimed that yes, he'd been eating dinner and heard two shots. Arriving at Marsden's side they shook their heads, wondering what had happened and what they should do, but agreed they needed to fetch the sheriff. Fine left Meng to guard the body and rode at a trot into Antonia for the law.

Meanwhile, local farmer Thomas Beckleg, who lived up Rock Creek, was heading into town to pick up supplies. He'd been driving his wagon well ahead of Marsden and Hensley without knowing he passed right by the spot where murderers lay in wait behind the big fallen tree. Entering the streets of Antonia, Beckleg was met by men walking toward him, then realized they were looking and pointing over his shoulder. He pulled up and looked back to see Marsden's lathered horse approach with its bouncing wagon and bloody passenger. Others on the street hurried to bring the runaway rig under control, and were shocked to see the shot-riddled Hensley, his battered head hanging over the hindgate.

Everybody talked at once. There was a crowd around the wagon carrying Hensley, and smaller groups on each corner, with a lot of pointing and giving of orders. "I must have passed right by them," Beckleg said. "They could have shot me!" The mood was serious, but noisy, with the clamor of excitement that can't be denied when people know they're part of something they'll never forget, something that will be forever woven into their community's fabric.

Just then mailman Fine rode into the crowded street and everyone looked to see what he was so excited about. "Mack Marsden's been shot!" he hollered. "His face is a mess and he is lying dead in the road two miles back."

"Mack Marsden," someone echoed, and that started the chatter anew. Yet the general reaction was not one of horror. No, it was altogether logical that Mack would come to a bad end.

A lot of people in the crowd knew Matthew Harrison Marsden and called him by his nickname Mack, and some had been friends with various members of his sprawling family for a long time. But some people preferred passing to the other side of the street when they saw him coming. Many believed his end meant the end of a three-year string of unsolved crimes, including arson, robbery, and murder, that had kept the whole northern part of Jefferson County on edge. Mack had been constantly under suspicion, and was repeatedly arrested and questioned by Sheriff John Weaver. Allie, his brother-in-law and constant companion, was guilty by association, even though he never got the kind of attention that would cause *The St. Louis Post-Dispatch* to brand Mack a "desperado."

Turning back to the more urgent matter of the wounded man in the wagon, many in the crowd knew Allen Hensley, who was called Big Allie, and whose kin were among the older families of the county. Now both Mack and Allie had met a violent fate, right here outside Antonia, and the citizens of the town found it impossible to look away. Yes, a bloody man hanging out of a wagon in the middle of the street was sickening, and these were decent people who would have preferred to have their criminals neatly processed through the courts. Still, they all knew it would be talked about for years to come, and each one wanted his own personal piece of the story to tell.

Before long, Antonia's mayor, George Edinger, came hurrying down the street buttoning his gray coat, and immediately contributed a sense of order. Someone ran to get the constable, and the mayor started organizing a street corner inquest. Beckleg, with a wagon full of men who insisted on seeing the corpse, headed back up Frisco Hill to see if it really was Mack, and to bring the body into town. A young man rode out southward to tell the Marsden and Hensley families. Another young man with a good horse mounted and cantered out the same way on a ten-mile ride to the county seat of Hillsboro, to tell Sheriff Weaver what had happened.

Later, when that sweat-soaked messenger cantered into Hillsboro, he didn't bother to tie his exhausted horse, but jumped to the street, bounded up the stairs to the sheriff's office, flung open the door and blurted out his news: Mack Marsden was shot dead up the other side of Antonia, and another man was badly shot too.

When Sheriff John Weaver stood up from his desk, the boy tried to read the slender face, which was dominated by a prodigious mustache. He searched the sheriff's deep, green, intelligent eyes, but they showed no emotion, and the man spoke not a word.

Weaver looked like a man capable of handling anything that might come along, and yet seemed unsure how to feel about this turn of events. In a way, he was relieved beyond measure. In another way that was really beyond his understanding at that moment, it was the end of his purpose. The crimes associated with Marsden had consumed him for three years. He scarcely knew who he was without the Marsden case.

Sheriff John Weaver, shown in retirement.

Weaver was in his mid-forties, strong and fit, with uncommonly broad shoulders. Before he became sheriff he rarely wore a necktie, but now he always wore one in the office, and kept his vest buttoned. Funny, he thought, when he took the job he only had clothes fit for a farmer, and now, he hardly had any farming clothes left. On the street he generally wore a business coat, even on hot summer days like this. It was just good to keep that look of authority, he thought, and the county fathers appreciated it. Besides, it concealed the pistol buttoned into a holster on his right hip. He didn't like to wave that around, but he did like his badge to be seen on his vest. He wore a big star and made sure his coat hung open, just to be sure nobody missed it.

Weaver sighed and tried to take in the impact of the moment, tried to decide how to feel, and wondered who did the shooting. His thoughts now started racing, but he couldn't take any time to sort it all out. He'd have to do that as he rode. Whatever happened on Frisco Hill, he had a feeling it wasn't quite over.

He methodically laid down his ink pen, put on his coat, grabbed his hat and a carbine, and left the office. As quickly as possible he gathered a couple of deputies to ride with him, knowing that even at a quick pace it would take them an hour to get to Antonia.

While the August sun blazed hotter with every minute, they rode without stopping, crossed the covered bridge, then pressed on north-eastward as the road rose gently but steadily. Nearing Antonia they rounded a curve when suddenly someone yelled out and they all had to pull their mounts up short to keep from plowing headlong into an oncoming mule team. Weaver and his men found themselves face to face with a wagonload of bearded, ill-tempered Marsden men headed south. Behind them Weaver saw Clay Moss and Gabe Johnston in Mack's green wagon, bearing the horribly wounded Allie.

Weaver had to admit to himself that he wasn't really surprised to see that the Marsdens had beaten him to the crime scene and taken charge of the victims without waiting for him. They blamed the law not only for hounding Mack, but also for failing to send someone else to jail for the crimes ascribed to Mack. In their eyes, Weaver should have protected Mack from the very attackers who had now taken his life. That was the thing about Mack. It had never been proven how guilty or innocent he was.

Now the lawmen and the dead man's family glared in silence as lathered horses heaved and harness leather creaked in the searing heat. Gabriel "Buzz" Marsden, Mack's big brother, was the first to speak. He impatiently explained to the sheriff that they were taking Big Allie home to die, and then had the unpleasant task of delivering Mack to their poor father, Samuel. If Weaver would get out of the way, they could get about their business.

Weaver was unsettled by the resolute Marsdens, and found himself at a loss as to how to take charge. Someone needed to show him the crime scene. He needed to interview the people who found the victims. He had to find out if there were any witnesses, or if Allie had named the killers. But now that Mack's body was moved, there was no good place to begin an investigation. He was as frustrated as the men in the wagons, and yet he also wanted to be sympathetic with the grieving family's mission. He rode over to the second wagon and looked down at Hensley, who was struggling to breathe. The standoff ended with Weaver agreeing to turn around, go with the Marsdens, and get Allie to a bed. After all, right now Weaver needed to stay with Allie and hope he stayed alive long enough to talk.

Allie was fading fast. The shotgun pellets made tiny wounds, but inside he was bleeding terribly, and every rock in the road sent him into painful, moaning fits. Not only had he bounced around over the seat and into the bed of the driverless wagon during the two miles from the crime scene to Antonia, but this continued trip had been even more arduous. The road took them along Dry Creek, then up over progressively higher ridges. Then it was a mile up to the big bald, and a mile and a half down, five miles in all. They almost had him home, but they'd kill him if they didn't get him out of that wagon. Someone said they didn't think his parents would want him, so they didn't know where they should take him. With no other obvious choice, they pulled in at the nearest house, surprising the farm family of John and Elizabeth Gillman. The men carried Big Allie inside as gently as possible, while Elizabeth ran to pull the quilt off the bed before they laid his bloody frame atop her crisp cotton sheets. The other wagon with its sad cargo continued down the gravel road toward Mack's father's home, less than a half mile away.

Horses and wagons in the yard told Buzz that family members had gathered to console Mack's wife and father and await their return. Buzz was almost as sad as he was angry, carrying his little brother's body into the house. Women sobbed. Voices were hushed. Somehow it hadn't seemed real until they saw the murdered Mack stretched out on the kitchen table. Then there was no way to measure the grief and frustration. They'd been robbed of a husband, father, brother, and son. So many had tried to protect him, to help him, and yet the end came when he and Allie were alone, beyond the reach of any help.

Back at the Gillman house, the men who stayed with Weaver now watched from the doorway as the sheriff bent low to look for signs of consciousness. He could hear the blood gurgling in Hensley's lungs with each breath. There was little hope, but nonetheless, a rider was sent to fetch Dr. Hull from Sulphur Springs, nine miles to the east on the Mississippi. He was the closest doctor, and since he had a partner in his practice, one of them was likely to be able to come quickly. Weaver pulled a straight-back kitchen chair into the bedroom and sat by Hensley in case he recovered enough to talk. As the others settled on the porch to wait uneasily and conjecture about the case, Elizabeth kindly brought some civility back to their day by pouring steaming coffee into white porcelain cups.

The sun was low in the sky when the doctor arrived in his buggy, came into the darkening bedroom, and bent over Allie to examine him in the light of oil lamps held close to the bed. He assessed the wounds, stopped as much bleeding as he could, but didn't bother to try removing all of the lead. That could wait. That is, if Allie lived long enough. After all, by the doctor's count he was hit with more than two dozen buckshot from the neck down. He told Weaver if he was going to get any information out of him, he better get it soon.

The men, who were now all surrounding the bed, continued to wonder in low voices whether Allie would survive. Would he be able to tell them what happened at the ambush? Who were the ambushers? Then slowly, Allie opened his eyes and started to speak.

Chapter Two
A Good Place to Raise a Family

Mack Marsden was born in a sturdy log house in the Sandy Valley in 1849. By the end of his life in 1883, Jefferson County had enjoyed eight decades of settlement by a hardy mix of French, Germans, Scots, Irish, Catholics, Lutherans, Episcopalians, Presbyterians, and Baptists.

The area was once Spanish territory, the Louisiana District, though there was virtually no Spanish presence, or any people besides Native Americans in that wilderness. On the south side of St. Louis the Meramec River was a natural and formidable boundary to travel. The Spanish governor wanted that problem solved, so in 1776 he called on the resourceful, red-headed French trapper and trader Jean Baptiste Gamache to cross the Meramec with a ferry, which was later operated by a François LeMay. To complete the plan, Gamache surveyed a road called "El Camino Royal" (The King's Trace) all the way south to the next major trading post, Ste. Genevieve. Suddenly the door to settlement was open.

People trailed in from both north and south along the Mississippi River, searching for a new home, and knew they'd found their promised land when they came to the rolling emerald hills where every ridgeline gave a view for miles and every hollow was a lush, cool sanctuary. Limestone outcroppings displayed layers of sandstone, flint, shale, hematite, and galena. The land was laced with fingers of crystal water making a winding descent to the east, where the land that would become Jefferson County was bounded by the Mississippi River for three dozen miles, alternately dotted with sand beaches and towering limestone bluffs.

The Osage, Shawnee, and other Native American tribes had been friendly enough with the early trappers and traders, but were only destined to be pushed aside. As more pioneers came, contact with the Indians increased, and so did skirmishes. It got worse, until a series of attacks drove the settlers back to St. Louis in the 1790s. But of course their incessant tide could not be resisted for long. At House's Springs (later called House Springs) in 1800 there was a massacre of settlers, followed by a massacre of Indians. And then, their time was over.

The government began welcoming settlers with land grants bearing the curious stipulation that they couldn't settle within fifteen miles of a town. The Spanish wanted them spread out, in an effort to cover as much area as possible with the few brave people willing to live that far from civilization.

Those early pioneers wore buckskin clothing because there was no place to buy cloth, and besides, they needed their land to raise food, not cotton. Their shoes were homemade moccasins with hard soles. They ate cornbread because corn was so versatile, and no one could spare enough land to grow wheat. Among the game they hunted were elk, bear, and buffalo. There were no eating fish in the streams, so fishing meant a trip west to Big River or northeast to the Meramec. Most families kept a milk cow, and as for other comforts of civilization, they simply made what they needed, or did without.

They were so remote, it took four months for the news of President Thomas Jefferson's election to reach them. But the Louisiana Purchase was soon completed, and they found themselves once again residents of the United States. Jefferson County was established in 1818, Missouri became a state in 1821, and while the political wheels were turning, the people kept coming.

Among the first white settlers, before 1800, were Captain William Moss and his brother-in-law Benjamin Johnston, both of whose fami-

Captain Billy Moss was among the first settlers before 1800. Courtesy of Nancy Moss Hollingsworth.

lies would figure prominently in Mack Marsden's life. Moss swam the Mississippi with his horse several times to court his future bride. Finally he took a canoe, married her, and brought her back to share his life in the wilderness.

Several Hensleys, including Fleming and his wife, Jane, came west from Virginia around 1830. He was a surveyor who took land for his pay, and so ended up owning a few hundred acres of Sandy Valley. Fleming and Jane instilled such a love for the county in their children that all seven of them stayed in the Sandy Valley as they grew up and married. Their son Leander married Cynthia Ann Williams, whose second child, Emma Jean, would one day catch the eye of neighbor boy Mack Marsden. He would become her second husband.

By the romantic's standard, the land was a fascinating tapestry of textures. By the farmer's standard it was hilly and rocky. So eighty years after the Indians, twenty years after the Civil War, when Mack had grown to manhood, wheat and beef cattle still remained in limited supply. Sheep did well in small numbers, and there were a few dairy farms. But generally, the farmers of Sandy Valley continued to favor hogs as their primary livestock, and corn as their biggest crop.

The ground was increasingly dotted with planted rows, houses, wells, irrigation ditches, footbridges, sheds, barns, and trails. Yet as much as the people shaped the land, the land shaped the people. It welcomed them to its bosom, then told them emphatically where they could build, where they could travel, and where they could farm. Their homes were scattered on the sides of hills in every hollow, reserving the best soil and the flattest land for crops. In those early years the biggest fields were no more than five acres, and most farming was done in little squares that could be cultivated between the rocks and gullies.

People got from one place to another by following the earliest inhabitants, the animals. Deer scouted the path and cut the brush, then everything else took that way, along the creek banks and around hills, finding the most level path through woods. Those game trails became Indian trails, which became settler trails, then roads that would accommodate a wagon.

Every home had a vegetable garden with tomatoes, squash, beans, potatoes, sweet potatoes, turnips, greens, and melons, and the women knew how to choose mushrooms from the damp woods. Their sweeteners were maple syrup and honey. Apple and pear trees did well, and blackberries abounded like God's own bounty every July. Autumn brought grapes, walnuts, chestnuts, and bright orange persimmons so sweet they were like candy on the tree. Milk and butter were cooled in the creek, or in a spring by those families fortunate enough to have one. Produce kept well in root cellars. While some were spacious, others were merely barrel-size pits lined with straw and covered with a board. For a child to finish chores in the spring and be allowed to get one of last fall's juicy, red apples from the cellar was a treat beyond measure.

After the Civil War, cotton, flax, and wool were providing yarn for weaving, and nearly every house had a spinning wheel, most of them homemade. Tables and chairs were made at home. The beds were high four-posters, and in those small houses, a child's bed was designed to slide under the parents'. Mattresses were stuffed with corn shucks, straw, and goose down, in whatever quantities were available, and laid on beds strung with ropes, rather than slats. When the ropes stretched, they were simply pulled taut, with the blessing, "Sleep tight."

Everyone had some sort of craft, which gave them things to sell or trade. Women canned food and made clothes, hats, baskets, and rugs. Men cured meat and made tool heads and handles, barrels, rope, chain, and cooking pots. Milk, eggs, and butter could be traded at the towns of Pevely or Kimmswick, which had small river ports, and later train stations. Almost everything not used at home was traded locally, because after all, shopping in St. Louis meant a thirty-mile trip, a long day's ride by wagon and not much faster for one person on horseback. Few families could afford hotel rooms and restaurant meals on such a trip, so for most people, Jefferson County's commerce was a home-grown affair. They not only traded together, but also knew one another, trusted one another, and over the years became kin to one another by marriage.

People walked everywhere. It was just their custom, and the life of the valley turned on a foot-paced schedule. If it took hours to walk somewhere, that's what it took. Every family had one or two mules, and some were considered quite beautiful, but they were chosen for work, not for riding comfort. Most of them were bigger, stronger animals, suited to plows and wagons, and of course every working farm had some sort of wagon. After the Civil War, big machines appeared on the more successful farms. Cultivators, combines, and manure spreaders amazed everyone, even their owners, with their noise, production, and complex efficiency.

Then the railroad was completed through Pevely to Victoria and points south, so forward-thinking farmers could get their livestock and produce to the St. Louis markets faster and easier. That called for more roads to connect more families to the trains. Still, shipping farm goods was expensive, and complex, so many farmers stuck to the tried and true methods of driving livestock and hauling produce in wagons. And agriculture continued to be a blend of old and new methods.

As transportation improved, so did county government and schools. Towns, complete with stores, banks, and barbershops, dotted the land, and a necklace of quaint cities lined the Mississippi River bank from Kimmswick down to Crystal City. Most children attended a few grades, learning the basics of reading, writing, and 'rithmetic, using spellers by McGuffy or Webster. School was in session from 8:00 a.m. until noon through the winter, roughly after the harvest until spring planting.

As rugged as the men of Sandy Valley were, by the time Mack was grown, they were living in a time and place that was trying to prove it had evolved beyond carrying firearms. Guns were illegal in town, and pistols were never seen on a man's hip anywhere. These were men who favored a long gun. Most of them didn't have a lot of money to spend on a collection of guns, so a man first had to have one that could bring home wild game. A rifle for deer, boar, and the rare elk or bear. A shotgun for turkey, goose, rabbit, possum, coon, and squirrel. And those guns were their families' best protection from snakes, mountain lions, wolves, and chicken-stealing varmints. Guns were for the homeplace, and if a man was seen on the road carrying a long gun, it always drew attention.

In Mack's era the county seat of Hillsboro enjoyed stagecoach service to St. Louis and wooden plank sidewalks in the business district, and boasted that its Thomas Fletcher had grown up to be Missouri's first native-born governor. And yet, Jefferson County had a dual personality. While leading families strived to emulate the fine life of the city, with its paved streets, theatres, and ice-cold beer, they contended with isolation and a lack of jobs. For all its progress, it was a country cousin to the bustling commerce of the St. Louis riverfront, home to frustrated subsistence farmers and rowdy lead miners, and still characterized by a certain sharp-edged frontier mentality.

Old and new, progressive and traditional, all things considered, Jefferson County was a good place to raise a family.

Chapter Three

Dreams

Marsdens operated tin and lead mines in England for generations. Then a few of them, including Mack's grandparents Matthew and Mary, brought their families to America and created a mining empire around Galena, Illinois. After Matthew and Mary's children were grown, rich lead deposits were discovered in Missouri in the 1820s. So the couple again packed up their English accents and big dreams and moved west, planning to build another Marsden mining operation. Three sons came with them: George, Samuel, and Richard.

Arriving about 1840, they came through St. Louis, crossing the Meramec River on the Lemay Ferry and continuing south on the winding and rutted Old State Road. Halfway from St. Louis to the county seat of Hillsboro, they passed through Bulltown, a community where cattlemen bringing herds to the riverfront would stop to water their livestock in Glaize Creek. They continued over one ridge and another, past Hillsboro, past the town of DeSoto, and all the way to Franklin County. There they settled and started working in the mines. But Matthew's sons couldn't forget one place they passed through.

Halfway between Bulltown and Hillsboro was the community called Sandy Mines, or simply Sandy, where travelers on the rutted road had to ford the deep and fickle Sandy Creek. Sometimes when it was high and fast, people had to wait for it to calm again. Sometimes when it was low and inviting, people would stop to drink and cool off

A pioneer home on the Old State Road.

in the shade of the willows. Friends, seeing friends, would unhitch their horses and take the opportunity to visit. There were almost always people at the ford.

Coming from the south, the road eased around Fort Hill, then dropped toward the stream. Coming from the north, the road descended from Bulltown, then was flat for about half a mile before it eased into the ford. That pretty little piece of bottom land was destined to become a hub for life in the valley. And best of all for the brothers, just a mile to the south were lead mines. Mines that they thought had promise.

So about a year later, Samuel and Richard went back to Sandy. They introduced themselves to Thomas Moss, son of the pioneer Captain Billy Moss, and he helped them settle on some nice farmland right along the Old State Road, just a half mile north of the ford. Between them and the ford was the farm of the stoic Leander and Cynthia Ann Hensley. In hardly any time at all, marriages would make the Marsdens, Mosses, and Hensleys kin in too many ways to count.

Most of the lead from Sandy Valley was smelted and moved by wagon the few miles over to Herculaneum, on the Mississippi. There Moses Austin, whose son Stephen F. Austin would become the father of Texas, built a shot tower in 1798. He had been successful in that business in Virginia, but was held back by a trickling supply of lead. Frustrated and broke, he simply packed up a wagon train, headed west, and started over on the banks of the Mississippi, trusting that the lead deposits of the Sandy Valley would be more sufficient than the ones he left behind.

His tower, and a second one built later, was at the top of a 100-foot-high overhanging bluff. At the top, molten lead was dropped through a sieve-like device, and as each drop fell, surface tension formed it into not teardrops, but perfect spheres. At the bottom, the spheres landed in a cushioning and cooling vat of water. By varying the size of the sieve, the men could make everything from the smallest shotgun pellets to .50 caliber rifle balls. It was a business crucial to a young nation, and supplied shot to her armed forces during the war of 1812.

The first of two shot towers built on the banks of the Mississippi in Herculaneum.

Unfortunately, Austin's business grew beyond his dreams, and he couldn't find enough employees. Acting on an impulse, he populated his lead factory with slaves, and in no time at all found that it cost him more to house and feed the slaves than it did to pay salaried employees. After two years in Jefferson County he was bankrupt, and moved on to what was then Mexico. In a twist of international irony, the towers continued to produce lead shot for American wars, including the one in which the States took Texas away from Mexico, resulting in the Austin name being forever enshrined in the capital city of the new state.

The ore of Sandy wasn't in the hills, but in the relatively flat valley floor. So mining was not the great mechanized operation that's often pictured, with shoring timbers, rails, scores of miners, mules pulling ore-laden carts, and yawning tunnels laying open the hearts of mountains. No, the Sandy mines were little more than holes in the ground. There was one major vein. It extended for nearly a mile beneath the farms, but it was narrow. So a south entrance was opened, measuring about 100 feet long and 50 feet wide, and a north exit, only about 5 by 7 feet. Then a line of shafts were sunk about eighty feet down, where the men would find pockets of lead at various depths. In those slender confines, the digging was the work of only a few men at any time. They descended on ropes and ladders, and the ore was lifted out in hoists, then dumped into barrels and casks for hauling.

Pit mining was also used to get at small deposits nearer the surface. The men would dig where they suspected ore, and if they found it, place a dynamite charge. The explosion would remove the soil and overlaying rock so the miners could dig the ore with picks and shovels. When it ran out, they'd simply move on to the next spot, leaving the land pockmarked with dozens of craters, each within its circle of debris.

Like most mines, the Sandy mines were plagued with flooding from the start, especially during spring rains. For many years the miners just hauled the water out in buckets, or if it was too bad, waited until the water went down. Then they re-entered the damp, cold shafts.

Top: The north mine exit measured only about five feet by seven feet. Right: View from inside the mine. Photos by John W. Linhorst. Used with permission.

It was all such tedious business, continually searching for tiny deposits along a stingy central vein, it didn't provide much of a living for many men. Very few were full-time miners, but rather most were farmers who picked up work in the mines during the cold months. Or craftsmen who earned extra money with short stints at mining, then went back to their primary job. It was a spotty business that attracted solid citizens in equal numbers with scalawags. A stream of men drifted in from St. Louis and the river, willing to work hard for a few dollars, but men who kept one eye out for easy pickings couldn't help but bring trouble with them. Constables and doctors made frequent trips to the mines to clean up after thefts, sickness, fistfights, and stabbings.

The Marsden brothers leased little plots of land and worked diligently mining them. But they were never mining their own land. The army and big mining companies headquartered in faraway cities controlled the Sandy Mines. No significant veins beyond the original one were ever found, and the lead deposits of Sandy Valley never turned out to be nearly as rich as everyone had hoped.

So Samuel and Richard found themselves employed not as mine owners as they had once envisioned, but as mining engineers and part-time hardscrabble farmers. Both were handy as smelters, melting the lead in charcoal fires, chemically removing the impurities, and forming the lead into manageable ingots. In an unusual complement to those skills, Samuel also worked as a cooper, building the hardwood casks used to haul the ore and ingots. Like almost everyone else, Samuel and Richard both worked hard from sunup to sundown.

But dreams have a peculiar way of redirecting the lives of dreamers. And while the Marsden brothers' hopes in mining met with only modest success, they led to unexpectedly rich rewards of romance and family. Samuel found Mary Johnston, and Richard married Elizabeth Shelton, both from solid, early Sandy Valley pioneer families. There in the Marsdens' little corner of the world, where the rutted Old State Road crossed Sandy Creek, they knew they were in the right place at the right time.

Chapter Four

The Road, the Bridge, and the Man

Samuel and Mary built a twelve-by-twenty-four-foot log home, with a second story over part of it, on the east side of the Old State Road. Their first baby was born in 1844. Then, in the 1850s, the federal government released vast amounts of public land to the states for sale. People with a little cash could buy farms cheap, and that's exactly what Samuel and Mary did. They moved to a beautiful spot at the head of a little creek called Metts Branch, originally settled by Henry Metts in 1804. It was just over the hill from Mary's father, Judge Gabriel Johnston. From that time on, the long lane leading in to their house became known as Marsden Lane.

The spot looked south onto one of the longest hollows and biggest cornfields in Sandy Valley. To the west was a gentle rise to a bald of several acres. To the east, the climb started toward Antonia. Behind the house was a nice orchard and a one-acre garden. Though they were embraced by trees and rising land on three sides, from their front porch they had an uncommon view south, all the way across the old, rutted road to their first house and the farms beyond. They could see almost all the way to the mines.

Mary gave birth to a daughter, Mary, then sons Gabriel—the one called Buzz—and Matthew, or Mack. Buzz was three years older, but the boys grew up as close as brothers ever did. Then there were four more girls and two little boys. All the children benefited from the blend of ambitious, hard-working parents and the wonders of life in the

Samuel and Mary's second home stood among the trees in the background and looked out on one of the longest, flattest cornfields in the county.

country. School was just enough to do the job, and not too much to keep them from chores and playtime. Their chores were often as much fun as work. In the fall they picked apples and nuts and helped tap the maple trees for sap that the men boiled down into syrup. In spring they beat winter's dust out of the rugs and took care of baby chicks and pigs. They could hardly wait for Friday night socials, when work stopped, families gathered at one of the bigger houses, and there were more cousins, food, jokes, and music than a kid could take in. When the music ended, sleepy heads couldn't help but fall asleep in the wagon bed before it was even out on the road home.

Young imaginations turned rocks into castles and sticks into horses. They made carved wooden guns and twisted up cornhusk dolls. They played along the creek, in the hills, and in the sandy bluff caves. There was one special place, a stump near some big rocks, that must have been an Indian camp, because the children found arrowheads everywhere. Summer or winter, they were on the go. When the creek froze hard, they skated and didn't even need skates.

The children played in the natural sand bluff caves.

Then everything changed when Mary died in the cholera epidemic of 1866. Buzz, a typical oldest son and always the serious one, was grown up and had a good job carrying the mail from St. Louis. He also had a girlfriend, Maria Strickland, to occupy his time, and a few months later he married her. The widowed Samuel was so busy trying to make a living that it was hard to care for the little ones, so the girls spent much of their remaining childhood with relatives. He sold off some of his land, including the original place with its log house, which went back to Thomas Moss. He kept the big field up Marsden Lane with its house, but left that empty, and moved with the two younger boys, Samuel J. and Clarence, to a smaller house on the other side of the Old State Road.

That's how, at the age of seventeen, Mack found himself a lonely middle child, old enough to work, but young enough to miss his mother's arms. He just didn't belong in the smaller house with those little children. He was different, and he felt different, and maybe that's why it's said that he suffered the most of all of the children from Mary's passing. Lacking his father's talent for engineering, he was convinced that he didn't want to work in the mines, but hadn't any idea what he did want to do for a living. He felt like an orphan and looked like a man.

During that time, even more than before, Samuel clung to this friendship with his father-in-law, Judge Gabriel Johnston. Mary's family was different from the Marsdens, but the two were always very comfortable together. Her father had grown up in a home served by a slave, Isaac, who handled chores like walking four miles to Rankin's store on the river. The shopping list varied, but almost always included "a jug of your good red wine and a quart of Tennessee whiskey." Though they weren't wealthy, they were lawyers, judges, big-scale farmers, and members of the Masons. They tended to be educated, outgoing, and, most important for Samuel, involved in politics. It was partly through those relationships that the county discovered what an engineering treasure they had in Samuel.

When he and Richard arrived in Sandy, the county seat had just been moved from Herculaneum, on the river, to Hillsboro. It was one of those towns that had no reason for being there. Oh, it had a nice spring, but no river, no intersection of major roads, no railroad or industry. So it took a while for people to start looking, thinking, and traveling inland. After a while they began to see how important the Old State Road could be to life in the county.

Around 1870 they commissioned Samuel to survey that rutted road and turn it into a wide, smooth, thoroughfare, the Lemay Ferry Road, paved with gravel all the way from St. Louis to Hillsboro. It was a life-changing, history-shaping event for the area.

Of course when that bumpy, wandering road was modernized, traffic picked up. Where it crossed Sandy Creek, the water could be twenty or thirty feet wide, depending on the season, sometimes running six feet deep, and prone to flooding. With so much traffic on the road, and with the creek often too deep to ford, a bridge simply had to be built. It was the kind of progress for which Jefferson County yearned, so the

Sandy came to be known as the site of a beautiful covered bridge.

money was quickly appropriated. The masterpiece was constructed in 1872, with Samuel as the commissioner. It was his crowning work. And that's how Sandy came to be known far and wide as the site of a beautiful, red, barn-like covered bridge spanning seventy-five feet.

For the folks around Sandy, progress called for more progress. Thomas Moss was among those who thought the place needed its own post office. It was silly that the mail carrier passed right by them on his way to Hillsboro, and the people had to go down there to pick up their mail. Most postmasters of that time were storekeepers as well, so if Sandy could get one, the other would probably be in the bargain. Moss had bought Samuel's original home, and now, with the bridge in place, that was the perfect spot for what Moss had in mind.

Back up the road, Bulltown had undergone a miraculous transformation. When the nation's cattlemen turned their attention west, to better grazing and Kansas railheads, the town focused on the vision of German immigrant Anton Yerger. He saw that the little village on Glaize

Creek would make a perfect stopping place for weary travelers between St. Louis and Hillsboro, and a trading place for all of the settlers to the south. So he gave it his wife's name, Antonia, and attracted other Germans who adorned the area with busy dairy farms, cooling their milk, butter, and cheese in the big spring at Pevely. There, they accumulated big shipments that awaited the next boat or train to St. Louis.

Anton's brother Joseph became Antonia's most successful merchant, so Thomas Moss turned to him with his idea for Sandy. He convinced Joseph to bring in a stock of goods for a store in the old Marsden log house and send a man to run it. In no time at all it was a post office too.

Then Moss's grandson Claibourn Thomas Moss and his friend Fritz Koch opened a blacksmith shop, specializing in wagon building and repair. They took over an empty log cabin next to the Sandy store, and added on a barn. That gave them plenty of room to work out of the weather. Yes, the little place beside the bridge was really beginning to grow.

Still, for Samuel, no engineering of roads or bridges could replace his love for the mine, the quest for lead, and the hope of a strike. He was a hillbilly philosopher who believed that hard work would be rewarded, that his family was good, and perhaps even that he was a hard-battling crusader in a tough and unforgiving world. Even while engineering roads and coaxing enough food from his little farm to feed his big family, he continued to work in the mines as long as he was able.

Brother Richard's imagination lay in another direction. Like Samuel, he engineered county projects to supplement his income. But he's the one who, in his early twenties, left Illinois to return to England on a horse-buying trip. He had a little money and dreamed of starting a famous horse ranch with hot-blooded English stock. On the ship sailing back to America, he even slept in the hold with his prized foundation stock.

Although that horse venture failed, Richard brought his love for the agricultural life to Missouri with him. He was willing to turn loose of mining and engineering in favor of seasonal, and no less difficult, results from farming. He proved to be very talented at it, and worked diligently to get better. And what made all the difference in Richard's life was marrying into the Shelton family. He acquired big parcels of land near the Sheltons, two miles south of the covered bridge along Jarvis Road. When he made money, he didn't sock it away in banks, but invested in more land. It was all in a broad expanse reaching south and east of Fort Hill, including several fields studded with woods, bordered by Lemay Ferry Road on the west, and good farm roads on the south and east.

Among the Marsden brothers, Samuel was the slender, talkative one who enjoyed technology, and Richard was the muscular one who chose his words more carefully and loved agriculture. They were educated and creative, unafraid to follow an idea to see where it would lead. The differences between them and their older brother George were apparent, even in the parcels of land they called home. George was the sullen one, and when the land patents became available, he settled for forty nondescript rocky acres about a mile west of the ford.

The failed expectations of a fortune in lead mining must have hit George the hardest. He was the most impatient, the most reckless, and a wanderer. He spent little time in Sandy, even going out to California to prospect for gold. He fathered at least eight children, but never provided a stable home to any of them, and died a relatively young man, estranged from his wife and children.

What makes someone disprove the scripture in Proverbs that says to train a child in the way he should go and when he is old he will not turn from it? How can the upbringing that instills values of hard work and faithfulness in one, fail to instill those traits in his brother? For some reason, George was different from the other Marsdens.

Mack Marsden was different too, but not in the same way as his Uncle George. What sort of impression did Mack make? He was uncommon, a man of few words, with a somber intensity that attracted some men and put others on guard. Mack's dark brown hair was combed back in a wave, and while many of the men sported bushy goatees that hung to their chest, Mack opted for a rakish, trimmed mustache. He was not characteristically Marsden. If the others were chiseled from granite, Mack was forged in the furnace. They were ruggedly handsome, with a square jaw, big head, and hooded, sincere, gray eyes. Mack's kind of handsome was lean, alert, and passionate, accented by his Roman nose and high, imposing cheekbones. But it was the eyes that transfixed everyone he met. Some saw a dangerously calculating glare in them. It's not uncommon for a serious, quiet person to be misunderstood in any number of ways. He might be thought shy, temperamental, belligerent, or scheming. And yet a more careful person would look into Mack's resolute countenance and see past the narrow brown windows of his eyes to the deep sadness there, a lost gaze that changed forever at the passing of his mother, just when he passed into manhood and needed her the most.

Mack was a bit above medium height and slender, which belied his great strength. Some men built muscle swinging axes and lifting hay, but Mack's frame was born of naturally good lineage. He was never afraid to bend his back to the hard and unending work of the farm. But for his life, he intended to be in business, making deals, making money, and wearing clean clothes. While others waited for a crop to come in, or sold their eggs and milk for pennies, Mack was determined to make his living on the quicker satisfaction of buying and selling at a nice profit.

In everything, from appearance to manner, he gave the impression of a man of money, even in times when he had none. He was no dandy, but he'd seen enough of men like his father wearing their years away like axe filings on the wheel, as the blade wore thinner and thinner. The farm, the mine, they were both a slow death to Mack, although he admired the men who were willing to slave at those jobs.

Some men in the valley wore shirts that were repaired using bits of fabric until they ended up pieced together like quilts. But not Mack. He wore nice shirts, and if he didn't have a clean one, he'd rinse one out.

Mack Marsden, ca. 1880.

He had one pair of muck boots, and one pair of ankle-high shoes that served for work, church, and social occasions. His pants were homemade but well fitted, held up by both a belt and suspenders. Completing his daily attire, he usually wore a dark coat and narrow-brim, flat-crowned hat. Other young men had one black necktie that saw daylight only on the way to church. When Mack wore a tie he preferred something with a little color and pattern to it. As he strove to establish himself as a businessman, it was important that when people met him, they remembered him. Indeed, he made sure they did.

When the Dakota gold rush hit in the mid-1870s Mack was among the Missourians who joined in, hoping to stake himself to a good business back home. Out West, his soul took flight. He loved the freedom and individualism. He enjoyed the camaraderie of other hard young men. Men who lived on the precipice of adventure. Unafraid to take a job or lose it. Always ready to try something new. Trusting in themselves. Mack's mental toughness and quiet manner, which were so different from most men back home, made him just one more personality in the stew of characters populating the gold camps.

But those camps also introduced him to a dark side of humankind that he'd never encountered in Sandy, and he didn't like it one bit. He was there for a couple of years before there was a dispute over the claim that he and some other men were working. Mack saw one of his partners shot dead, face down in a badlands creek, and that was enough for him. That night there was heated talk in their tent, but Marsden only listened. Though the others agreed to stick together and make a stand for the claim, he slipped out that night and headed home.

The experience hardened him. He didn't get rich, but neither did he return penniless, as so many seekers did. He came home satisfied, with $100, which bought his spring wagon and a black horse named Coal. He was a handsome black Fox Trotter with a little star and two opposite white socks, perfect for riding the hills, and just as valuable for a smooth trot before the wagon.

Mack also brought back a .44 Winchester rifle and a beautiful nickel-plated, pearl-handled pocket pistol. It was a genuine Smith & Wesson Model 1½, .32 caliber spur trigger single action, adorned with delicate New York–style engraving. In the hills of home, where utility was prized, such a decorated item was a true rarity. That pistol spoke volumes about the kind of man Mack was, a man who aspired to fine things, handsome things, things owned by business men.

That .32 was his personal favorite, small enough to tuck away, big enough to do the job. Out West he always carried it in the holster with the flap buttoned. That was the custom in Dakota, where a weapon on the belt served as fair warning to claim jumpers and other thugs. In Sandy, that kind of bravado wasn't necessary, but everybody knew he was never without it. The holster might be under his coat, or the .32 might be tucked into a pocket. After all, there was plenty of trouble about the neighborhood, and if trouble came, he'd rather be ready than find himself an unarmed victim. A year in the diggings of Dakota had that kind of effect on a man.

By the time he was almost thirty, he had left no mark on the world, and was on no course to make one. So as might be expected, when Emma Jean Hensley fell for Mack, the Hensleys preferred that she'd choose a different sort of man. They were a staunch people, puritanical, with a view of the world that was limited to family, farm, and church. In fact, in the eyes of Emma Jean's father, Leander, there was no distinction among the three. He worked the land his father left him, intended the same for his sons, and fully expected his daughters to settle down with the same sort of man.

Emma Jean and Mack grew up together in a hotbed of religion. Her parents were among the founders of Sandy Baptist Church, which had just moved from its original log building into a beautiful new all-brick structure. It was exciting, watching the clay being dug from the hillside across the road and the bricks fired right there on the site, the church

Top: A rifle like Mack's, a Winchester 1873 in .44-40 caliber. Courtesy of joesalter.com. Right: Mack's engraved, nickel-plated Smith & Wesson pistol. Courtesy of Terri Rae Round.

rising to overlook the valley. On top was a stout little cupola, rather than a steeple, because some of the old timers thought steeples were pretentious.

Through her mother, Cynthia Ann, Emma Jean was also kin to Elder James Williams, a well-known, church-planting, Missouri Baptist evangelist. Her uncles, Joel and William Hutson Hensley, were both preachers who spent some years traveling and evangelizing together. It was Joel who baptized her and countless others in the waters of Sandy Creek, while the gathered faithful sang "Shall We Gather at the River" and "Amazing Grace." The weather didn't matter. When somebody got saved, they got dunked, sometimes the same day, even if Pastor Joel had to break the ice to get them in.

When she was younger, Emma Jean had married Jeptha Kite, who divorced her, and she had her Hensley name restored. But that did little to salve the embarrassment her parents felt that their daughter had wandered so far from the fold. The Hensleys were a people who raised their children in the shadow of an angry, punishing God, and the Scriptures clearly prohibited a divorce like Emma Jean's. Since she had no place else to go, they took her back into their home, but from that time on, she was regarded more like a boarder than a daughter, and left to her own choices.

She not only dreaded the thought of becoming a spinster, as all women did, but also genuinely wanted to be married. The years showed in her eyes, and she lived under the glare of her judgmental parents. Still, while she worked around the home, she remained conscious of her womanhood and the toll the endless chores took on her face and body. In the garden she shaded her face from the drying rays of the sun with a bonnet and soothed her hands with bag balm, the same lotion they used on the cows' irritated udders. She and her sister Lydia would slip off to the barn every morning to pray and read their Bibles. As Emma Jean listened for divine answers, she heard a different message from the one her parents heard on Sunday mornings. Bathed in her

Top: Sandy Baptist Church. Right: Rev. Joel Hensley, who baptized Emma Jean, Mack, and countless others.

sister's kindness, she began to feel loved and encouraged, and in time, hope was reflected in her face again.

She had to admit that as a thirty-year-old divorcée, her prospects were none too good. And yet, she was a strong woman in excellent health. She knew how to make a home, and she knew how to smile when Mack came around. The returned gold miner found himself at loose ends too. And at that point in their lives they rediscovered each other. Their parents were practically next-door neighbors, so they'd grown up almost like brother and sister. For Mack and Emma, being together again when they were grown up, after being out in the world, was like coming home. It was familiar and good. When they married, they had the kind of romance that's solid, long-standing, and grounded in trusted friendship. Samuel Harrison Marsden, who would be called Sammy all his life, was born to them nine months later, in 1879.

Chapter Five

A Visit from John

One of Mack and Emma Jean's favorite jokes was that their marriage made them kin to everyone in the valley. So many Hensleys were married to Mosses, and Marsdens married to Johnstons. Then there were Kings and Thomases and two lines of Williamses who married into all those lines.

One man who said he was Mack's cousin was Allen Marsden. Allen and his little brother John were younger than Mack, and he had met them when they were kids, but never spent any time with them. They said they were the sons of Samuel and Richard's deceased brother George. Mack wasn't sure about the kinship, but nonetheless, he and Allen became friends after his return from Dakota Territory. Samuel Marsden didn't much like his son's association with Allen, but said little about it.

One day Allen saw Mack at the store and told him he was getting ready to make a fresh start for his family by renting a few acres outside Crystal City. A thriving town was growing up around the glass plant, and the talk was that a man could make money there. Before long, Allen talked Mack into making the move too, and taking one more try at farming. After all, Mack and Emma Jean had baby Sammy, Allen and his wife, Elizabeth, had two baby boys, and the women could help each other. So the two men went to Crystal, rented a couple of houses, and moved their new little families.

When Mack moved to Crystal, one of the people who missed him most was twenty-two-year-old second cousin Gabriel Jesse Johnston.

Gabriel (Gabe) Jesse Johnston, faithful defender, baseball teammate, and younger cousin who looked up to Mack.

He was a hot-blooded one, with flashing ebony eyes he inherited from his French mother. It hadn't been easy for Gabe, growing up as one of the oldest in a family of fourteen children. His parents just didn't have enough time to devote to any of them. Yet somehow it forged in Gabe an uncommon level of loyalty to his family and friends. It got him into trouble more than once, but also won him a reputation as a rock of devotion.

Once Gabe was out on his own, he liked being among his cousins, the Marsdens of Sandy, especially Mack, who was a few years older. So after Mack moved, Gabe was lost, agitated, and anxious. Fortunately, it was only a few weeks until he gained an even closer companion when he married Mack's sister Isabella.

Ten days after his wedding, on a cool, early May morning outside the Sandy Store and Post Office, Gabe sat on a bench whittling. Other men smoked their pipes and talked lazily, looking out on the broad fields, just greening with young corn shoots. A quarter mile to their left stood the covered bridge. From the south up Sandy Mines Road a horse approached, its hooves thumping, then crunching, as it stepped from the dirt road to the gravel road.

Even at a distance Gabe recognized the rider, Dorsey Hensley, also in his mid-twenties, as he approached the blacksmith shop. He was a distant cousin of Emma Jean, and in three weeks his sister Hattie was going to marry Gabe's cousin Eugene Johnston. Sandy was full of kinfolk, indeed.

But when Gabe saw Dorsey, that wasn't family love in his eyes. Some disagreement was lingering between them, and Gabe muttered, "He's been telling lies about me, and it's time I brought him down to size." It only took Gabe a few strides to cover the distance to the blacksmith shop and confront the other man when he dismounted. They exchanged a few hot words, then Dorsey suddenly slugged Gabe in the face, and they pitched at each other in a rolling, punching fight that kicked up a thick cloud of dust. Scuffles among rough young men were common enough, so the other men just watched like they would any sporting contest until someone shouted, "He's bleeding!" and someone else yelled, "Gabe's got a knife!" They jumped in and broke up the action, but Hensley lay motionless and groaning. He was loaded into a wagon and hurried off to a doctor with stab wounds, three in the neck, three in the chest, and one in the stomach.

A warrant for Gabe's arrest was issued, but he turned himself in before it could be served. After all, there was no point in hiding in Sandy.

Attorneys at that time often served as justice of the peace, wearing the title of "Esquire." One such man, 'Squire French, heard Gabriel's plea, and had no mercy for him. Using a knife against an unarmed man? French called for a $1,500 bond. Well, Gabe couldn't post that amount, nor could his parents, so he had to stay in jail for two weeks. But in the end, he got off with a fine of only $100.

Maybe the judge was lenient with him because the doctor was able to nurse Dorsey through his wounds. Maybe the fact that Dorsey threw the first punch had a bearing. Still, Dorsey would have been dead if Gabe had his way. That $100 fine was pretty good treatment for a man who was guilty of attempted murder.

The family told 'Squire French that Gabe would be okay if only he weren't around such ruffian friends. He'd been running with John Marsden, and he was a bad influence. So Gabe's parents suggested to the judge that if the charges disappeared, Gabriel would too. That was a common way to deal with troublemakers at the time: just get them to move on down the road. The judge agreed, so Gabe, his bride, his parents, and the other children who were still living at home, all packed up and moved to Texas County, where they had other kin.

It was a good time for Gabe to leave. When he returned a year later he was going to find things had changed in northern Jefferson County, especially in the vicinity of Mack.

Over in Crystal, the two young Marsden families were experiencing problems of their own. All four missed their families, both couples wished they had someone to help care for the babies, and as if that weren't trial enough, Mack and Allen weren't very good farmers. Allen was determined to stick with it, but Mack saw a different future for himself back in Sandy. What he didn't realize at the time was that the circle of friends he made in Crystal would follow him back, changing his life forever.

At that time, Allen's brother John was still living with their mother over in Sandy, but he was a frequent visitor at Allen's house. Whenever he came to Crystal, he made it a point to spend time with Mack, gabbing endlessly, while Mack tried to work. Obviously, Mack thought, John didn't have any idea what it took to keep a farm going. Also among their new friends in Crystal were Allen's neighbor John Gillman and his wife, Elizabeth. The meeting of all those men was like whiskey from a still, starting with a tiny drop, but pure poison.

One fall night, under a clear, star-filled sky, those four, Allen and John Marsden, Gillman, and Mack, sat on the fence passing a bottle of riverfront wine and discussing the eternal verities of Jefferson County. As they bemoaned the farmer's life, John started to talk about other ways to make money. Ways that were decidedly not legal, but decidedly more exciting and profitable than digging potatoes and slopping hogs. He talked about how easy it would be to take a calf or a pig from the valley and sell it up on the river. Those farmers, he said, if they say anything about it, you shake a fist in their face they'll back down. John had it all worked out, and claimed he'd already done it.

Allen and Gillman were going right along with him. "You've already done it?" they repeated. John smiled and told them Gabe Johnston helped him, unaware of the frown that crossed Mack's face at the mention of his old friend in such a tale. "You remember Dorsey Hensley? Gabe made the mistake of bragging to him about it. Then he told somebody else Gabe did the stealing, and that didn't worry me any, but Gabe jumped him with a knife."

"No," the men chorused.

"Sure as I'm sitting here," John affirmed. "Dern near killed him too. Stabbed him seven times!" John laughed, reaching for the bottle.

Mack was surprised at the turn the conversation had taken, and didn't like it at all. So, Mack mused, young Gabe had replaced his friendship with that of John, who dragged him into his escapades. But then again, Mack wasn't sure he believed it. John was a braggart. Looking down the fence he thought those fellows wouldn't do those things any more than he would. He smiled, reassuring himself it was only the idle talk of young men drinking wine, and he gave it no more serious thought. But Mack misjudged the men beside him, and in fact, it was truly dark and deadly seed John Marsden was sowing.

In the spring of '81, John Gillman moved to a little farm on Lemay Ferry Road right beside Marsden Lane. That's also when Mack gave up the idea of being a city farmer and returned to Sandy. With a little asking around, he found out John Marsden had been telling the truth about the stealing. Gabe returned from Texas County about the same time, and Mack set him straight. Though Mack was only a little older, Gabe listened to him, and that was the end of his friendship with John.

Mack and Emma moved back to Samuel's second house, the big one at the head of Metts Branch, which had stood empty since the widowed father moved down on the other side of Lemay Ferry Road. Back in the home where he grew up, Mack could walk out in the yard after supper and see familiar scenes through older eyes. While Emma Jean washed little Sammy in a washtub, Mack gazed south on the long cornfield, the gravel road beyond, and the world beyond that, hoping to gain a vision of his life.

A flock of over fifty turkeys stretched almost all the way across the field, heading for their roost, and he smiled to be in such serious thought, while the birds went about their business so carefree. Like it says in the book of Matthew, they don't plant or harvest, but God feeds them. It sounded good, and he wished God would give him a plan that would feed him and his family.

He'd always been outdoors, and still loved it. He liked using his head, figuring things out, with his singular mix of creativity and determination. He was more convinced than ever that he lacked the patience to watch a crop decide whether it would flourish or languish, and felt the same about waiting for calves and piglets to achieve market size. What he needed was a line of work that would let him work with the livestock, and use his deal-making imagination. He had to admit that he wasn't the kind of salesman who had a glad-handed smile and a joke for everyone he met. But what he lacked in friendliness, he made up for in the courage to look people in the eye. He could talk to anybody and offer them a price, whether it was what they wanted to hear or not. In the long run, that should be good for business.

It would help to have a little money to get started, and he wasn't afraid to borrow a few dollars to finance a deal. Don't try to make a killing all at one time. Borrow a little, pay that off with a little profit, then borrow for the next deal, and just build it up. He could see himself running a business like that, but just had to figure out what to buy and sell. If he could figure that out, he knew he could make it pay.

Fortunately for him, his Uncle Richard was becoming a very successful farmer. In fact, too successful. It was more than he could do to manage the fields and livestock and get it all sold. He'd been talking to Samuel about how a man might make a nice living as a livestock trader. On Sunday after church there was dinner on the ground, and that gave Samuel a chance to arrange for Mack to talk with his uncle about that line of work.

The next morning Mack rode Coal over to Richard's place, and his uncle welcomed him inside. Elizabeth brought them lemonade on the back porch, and it didn't take much of a conversation to convince Mack that stock trading was for him. Richard did some buying and selling with him, and taught him how to bargain for cattle, horses, and hogs

Richard and Elizabeth Shelton Marsden.

from the local farmers at the peak of marketability, then drive them to market and sell at a profit. One thing he cautioned Mack was to always get a bill of sale.

"You'll notice," he said, "when you sell your stock, the slaughterhouses always get a bill of sale. There's a reason for that, and we have to do the same thing. It's too easy to buy stock that's been 'borrowed' from a neighbor. No matter what, even if you're buying from a friend or family, always get a bill of sale." Mack nodded, and from then on, that was one of the underpinnings of his business.

Emma Jean had a younger brother, Allen, who had little ambition, and had no interest in either farming or the church. He was uncommonly big for a Hensley. In fact, he was tall and broad, and known as Big Allie. But for all his size and strength, he just couldn't seem to put it to any purpose.

Big Allie just didn't fit the Hensley mold. They spawned preachers and churches. They acquired property so they could build a highly moral country empire. For them, there was no distinction among religion, work, family, conduct, and money. In fact, they weren't given to seeking office or raising their profile, except in the church. The Hensleys had a rigid code of behavior, and Allie violated it.

No one outside the walls of the home knew whether Allie's banishment was his own doing, or a twist of circumstance. It might have been some unreported legal trouble, or something as simple as his refusal to be a farmer. But it was general knowledge that their dour father, Leander, got fed up and sent him down the road. From that time on, no matter what kind of trouble Allie had, the Hensleys never once rose to his defense.

So he was too ornery to live with his parents, but not too proud to live with his Aunt Ella Hensley. She was a widow who shared her spacious white house with five of her own children, assorted nieces and nephews, and a servant girl. Allie knew that beggars can't be choosers, and he was living there for free, but still, he couldn't stick with that arrangement. It was just too crowded. Besides, there were too many females, and he didn't much like being a member of the little composite family in which everyone shared the endless farm and home work. No, he needed something different.

Allie just happened to be mulling his none-too-plentiful options, when Mack took up stock trading. Mack didn't want to do all the dirty work himself, but was in no financial position to hire a man. So when he and Emma Jean moved into Samuel's old house, Mack also acquired Big Allie, a live-in business partner, brother-in-law, and sidekick.

Since he had no direction of his own, he jumped any time Mack said frog. Wherever Mack went, there was Allie. The two of them were a common sight, out on the roads in Mack's spring wagon pulled by the trusted Coal.

The rig was what folks from New England called a mountain wagon. It was about seven feet long, painted bright green, with yellow wheels and prongs, low sideboards, and a short bed, just big enough to hold a little cargo. Many's the time Mack was glad he had that light wagon when he met farmers on the road in their heavy, high-sided, two-mule wagons, working hard to get up the hills and riding the brake to keep them from running away on the down slopes.

To Emma Jean's delight, her younger sister Lydia also came to live with them and help care for baby Sammy. That was fine with Mack, knowing the women were busy at home when he and Allen took off in the wagon. It was the happiest time for Emma Jean, a sort of grownup, rediscovered childhood. Regardless of his mood or state of mind, Mack looked and acted the same, always intense, so it was hard to say he was happy. But he was at least content, and certainly had more hope than he'd felt in a long time. It did his heart good to see the old home place filled with love and hear it ring with little Sammy's voice.

Then some cattle started disappearing from Sandy Valley farms. And a few hogs. At first nobody was sure it was rustlers, because it was just one or two here and there. But as it continued, they knew there was a thief at work, and some thought they knew who it was. But it wasn't enough trouble to do anything about, and besides, people were busy.

Nobody paid much attention until June, when a fire consumed an unoccupied cabin on the farm of James Thomas Moss, whom everyone called J. T. It happened over in Moss Hollow, between Sandy and Sulphur Springs. There had been no lightning, and since it burned from the ground up, the blaze was clearly the work of an arsonist. When someone mentioned it to Sheriff Thomas J. Jones, he wondered not only who started the fire, but why J. T. didn't send one of his sons to fetch the law right away.

The day the sheriff rode out to see about the fire, he passed by the blackened pile of logs and continued to the house, where he found J. T. sharpening tools in the shade of his shed. Happy for a reason to take a break, the farmer shook Jones's hand and walked with him over

The home of James Thomas (J. T.) and Eliza Moss.

to the house for a glass of cool buttermilk. After some small talk, the sheriff got to the point of his visit, and J. T. just smiled. It was nothing, he said. Maybe some kids thought it would be funny to watch it burn. Jones took a sip of the refreshing milk and thought something very different.

Jones rode away thinking J. T. knew who set the fire, or at least why it was set, and it wasn't an act of idle playfulness. Somebody intended for that fire to strike fear in somebody else's heart. Maybe it was a threat to J. T. Maybe a threat to someone close to him. Maybe it had something to do with the stock thefts. Whatever the facts of the fire, it certainly worked well enough to keep Moss's mouth shut. The farmer put on a good show to get rid of the law, and Jones rode away unsatisfied. He was no detective, but something was wrong. That little fire had been out for a week, and still it continued to smolder.

Chapter Six

Arson to Cover a Murder

Abraham Anson Vail slipped into the Sandy community without fanfare in 1875. He was a recluse in his sixties from back East who didn't like to talk to anybody, and especially not about his previous life. One thing everybody knew is that he had plenty of money, because his tiny farm was home to an uncommon herd of eight horses, including a nice stallion, plus a mule, sheep, and more than a dozen hogs.

There was a good deal more to Vail's story than ever was known in Sandy Valley, because back in Masonville, New York, he was on relief for the poor as late as 1871. How he came from that lowly status to the life he lived in Missouri remained a mystery. He would only say he was born in New York, got fed up with his spendthrift wife, lived in Boston for a while, and then took off for the West. Rumors soon began that he had to leave Boston in a hurry with an ill-gotten fortune. But they were only rumors, and he never said more.

Vail holed up in a sparse fourteen-foot-square cabin four miles from Hillsboro, a mile due west of the Sandy Creek covered bridge. He never saw the neighboring farm families unless they had business with him. Of course, plenty of them had business with him, because as soon as he arrived he became a neighborhood lender, a source of quick, high-interest cash loans. Some of his borrowers needed cash to buy from other farmers. Some were on hard times, had reached the limit of their credit at the local store, and adopted the common but sorry practice of using one debt to pay off another.

To avoid taxes or any other scrutiny, he dealt in cash and barter, always with collateral. It was usually a mortgage or lien, but sometimes livestock or other chattel. In fact, the stallion was once chattel, and so became Vail's. He kept no formal books, but only jotted notes about his many deals, and his gruff manner didn't win him any friends. He filed one lawsuit after another to recover his due from debtors, some of whom were simply too broke to borrow, much less pay back.

One poor customer of Vail's named Burkhardt had borrowed wheat on a promise to repay the loan in wheat. When he put up a fair store of wheat in his barn, and still hadn't paid Vail back, he came face to face with the old man's determination to collect. Vail simply drove his wagon over to Burkhardt's barn with his rifle across his lap. Then he started loading bags of wheat into his wagon, while the irate farmer stood a few feet away, flailing his arms and screaming at the top of his lungs, threatening, swearing, all of which Vail appeared not to hear. Expressionless, he loaded exactly enough bags to pay the debt, climbed into the wagon seat, and took them home, his debtor's screams fading in the distance.

Burkhardt immediately hopped on his mule, rode into Hillsboro, and complained to Sheriff Jones that Vail had stolen his wheat. The sheriff had no choice but to arrest the old man. However, Vail knew his way around both the law and intimidation, and was more than happy to explain the situation to the justice of the peace. The justice had to admit that Vail had a pretty good case to justify helping himself to the wheat, but scolded him that there was no excuse for taking the law into his own hands. Seeing that he wasn't going to be set free, Vail simply posted bond, and then turned around and sued Burkhardt for nonpayment of the debt.

The whole case was clearly a matter that should be settled with a little common sense, rather than jail, lawsuits, and trials. So the sheriff wisely went out and reasoned with the farmer, who dropped the theft charges, and Vail dropped the lawsuit. He really didn't care that

Burkhardt continued telling everyone he met that Vail had stolen his wheat. That's the way Vail operated for years, making enemies on his way to making a living.

The worst drought in memory came along in 1881, bringing pitifully poor crops. Wheat heads were small and hay was scarce. Corn ears were short and melons failed altogether. People found it hard to feed themselves, much less their livestock. They were living on bank loans and store credit, and some had put up their property for cash from Vail. It seemed like every family was up to their necks in debt, and many couldn't pay on their loans.

Then one cool Sunday night in early November of 1881, just after dark, dogs on the farms west of the covered bridge started barking and wouldn't stop. Frank Meyer, who lived just up the rise across the road from Vail, looked out the window and saw his dogs run halfway down to Vail's place and back a couple of times. Something was going on over there, but a slip of woods cut off his view, and besides, it was just too dark to see what was going on. More important, he and the old man had had some cross words one time, and Vail warned him never to set

Henry Brady's home (above) was about a half mile away from Vail's, which was nestled among the trees at the center of this photo.

Lewis Meyer and family.

foot on his property. Meyer decided that whatever the dogs were fussing about, it wasn't his business.

About a half hour later Henry Brady was walking to his woodshed and noticed smoke rising from the direction of Vail's place. He immediately struck out down the road, gathering Lewis Meyer, Frank's brother, who rented the cabin on Brady's farm. At the same time, Frank glanced out his window again and saw the gray smoke rising from behind the trees into the black of the night sky. Just then Brady and Lewis came hurrying from the west, pointing and yelling about the fire at Vail's. Frank refused to go with them to check on it, so they went on without him. They cut through the slip of woods, coming in full view of Vail's cabin, normally a beautifully pastoral place cradled in the broad hollow between two branch creeks, but now alive with flames leaping high into the clear autumn night. The cabin had burned from the ground up, and when the men got there the roof was just collapsing into the charred structure. The flames had also jumped to a new cabin Vail was building nearby. Since the men had no buckets, and not enough hands to stop the blaze anyway, they settled for pulling a pile of new lumber out of harm's way. After waiting long enough to be satisfied that the fire would safely burn itself out, they returned to their homes.

In the early morning mist, the two pulled on their coats and went again to check on the damage from the blaze. As they peered into the ashes they saw Vail's blackened rifle, the stock burned away, near the back wall. A shocking a sight as that was, the men had the presence of mind to realize that the rifle wasn't where it should be. They knew it always hung above the door. Looking closer, they found that the gun was surrounded by bones, human bones, and it was all on top of a stack of charred bags, like a backwoods funeral pyre. Aghast, they realized that Vail had burned up atop the very bags of wheat he took from Burkhardt.

Leaving Meyer to guard the grisly scene, Brady immediately went back home to get his horse, and rode into Hillsboro to tell Sheriff Jones. He fetched deputy John Weaver and Dr. Brewster, the county coroner. Arriving at Vail's still-smoldering ruins, they investigated the smoky mess as well as possible, but the fire scene yielded up no secrets about what had happened. They made a thorough search for Vail's fabled stash of money or gold, and found none, which made it clear to Jones that somebody killed the old man and robbed him of his fortune. With all the trampling around by the neighbors, there were no tracks to follow, and besides, neither horse nor man would leave prints in that drought-hardened ground. Jones simply found no other evidence to help in an investigation. So the doctor picked up Vail's bones and put them in a blackened soup pot. A curious neighbor who had stopped by, Will Clark, was enlisted to take the pot and what was left of the body in his wagon to Brewster's office in town, with the promise that the county would pay him two dollars for the mission.

About that time the sheriff was beginning to see a story in the way everything in the cabin was arranged. Vail knew his murderer, feared him, and had his gun in hand to defend himself before the man came in. Standing in what used to be the doorway, looking east into the ruins, Jones pushed his hat back on his head and folded his arms. He pictured the scene, with the bed to the left against the north wall, and the grain bags at the foot of the bed, the northeast corner. In the middle of the room was the table, and to the right, the fireplace, which served for both warmth and cooking. He imagined the visitor knocking and Vail calling for him to come in. But first he cautiously took down the rifle and stood it in the northeast corner. When the man came in, the table was between the two. The visitor demanded money, the trouble started, and Vail grabbed up the handy rifle, but was overpowered by his younger, stronger assailant. He was beaten or strangled to death, or maybe even shot, as he clutched his useless gun.

And what about the fire? In an effort to cover the murder, the thief pulled burning logs from the fireplace, knowing as he ran away the fire would continue to spread. By the time anyone discovered it, the cabin would be engulfed in flames and he'd be well away. He hoped investigators would assume that Vail simply burned to death accidentally, and nobody would even suspect that a murder had taken place.

The culprit was probably one of his borrowers, Jones figured. Did Vail pull out his cash box to make a loan, or take in a repayment, only to have the man murder him and take the whole stash? Did it start out amicably, or did the thief show up demanding money from the start? Jones's only hope was that maybe, just maybe, the killer would brag about it in a tavern. Or go on a spending spree and reveal himself.

As the coroner's buggy pulled out, the other two mounted their horses and Jones thought back to a similar case back in, what was it, March? Yes, just last March. You recall? he asked Weaver. The deputy nodded, but Jones recounted the case anyway. Frank Spaulding was known as a perpetual and violent drunk. He became friends with a father and son, and a man named Stechem, St. Louis men who came to do some work in the town of Pevely, where Spaulding lived. The three shared a little cabin, and Spaulding joined them there one night for a poker game that became a very drunken poker game. Spaulding and the father argued and scuffled, so the son and Stechem got fed up and left. They later returned to find the house ablaze, with Spaulding and the father dead inside. At least that's the way they told the tale, and the fire left nothing to contradict them.

The son and Stechem were tried for murder and arson, but it was just as likely that the two victims fought, upset a lamp, setting the house ablaze, and died just because they were too drunk to escape. The accused men were acquitted, and hadn't been seen in the county since, so Jones didn't think they were involved with Vail's death. Still, it was frightening to think that maybe some ominous mind had learned from that case, maybe even been inspired by it, and decided that was a good way to deal with Vail.

In a community of log and frame houses, wood heat, and coal oil light, fires were not uncommon. For the criminal, a good fire destroyed evidence of who had been there and what they'd done. It might conceal gunshots, beating, strangulation, and stab wounds. Since money and property were destroyed, it might even wipe out evidence of theft. A good fire could be a method of erasure so complete that investigators couldn't tell if there had been any wrongdoing at all. That's exactly what happened to Vail. Had the dark element of Jefferson County discovered the perfect crime? It was a chilling thought.

As Jones and Deputy Weaver asked questions at the neighboring farms, suspicion fell on Mack Marsden because several people knew he went to Vail's cabin that night. The next day, Coroner Brewster convened an inquest with jurors and an attorney from town. Testimony included Mack, Brady, the Meyers, Mr. Kurz, who was Vail's neighbor to the northeast, and John Marsden, who'd been at the home of his mother, Louisa, directly north of Vail that evening.

Kurz and John testified that they saw and heard nothing. The others told their stories for the coroner. Then it was Mack's turn.

Sure, Mack admitted he had been there the night of the fire. Vail had loaned him $90 to buy a couple of steers, and he went over to repay the advance that evening. Mack's alibi, as well as the sheriff's suspicions, both depended on the timing. Mack was at Vail's house about 6:00 p.m., which is just after dark in November, coinciding with the time Meyer's dogs raised a ruckus. The fire was discovered in full force around 7:00. So Mack's visit was close to the time the fire was thought to start, and yet far enough in advance to cast some doubt in his favor. Besides, if a man were going to commit such a crime, wouldn't he sneak around in shadows and do the deed at night, rather than walk casually down the road in full view, speaking to neighbors, as Mack did? Wouldn't he keep the visit a secret, rather than tell several people he was planning to repay a debt to Vail that night, as Mack did?

Sheriff Jones also had to remember that lots of people disliked Vail, and maybe several hated him enough to kill him. Or maybe it wasn't hate, but desperation for money that drove someone to kill him. What about the wheat farmer Burkhardt, on whose bags of grain Vail died?

Back at the office, Jones put his feet up on the desk and studied Vail's list. The dead man kept a neat list of his debtors. Not in a ledger book, but just written on a piece of paper that he kept in a metal box, which saved it from the fire. Of course it was a metal box that probably also had a good bit of cash in it at one time.

The probate court clerk copied the list of outstanding loans for Jones, and he was going to use that to collect the debts for Vail's estate. Jones hadn't paid too much attention to it until now. Thirteen people were on the list, along with notes on how each loan was secured. When he set about collecting them, he planned to mark the amount he collected, or if there was nothing to collect, mark them "lost."

Some of the loans were dated as far back as 1875. None of them were staggering amounts, just $18 to this one, $75 to another. But on

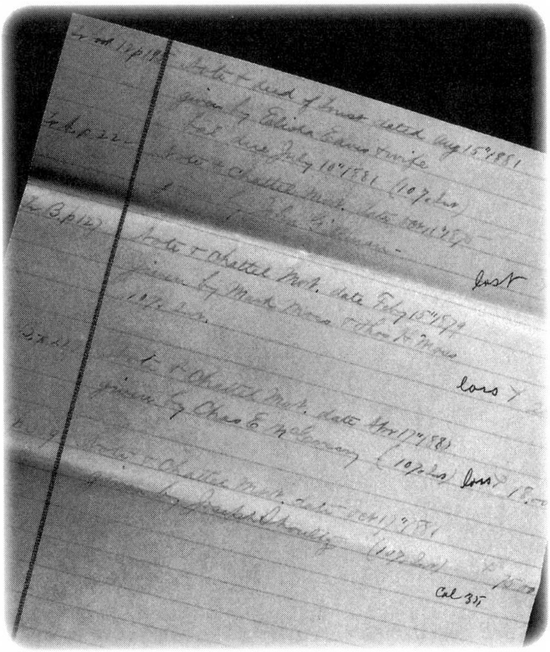

The county clerk provided a list of debtors to the sheriff so he could collect Vail's loans for his estate. Weaver's notes on what he collected are in the darker ink.

the other hand, $18 was a lot of money to some of the folks in Sandy. So could any of these debtors have been desperate enough to kill Old Vail? Could one of them have just been there, seen an opportunity, and taken it? Three of Vail's neighbors, Brady and both Meyers, were on the list. So were two of Mack's uncles.

Jones filled his pipe and lit it. Took a few puffs. Combed his hair. That always helped him think. It looked like everybody was a suspect. What about Mack? Mack was the one person he knew was there that night. Funny thing though, Weaver sat up and looked hard at the list, flipped it over and scanned the other side. Mack said he went to repay a loan, and sure enough, he wasn't on this list from the court clerk. That meant Mack was telling the truth, and Old Vail marked him paid right then and there. That was a point in Mack's favor, Jones thought, but he still had to be considered a suspect.

Word of the crime spread like dandelion seeds, so there was a pretty good crowd at the estate sale. Everybody was curious to see how the old hermit lived. Among the bidders was Mack Marsden. Hardly behaving like a man suspected of killing Vail, he was right there, checking the condition of the livestock. He ended up spending $86 making purchases that included all of the chickens and hogs, and the stallion. He didn't need a stallion, but saw a good chance to buy the horse cheap and knew he could sell it at a profit. Where did a guy like Mack get that kind of money? It was whispered that he was spending Vail's own money. But the truth is, the sale happened to come at a good time for him. He had just paid Vail back the loan of $90 after using it to buy two steers, which he sold, more than doubling his money. He was back at the sale, reinvesting it in Vail's livestock, and would probably more than double his money on that. He was good at making deals, and possibly even better at spotting opportunities.

As time passed, folks didn't forget about the crime, but rather grew more upset about it. Not that anyone was particularly close to old man Vail, but they had a vision of the kind of life they wanted to create in Jefferson County. Good schools, jobs, roads, commerce, and a safe place for families. They wanted electric lights, like folks in St. Louis had. And ice cream parlors. Murder and arson upset their plans for progress, and they wanted someone blamed. Sheriff Jones wanted to solve Vail's murder too, but pretty soon he had something else to worry about.

Chapter Seven
Midnight Ambush

"Fire! The house is on fire!" It was just after midnight when eighteen-year-old August Edinger awoke with a start, smelled the smoke, then burst into his aunt and uncle's bedroom to alert them to their mutual peril. Joseph and Louisa Yerger jumped from their bed. As she ran to their four children in the next bedroom, Joseph hurried barefoot down the oak stairs in his nightshirt and cap to find the flames well established throughout the downstairs. Wood floors, wool rugs, and Italian damask curtains were prime fuel for the hungry fire. There was nothing he could do but make sure everyone got out. How could a fire have surrounded the house so completely? There's only one way, arson, and the smoke was thick with the smell of the coal oil some devil had poured all around the walls of the frame house.

It was a life-saving stroke of good fortune that an alert, strapping young man like August was living in the home and working for his Uncle Joseph, the most prominent retailer in that part of the state. The two-story building housed not only the family, but also Joseph's combination saloon and dry goods store. Another employee and a hired girl boarded there, and a lightning rod salesman and his helper happened to be sleeping there that night too. While August and Louisa roused everyone, Joseph ran through the flames that blocked the front door, down the steps and into the yard. His senses were assailed by the stench of smoke, the searing heat, and the startling crack, pop, and sizzle of the inferno. Only then did he realize his nearby feed store and barn had also been set ablaze by the arsonist.

Joseph yelled to the neighboring houses for help. There was no time to spare. He had to think the whole farm business was lost, but the more hands that were put to the task, the better their chances for saving something of the beautiful and spacious Yerger home and store. Six neighbor men came running from their beds to lend a hand in fighting the fire as Joseph took up a post at the pump, just outside the kitchen door, and started filling buckets.

Little did they know a pair of evil eyes watched their every move from an alley across the street. Joseph had been moving quickly, and had been too far for the man to get the advantage he sought. But once Joseph stopped running and took up a post at the pump, filling buckets, the shadow man had his chance. He slipped a few steps to the side, always in darkness, to get just the right angle and as close as possible without being seen. He found a spot no more than fifty feet from the pump.

"Blam!" came from the blackness. Yerger whirled, screaming, "I'm shot!" He felt the sting of the blast, but his adrenaline was pumping so fiercely that he didn't realize how seriously he was hurt. Peering into the darkness he shouted, "Who's shooting there?!" It wasn't the pellet that pierced his side, or the one in his thigh, but the one that entered his heart that did the deed. As blood gushed into his chest cavity with each weakening contraction, Joseph Yerger slowly slumped to the ground.

The other men heard the shot too, and turned toward it, but could see nothing in the dark. Then they realized that Joseph had fallen, and ran to him just as Louisa and the children made their escape from the burning house. Louisa dropped to his side and the children saw their father lying in the grass, looking up at the fire, and making feeble attempts to draw shallow breaths. The men carried him out of the dusty street and into the neighboring Heiligtag home, laid him on the dining table, and lit the lamps, but by then he was dead.

Joseph Yerger, successful Antonia merchant and younger brother of Judge Anton Yerger. Courtesy of Glee Naes.

While the fire continued to feast on the house, store, and barn, the murderer was swallowed up by the night. He stayed off the road, skirting the fields, making his way home undetected and unhurried.

Joseph and Louisa Yerger were part of the close-knit, yet outgoing community of Germans who had made their way to this promising place in the heartland of America. They were skilled and industrious craftsmen, farmers, and dairy producers, but Joseph was perhaps the best known and most prosperous young man of his generation, the first of their families to be born in America. He came to Jefferson County with his parents, but was left an orphan at an early age. As a result, he developed a fearless, enterprising spirit that later led him to work on riverboats while saving his money for the day he could have his own business. He had a knack for a good deal, and gradually built up a trade in farm machinery, which evolved into a feed and farm equipment store. For the location, he chose his busy hometown of Antonia. Situated ten miles north of Hillsboro, and about the same distance from

Yerger's flour and feed store, along with the stables.

St. Louis, it was a central location, just an easy wagon ride from dozens of family farms.

Around the store Joseph added corrals for livestock and stacks of cleanly cut lumber, even a sawmill powered by a steam engine. Then he built a separate business, a colossus of a building that housed the combination saloon, grocery, and dry goods store. That's when he and Louisa left their farm and made their home above the store. Then he leased the old Marsden home in Sandy from Thomas Moss and opened a store and post office there, just five miles down Lemay Ferry Road.

Louisa was one of the most desirable young women of the German families. She and Joseph had known each other since they were children, crossing paths at community events and the German Evangelical Church. Their marriage was different from most, the difference being money. While their neighbors scraped a living from rocky farms, planting small gardens, raising a few hogs and chickens, making iron tools, barrels, and cheese, Joseph bought those products from his neighbors at the best price he could, for resale in his store. And he sold the same neighbors the wonders of the world's industrial centers that came up the river. The newest plow designs and the best shovels. Seed. Feed for livestock. And an ever-expanding offering of dry goods. They all came into the St. Louis port, and Joseph was quick to get them to his store.

Yerger's combination general store, tavern, and post office, with the family's home upstairs.

Clearly, as his business grew, he knew how to put money back into it so it would keep growing. That meant he needed more and more employees. And with the hiring of employees comes the firing, the ones who don't work out, and the ones who leave disgruntled. Also comes the credit account that's not paid in a timely manner, the demands for payment, an occasional lawsuit, and a string of tattered relationships that parallel all of the good relationships Yerger had built. Yes, there were hard feelings, but on the other hand, everybody appreciated the good things Yerger brought to those Missouri hills, including jobs, both steady and temporary. There was simply a distance naturally created between employer and employee, between the merchant and the customer on credit. But nothing at all that would prompt the life-threatening arson.

Credit was a way of life in that era, especially in a farming community like northern Jefferson County, where they all knew each other, and almost everybody was somebody's cousin. Yerger's store could not have achieved its singular success without granting credit to the farmers, who could only pay their accounts months later, after their calves, hogs, mules, or corn had been sold in St. Louis. Or when their wives' quilts, baskets, and other crafts were sold. Still, there was no one with whom Yerger had quarreled to the point of violence. No one that any reasonable person would suspect of torching Yerger's home and business while he and his family slept.

Could it possibly have been the arsonist's intention to kill the whole family, their visitors, and boarders? If he meant to get Joseph alone, there were plenty of chances to do that. He must have known that Louisa and the children were asleep, and it was a possibility that everyone in the home would perish in the blaze. What awful disdain must he have harbored to set such a lethal trap? Who could have hated the merchant that much? Who could have been that heartless?

On the surface it seemed unrelated to the livestock rustling in the valley. But when Jefferson County's weekly newspaper, *The Democrat*, told of Yerger's murder, it reported another cowardly crime. Mack Marsden's father-in-law, the widowed Leander Hensley, was out working in his field when someone slipped up to his house with a can of coal oil and set the place afire, leaving it a near-total loss. To add to the tragedy, just a few days before, one of Leander's sons had fallen on hard times and moved back into the house with his family, so they too lost everything.

Sheriff Jones and Deputy Weaver knew the Hensley fire was arson, and there was some sort of unseen web that bound Vail, Yerger, and Hensley. But when they talked to Leander the older man shook his head. "No," he said, "it was a chimney fire. Started in the stovepipe. It happens sometimes," he added offhandedly. But that didn't satisfy the sheriff. He had the feeling that Leander knew something. And somebody had set the fire as a warning to keep his mouth shut. And there was still the unsolved arson of the empty cabin at the Moss place. There was a thread. The lawmen just couldn't see what was connected to what.

Chapter Eight
Weaver Takes Over

Yerger was killed only three months after Vail. Community leaders were aroused, a $3,000 reward was offered, and plenty of attention was focused on finding the criminal. But six more months went by with no break in either case, no suspect arrested, not even a motive discovered, and public concern continued to grow. It was terrifying for the community to think there was a homicidal lunatic at large.

Part of the reason there had been no progress is that Jefferson County's sheriff had first virtually, and then literally, disappeared. One by one his four children came down with scarlet fever in the winter of 1882, shortly before the Yerger murder. A young woman, Minerva Meyer, was hired to help with the household. Then when the family was healthy again, she moved to St. Louis. Only when Mrs. Jones discovered some letters and telegrams in the sheriff's pocket did she realize that Minerva took his heart with her when she left. He had been away from his duties, visiting her in St. Louis as often as he could get away with, and keeping her in fine big-city style. How did he afford such a lavish indulgence without his wife seeing the decline in his meager lawman's salary? By borrowing hundreds upon hundreds of dollars, until at last his debtors could not be kept at bay any longer.

The public outcry was loud, and the courts were demanding. When judgments were issued against him, *The Democrat* described Jones as "a man who has had the confidence and respect of everybody, abandoning his wife, children, father, mother, brothers, sisters, and many friends—all who ever cared or did anything for him—all for the sake of a lewd woman who will have no further use for him after his money is gone." Of the several courses available to him, none were attractive, so he simply chose to run away.

Judge Anton Yerger, older brother of the murdered Joseph Yerger, had ascended to the bench after being a county commissioner. It was a natural transition for him following his service in the Civil War, both in the Union Stuarts' Cavalry, and later as colonel of his own regiment of Enrolled Missouri Militia. He was a man of loyalty and action, and he expected loyalty and action of others.

With Jones's criminal indiscretions fouling life in the county, and his beloved brother's murder unsolved, Judge Yerger was furious. He removed Jones from office and appointed the trusted deputy John Weaver to finish the term. Finally, Yerger said, shaking Weaver's hand, after Jones's distractions from his job there would be some new action on

Judge Anton Yerger, builder of the town of Antonia and older brother of merchant Joseph Yerger. Courtesy of Glee Naes.

the murder cases, and he let Weaver know the expectations were high. As if Yerger's pressure on Weaver wasn't enough, the young man who discovered the fire in Yerger's house, August Edinger, was the son of Antonia mayor George Edinger, and the mayor was Louisa Yerger's brother. Weaver knew he was going to dread seeing the judge or the mayor in public because they'd ask him what he was doing to solve the murder.

Jones did put some effort into the case. One man he considered a suspect was tall, brown-haired farmer Fidelo Rogers, called simply Delo. Born in 1855, Delo had come to Jefferson County as a young man with his family, married a nice German girl, and set about quietly making a home with her on Glaize Creek south of Antonia. They lived just a few houses away from Joseph Yerger.

Like most folks thereabouts, Delo and his younger brother John had bought seed and other goods from Yerger on credit, banking on being able to pay him back with their next crop. John is the one who had a problem repaying, and Delo had risen to his brother's defense, exchanging angry words with Yerger when the merchant demanded that John's account be cleared. That story was nothing new to now-sheriff Weaver. The investigation had revealed it early on. In fact, Yerger was also threatened by another farmer, John Thistle. But all that was over trivialities, the kind of argument that was common and quickly forgotten among hard-working men, and not the kind of thing that would spark murder. The financial problems behind the harsh words were long ago resolved.

That's the edge that a lawman like Weaver has. He knew the people, knew how they thought and talked, and knew the difference between idle threats and murderous intent. He knew Delo Rogers had not suddenly turned from earnest farmer to stealthy and cowardly ambusher. Of course former sheriff Jones could have reached the same conclusion, but he had other things on his mind.

Another of Jones's unlikely suspects was a Yerger employee, one Martin Zimpfer. Like Joseph, his saga was a perfect example of the immigrant's dream of the mid-nineteenth century, coming to the United States with his parents. Their deaths during an epidemic left him on his own, an orphan at the tender age of nine, much like Joseph, which must have created a natural bond between them. He worked hard and proved an able hand with horse and wagon, serving as a teamster for Joseph before leaving to become a coachman in St. Louis. When he returned to Jefferson County in 1880 he managed the new store for Joseph in Sandy and became the first Sandy postmaster.

After Joseph's murder, Martin rebuilt the big stores in Antonia in partnership with Louisa Yerger. He rented one of the rooms as his home, closed the little Sandy Creek store, and moved the merchandise to the rebuilt Antonia store. A little retrospect might make the ambitious Martin a prime suspect in Joseph's murder. He had everything to gain, including a chance to take over the business, not to mention the wife. But he was never in trouble with the law before, never showed anything but loyalty to Joseph, and so was never investigated.

Could he and Louisa have been carrying on behind Joseph Yerger's back? Certainly Joseph and Louisa never spent a lot of time together. A man with his responsibilities was on the job from before dawn until well past sunset. At home he was busy with his accounts and planning. He had people to meet, goods to buy, trips to St. Louis, and an endless string of details to which he must attend. As much as he loved her, the attention some men paid their wives was simply not available for her. But Louisa was a devoted and busy mother. And if Martin and Louisa had been romantically involved before the murder, they surely weren't showing it after the murder. When anyone saw them together, they were all business. Besides, if Martin wanted to kill Joseph to get the wife, he wouldn't have endangered her with the house fire.

Weaver wasn't interested in that kind of gossip. What Judge Yerger and Mayor Edinger didn't know was that even while he was a deputy, Weaver had already been working hard on the murders. In fact, he might have moved things along faster if he didn't have to wait for Jones to discuss every idea he had and every person he questioned.

Now it was his case. The oath of office was barely out of his mouth when he left Judge Yerger's office and walked directly to the office of County Prosecutor James F. Green. The attorney shook his hand and told him how glad he was that they could start working together. Weaver sat down and they started patiently building their case in the murder of Anson Vail. Even though Joseph Yerger was more respected in the community, and as horrific as his murder was, Green saw it as a footnote to solving the Vail slaying. Both killings were done by the same hand, he was sure. Yes, by the summer of '82, after watching Jones piddle away precious months thinking about a long list of suspects, Green still had his sights set on one man. He was eager to prove who murdered Anson Vail: Mack Marsden. His objective was not the solving of each individual crime, but getting Mack, the man he believed to be behind all of them.

Weaver came to his new job ready to do some digging, and he was surprised to find Green so set on hanging Mack. Of course, everybody in the county believed he was the guilty one. Even before Yerger was killed, folks were saying Mack killed Vail, he stole livestock, and he was a man to be feared. Then a new piece of evidence came along that persuaded Sheriff Jones and Prosecutor Green that it was Marsden who murdered Yerger too, and he did it to shut Yerger's mouth. There was plenty of motive in the testimony Yerger took to his grave, a testimony that would have hung the Vail killing firmly around Marsden's neck.

Back in the fall, right after Vail was killed, Yerger had come to Sheriff Jones, saying he had information about the case. Vail, like everyone else, shopped at Yerger's store, and Joseph remembered one particular time that Vail had been in to buy lumber for his new cabin. The man always dealt in cash, and when Yerger counted out his change it included a couple of five-dollar bills Yerger had patched. He noticed them in his drawer earlier that day, two bills with similar tears across them. So he picked up the mucilage and tape kept at the desk for sealing packages, put a swipe of the sticky glue on each bill, and cut a slip of tape to patch the tears. The stiff spots got his attention when he pulled the bills out later, so he remembered giving them to Vail.

A few days later, following Vail's murder, Mack Marsden paid for some things at the store. Yerger held out his hand and was stunned when Mack paid him with those two patched bills. Without a second thought the fearless Yerger accused Mack of having Vail's money, and said he was going to the authorities with the information.

Yerger was the man who a few years before had confronted a stranger who showed up at the store wanting to sell a brace of mules. The man had no proof of ownership, so Yerger locked up the mules, saying they could all go to the county seat in the morning and see if anyone could vouch for the man. Of course by dawn the traveler was long gone, and with a little advertising, Yerger was able to locate the owner of the mules that had been enjoying his hospitality. Sure enough, they'd been stolen. That's the sort of man he was, so he wasn't going to let Mack Marsden get away with murdering Vail.

Mack was livid when Yerger accused him. "I could have gotten those bills from anyone, anytime," Mack growled. "That doesn't prove anything," he went on, and Yerger would be sorry if he continued accusing Mack of anything. It was a natural reaction of which anyone might be capable when wrongly accused. It meant nothing of guilt or innocence, but Yerger took it as the feigned protest of a guilty man.

When Yerger told that story to Sheriff Jones back in November, the lawman knew it was the kind of break he'd been looking for. Sure, the patched old bills were circumstantial and flimsy evidence. Certainly not the proof the prosecutor needed to perfect a case. And as for Mack's reaction to Yerger's accusation in the store, angry indignation was perfectly normal for a man accused of such a horrible crime, whether he was guilty or not. Still, the story of the marked money might be used to pry a confession from Mack, or to somehow turn the case.

Green had been planning to bring Yerger's testimony to the next grand jury. He hoped that would be enough to get Mack indicted, which would help Jones build a case strong enough to convict him. Meanwhile, however, Yerger was in the gravest of danger because he had already told Mack he was going to the law. Unfortunately, Jones was too busy with his girlfriend to press the case while it was hot, and too busy to protect his star witness from his violent end.

The fire and shotgunning of Yerger did just what they were supposed to do, leave Jones with nobody to testify about the patched bills. So he simply gave up that whole line of investigation. But now that Weaver was in charge of the case, Green was ready to jump back into working the "marked money" angle.

Because Weaver was new to his job, he had to respect the younger man Green's experience with the finer points of law. But Weaver was also a man who trusted his own instincts. Mack could have gotten the patched bills from someone else, the new sheriff observed. If he did, the law had to know who that was. Yes, of course, Green humored him. But he didn't think there was anybody else. His sights were set on Mack. He simply couldn't prosecute until Weaver got him something more to work with. Better evidence. Or a witness who wasn't afraid of Mack.

So Weaver left the meeting reminding himself that he wasn't Green's errand boy. And he wasn't Judge Yerger's or Mayor Edinger's servant either. He had to work the case in his own way. He was a farmer, and he knew about being patient, about planting seeds and waiting until they produced. He was going to talk to people, including Mack.

But Green was through with being patient. He decided everyone should know that Vail's bills had showed up in Mack's hands, so he took the story to R. W. McMullin, editor and publisher of *The Democrat*. And in its next issue *The Democrat* reported that Yerger was the state's prime witness against Mack Marsden in the murder of Vail. It went even further to implicate Mack in both slayings, saying Yerger's evidence "made it a matter of necessity on the part of Marsden to put him where he would tell no tales."

There it was in print. Suddenly Mack was a suspect in two murders. When Weaver saw the story he was plenty mad and went directly to Green's office to see if he knew how the newspaper found out about the marked bills. The story was an injustice to Mack, and it tipped their hand, he said, shaking the newspaper at Green. Now everybody knew what they knew. Besides, how could he get the truth if everybody in the county already thought Mack was guilty?

Green admitted to Weaver that he planted the story. But he didn't reveal the details about the packing tape. He simply said Yerger had marked the bills. So if anyone turned up who knew how they were marked with packing tape, that person would know the inside story, something that was never leaked to the newspaper.

Weaver had to take the cards Green dealt, and play them out. But before he left, he reminded the lawyer that two mules in the same harness don't get very far pulling in different directions. Green agreed to work more closely with Weaver from that point on, and they shook hands.

With the star witness Yerger dead, they had to find someone to take his place. Maybe if they could make a case in one murder, that might also make a case in the other. Would the newspaper story light a fire under Mack? What would be his next move?

Then pretty soon the new sheriff had a lot more than murder on his plate.

Chapter Nine
The Shadow of Crime

The hogs of Jefferson County dominated the dinner table and the economy just as cattle did on broader, flatter lands farther west. Swine didn't need much land, and were well suited to small pens along rocky hillsides. They were natural foragers that would eat any kind of vegetable, fruit, or even meat scraps, and if the farmer had nothing to feed them they could dig for their own food. They provided ham, chops, bacon, sausage, salt pork, ribs, loins, chitterlings, chewy pickled tails and feet, organ meats, and tough hides. The dogs got the ears.

Every farmer had hogs to sell, as well as hogs to butcher for the family's main meat throughout the year, and December was hog butchering time. With Christmas in the air, there was an annual hog killing day when people would go from farm to farm, turning the heavy, dirty work into a neighborhood social. Some preferred to dry-cure the meat by rubbing salt and sugar into it and letting it dry. After a month or two it was cured. Some used pickling brine, packing it in barrels of salt water for a couple of weeks. Then the family would take enough for a big feast and hang the rest in the smokehouse, where the hickory fire smoldered day and night for weeks. If the brine-cured meat grew mildew on the outside, that was easily trimmed off, and the meat inside was salty and delicious. Once smoked, it kept for a long time.

Though domestic breeds were becoming more common, especially on the bigger farms, most of the hogs of the 1880s were not far removed from the feral hogs that were roaming America's woods. They were short, slab-sided creatures that still carried the razorback, a strip of long, coarse hair along their upper spine, so characteristic of their ancestors. Highbred or not, one of pigs' best traits was that they had no interest in running off and were willing to stay behind the crudest of fences. On the other hand, they were easily spooked. Sometimes the slightest surprise could send them off on a short sprint in any direction, which made them difficult to drive in any number. Another annoyance was that it was their nature to forage as they walked. They'd meander, nose to the ground, instead of watching where they were going, so drovers had to constantly remind them with long sticks to get back in a bunch. A trip to market with anything more than about three or four pigs required a couple of men just to keep them going in the same direction. And it couldn't be done from the back of a horse.

They could be sold to the meatpackers up toward St. Louis any time of year. It was a long walk and strenuous work, so lots of farmers, especially the older ones, depended on the young men to drive them. Sometimes they'd go from farm to farm collecting a sizable herd and drive them all up to market.

Farther west, where prairies were broad and unfenced, stolen cattle were run off in herds, sometimes in wild and dangerous stampedes. With the Jefferson County hogs, tucked away in hollows far from the roads, it was one stolen from this farm, two from that one. That's how it started back in the summer of 1880. It's not that the Sandy Valley had no cattle. There were some small herds; most families raised a calf or two every year, and yes, the thieves got a few of those. They got a few sheep and goats too. But all those animals were harder to steal because they were usually pastured behind good fences, and they could make a lot of noise.

Pigs, on the other hand, were nice and quiet, easy to take, easy to sell in neighboring towns, and hard to trace. In fact, until the trouble started, some farmers let their hogs run loose, and most others kept them in rustic fences that worked more intimidation on the hogs to stay in than on crooks to stay out. But that bucolic approach ended with the advent of a new breed of hog thief who struck like the fox that slips into the coop and snaps his jaws tight on the throat of one chicken without even waking the others. It was nothing for a thief to come in the night and just kick off the bottom fence rail. A little quiet hazing, a little prodding with a stick, would move a couple of hogs out. The bandit would shoo them over to the road and into the night while the others stayed right there in the pen. Best of all for the crook, they could be driven undetected through the woods until some ground had been covered. Then, once the thief put some distance behind him, he might get back onto the road and pass unrecognized or without drawing attention. After all, one spotted pig looked pretty much like another spotted pig.

Hog stealing was common throughout Missouri. It was an odd sort of crime, a small, pesky bother to the law. For that matter, it was so subtle, a farmer might think a missing hog just wandered off. Maybe that old fence rail fell down from age. If some drifter had come through and taken a couple of hogs, that would have been a thing to curse, dismiss, and easily forget. But this was a recurring nightmare lately, so the people of Sandy knew the culprit was someone local, and that made it a constant worry.

And the dirt-poor farm families who were losing their livestock were suffering. For them, the loss of one hog could be the difference between shoes for the children and no shoes. It could be the difference between having some extra meat to trade for potatoes and cabbage, or feeding the family nothing but pork and cornbread through the last months of winter.

Weaver, who had just been elected to a new term as sheriff in 1882, went through the same puzzle over and over again. A thief who lived in the neighborhood wouldn't take contraband hogs home to his own pasture, because the owner might come looking and recognize them. He wasn't slaughtering them, because that's a lot of work, and he'd wind up with a huge quantity of meat that still had to be sold. Nope, he was selling them as quick as he could.

There was no likely place to sell hogs to the south. Anyone driving hogs would have to pass through Hillsboro, then Victoria, then DeSoto, where any questioning by Weaver would turn up some kind of a lead. But to the north there was only Antonia, and then he'd be among strangers, and in busier places where people didn't take so much notice of who was passing where and when. He'd get to Carondelet, an old French settlement that grew into a town before becoming part of St. Louis in 1870. From the River Des Peres north, that part of town was pretty sophisticated, while the south side was rough as a cob, populated with businesses, warehouses, and the riverfront docks. There, a man selling livestock could find plenty of meat packers and shippers. He might make easy sales to busy butchers with few questions asked.

When the trouble started, it was always one or two hogs that one man could drive away. Then it escalated to three and four, and began to look like the work of more than one man. And what about selling them? Weaver wondered. One man can't keep going back to the same butcher without drawing a little too much attention. Also, if he drove them twenty or thirty miles to market, did he walk back home, or did he ride? Yes, Weaver thought, this is a gang, with horses and wagons. They're selling to first one packer, then another, and somebody's giving them a ride back home. Of course if it was a gang, that raised the question of who was in it. And at that time, Weaver had no good reason to think the livestock rustling had anything to do with the murders and arson of the previous year.

Wherever men met at the store or church they grumbled about the disappearing livestock. Some had toughened their fences, but others just gave up keeping hogs altogether. And they grumbled about Weaver. Was he doing anything at all about the thefts? Was he any better than Jones? Months went by, and it seemed that every time farmers gathered to talk, someone had lost hogs. And still, no progress from the sheriff.

Who was this man they trusted with their protection? Weaver was as common as any of them, born on riverfront land, to parents from back East, and raised on hard work. He served in the Confederate army, married, and lived like many of the people in the area, raising crops, livestock, and children. Veterans of either side in the Civil War were in demand for law enforcement. It was partly for their familiarity with firearms, partly because they knew a little about organizing and directing men, and partly because they'd shown some courage and fidelity to a code of honor. So John L. Weaver was recruited as a deputy for Sheriff Jones in 1876. He then gave up full-time farming to take on a second job as public administrator. This had the duel benefit of keeping him in Hillsboro, where he was handy when Jones needed him, and keeping him aware of what was going on all around the county. By the time he finished out Jones's term, everybody knew him, so he was elected in '82.

There was never any hint of impropriety about his time in office, but there was a good bit of grumbling. People wanted action, and Weaver was a thinker. After all, he had warrants to serve, delinquent renters to evict, and piles of paperwork to complete. He had a force of men to manage, including part-time deputies, plus a constable in each township, the six major divisions of the county. It was even the sheriff's job to collect taxes. He couldn't spend all his time tracking down a missing hog.

So he was working on the hog stealing problem in his own way. And he hadn't forgotten the two murders. What the Sandy Valley farmers didn't know was that Weaver had been taking little trips up Lemay Ferry Road, asking questions, telling the meat packers in the distant towns to be on the lookout, alerting the city police and town marshals all up and down the line. If you suspect a stolen hog, he told them, even one, tell your local constable, then come get me right away.

Weaver's conclusion from all his interviews was that people knew more than they were telling. Maybe they saw livestock being driven in the night, or maybe they just saw somebody flashing an unusually large bankroll. Whatever it was, they were afraid to tell. Of course it was an easy fear to justify, because most of what the thieves did looked perfectly normal. How could a farmer report a possible thief driving hogs up the road when lots of people drove hogs up the road every day?

As for Mack, his stock trading business was going well, but he still wasn't making enough money to save. When Yerger's estate was settled, Weaver was charged with collecting the outstanding debts among his many businesses. Mack had run up a sizable tab of $206 at the store, and he couldn't pay, so the court issued a judgment against him. Of course lots of people were in the same situation.

Then in early July of '82, the home of Leander Hensley's eighty-three-year-old father, Fleming Hensley, burned to the ground. The only thing he saved was his trunk. Weaver wondered if the blaze was set to cover a burglary. If so, it did the job, leaving any evidence of an intruder in the ashes. The old man wasn't even sure whether anything was stolen, so maybe it wasn't a burglary at all. One thing for sure, this fire, together with the one at Leander's house, made it clear that someone was targeting the Hensleys.

Did Leander and Fleming know something about the livestock rustling? About the murders? Or did the arsonist burn their houses to close the mouths of someone else? Maybe a loved one? That could include scores of friends and relatives. Weaver still couldn't say which crimes and which people were connected, but everything—the fires, murders, and livestock rustling—all happened within a year, and all within a distance of about seven miles.

It got worse. Since his charred home was uninhabitable, old Fleming moved in with another son, Rev. William Hutson Hensley, his wife, Pauline, and their two great-nieces. One Sunday morning when they all pulled away from the house in a wagon headed for church, a man watched from the trees until they were out of sight. Then he came strolling up the road as casual as you please, and turned in to the yard.

Doors were never locked in Sandy Valley, so he walked right in. The pretty dishes, silverware, and William's hunting guns were in no danger. This man was after cash and had a pretty good idea where it was. He could smell the smoke that had soaked into Fleming Hensley's trunk. There it was, under the bed.

Better to get it out of the house just in case someone showed up, the thief figured. He dragged it out the door, around the side of the house, and into the trees. About a hundred yards from the house he set the wooden chest down and opened it up. There was nothing he wanted in the tray, so he threw that aside and dug deeper. There were Fleming's personal things, winter clothes, and a couple of books. The robber dug clear to the bottom, strewing the trunk's contents around, and didn't find what he was after.

When the family got home, they immediately saw the open door, then the rumpled rugs, and knew someone had been there. Old Fleming and William could clearly see where the trunk was dragged out, and that the grass was trampled in a path leading toward the woods. They followed the trail into the brush and found the trunk under the trees, in plain view and not far from the house, with its contents pulled out and left scattered. Everything was there. But not the cash.

The cash. That trunk was where old man Hensley kept the precious bit of money he had set aside so he wouldn't be a burden to his children. Fleming rolled his eyes, and lifted a quiet, thankful prayer that only the day before he had given the cash to Leander to invest in some farm supplies.

As he and William talked about it, there was something about the odd attempted burglary that made them very uncomfortable. It was someone who knew the family well, and knew that Fleming had moved to William's house. The would-be thief was someone close enough to the family to know that the old man had a money stash. Fortunately, it was someone who didn't know the money had all been loaned to William's brother.

Who could have been that close, and that dirty? When Sheriff Weaver got the Hensleys' report he immediately had his suspicions. But he didn't push it. After all, he didn't think the Hensleys would be very receptive to the idea that Mack Marsden would try to rob his own wife's grandfather. Especially since Allie was his sidekick. Big Allie wouldn't burn out his own father and grandfather. Would he?

In fact, Weaver was having trouble with the whole picture. This little attempted burglary had to be connected to the other crimes, especially the fires at Fleming's and Leander's houses, Weaver thought. But why didn't the intruder set a fire this time? It didn't make much sense, and yet Weaver suspected it was all the work of the same twisted mind. If Mack were stealing livestock, and if he murdered Vail and Yerger, as people were whispering, why would Mack also set the fires? The more he thought about Mack as a suspect in all that, the less sense it made.

Arson was a cowardly act. It was a holdover from the Civil War era, when bushwhackers and guerrillas of both sides used arson as intimidation. A fire might carry a message to keep quiet. Or, "Tell us where the deserters are hiding." Or, "This could happen to you too."

By that time everybody in Sandy Valley was saying a gang was at work, with Mack at its head, and they would deal with anybody who exposed them. "He carries that pistol, you know," they would say. Even with the reward of $3,000 for Yerger's killer, nobody would risk burglaries, arson, and their family's lives by telling what they knew. If the gang was capable of the horrible atrocity against Yerger and his family, they were capable of anything.

The case simmered for months, and still Weaver had no witnesses. Then he had an idea. Maybe his best hope of witnesses was to get the gang's own members to testify against each other. The big question was, if Mack was as guilty as most folks thought, could the gang be persuaded to testify against Mack, their leader, the one man they all feared? Of course the other problem with Weaver's idea was that he didn't even know who was in the gang.

Chapter Ten
The Other Side of the Family

'Squire J. F. Green, the county prosecutor, was Weaver's closest ally. The two of them wouldn't give up, but neither could they make much progress. Green was sure Mack was the man they were after, but Weaver was unconvinced, and Mack was cool as a cucumber. Weaver had talked to him several times, and in every interview he maintained his innocence, leaving that nagging feeling in the back of Weaver's mind that Green and everyone else could be wrong. In spite of public opinion, Weaver still didn't believe Mack was their man.

Keeping Weaver's doubts alive, Mack's family was accusing other men. The Hensleys might have been afraid to talk, but not the resolute Samuel Marsden. He angrily pointed to some people whom his family didn't consider worthy to wear the name Marsden. They were John Martin Marsden and Augustus Allen Marsden, who lived nearby but were seldom seen and rarely even mentioned by those in Samuel's camp.

George Marsden, the third brother who came from Illinois, had compiled a colorful history in Jefferson County. Was he the black sheep? He was, at least, embarrassing. Even so, the three brothers had been close, faithful, and willing to walk through fire for one another. However, with the law closing in on his precious son Mack, Samuel Marsden had no choice but to point the law in the direction of deceased brother George's branch of the family.

Although George had his little home in Sandy near his brothers, he disappeared from the area for months at a time. He married Eliza

Peppers in neighboring Franklin County, and they had a daughter and five sons. Eliza died giving birth to the last boy in 1849. Unable to be a fitting father to all those children, George left the girl with his parents, Matthew and Mary, and returned to Jefferson County. There, he left his sons with brother Richard and his wife, Elizabeth. Even though they were just getting started making a life together, George knew they couldn't refuse to care for the boys.

After depositing his children, George was off once more, this time to the California gold rush. When he returned two years later, rather than embrace his daughter and sons again, he chose to start anew with a willing girlfriend, the much younger Louisa Williams Owens. Louisa married Orvid Owens in 1846 and by 1851 had three children, Marian Chandler, Thomas E., and Nancy Ann. What happened to Mr. Owens is lost to history, but divorced or widowed, Louisa had two more sons out of wedlock, Augustus Allen Owens (who went by Allen) in 1856 and John Martin Owens in 1858.

Was George Marsden the father of Allen and John? According to some Marsdens, George was never around long enough. Some branches of the family referred to the boys as "George's bastard sons." George didn't care what people thought, and he continued living with Louisa off and on until 1860 when she was pregnant again, and the neighbors filed morals charges against them for cohabitating. It was either go to jail or get married, so George and Louisa got married. They had two more daughters, Amelia Elizabeth, called Bessie, and Barilla. After they married, though none of Louisa's seven children were legally adopted, all of them except Tom started using the Marsden name. Tom was grown and saw no reason to take on the name of a man he detested.

George's escapades had been bad enough, but for all "those children" to take the family name, well, that was just too much for the Samuel and Richard branches of the family. They never thought it was right, and George never said anything to confirm which of the children were truly his offspring. If Allen and John were his sons, why hadn't Louisa given them the last name of Marsden from the beginning? Of course that question raised the next troubling question: If George wasn't their father, who was?

Long before Mack's troubles, George left his family again, moving back to Franklin County, where he died in 1869, leaving the young boys, John and Allen, to fend for themselves, wild and unsupervised. Louisa had no handle on them and was plenty busy raising the two little girls. Samuel and Richard's families shunned the boys because they didn't believe those two boys were any blood kin at all. John and Allen were sandy-haired, blue-eyed, and fine-featured like their mother. Smaller in frame than most Marsdens, they faced cruel teasing from other young people about the morals of their parents. It's no wonder they rarely darkened the schoolhouse doorway, got into frequent fights, and turned into hard cases. However, they also learned to avoid trouble by keeping to themselves, and as a result were never afoul of the law. That is, until Samuel Marsden got fed up with the accusations against his son Mack.

None of Samuel's other children had any trouble like Mack had. The oldest boy, Buzz, was married and put together a decent living with farming and various jobs. He and Maria were raising their children in a nice two-story clapboard home and doing all right. Buzz and Mack loved their sister Priscilla, who was a mother and the wife of the well-liked farmer Clay Moss. All of the girls were married or about to be, and the whole bunch of them attended Sandy Baptist Church.

So Samuel couldn't understand why, with such a fine family, Mack would be suspected in all those crimes. He told Sheriff Weaver flatly that the law needed to look at John and Allen Marsden. He had a point, Weaver had to admit. They were worth considering. And once he thought about where they lived, it was as if someone threw cold water in his face. When Vail was killed, John lived with his mother, Louisa, on the farm right across the road to the north. How did I miss this? Weaver wondered. These guys knew Vail, his farm, and his habits very well.

Clay Moss, farmer, Mack's neighbor, and husband of his sister Priscilla. Courtesy of Nancy Moss Hollingsworth.

Louisa's house faced south, with its back to a little fruit orchard and a broad, uncommonly flat cornfield that stretched and spread like a green comforter that faded every summer to a golden fleece. There was a little garden that always needed tending, and a small, low-roof barn that sheltered the milk cow, with a little room for other livestock when they could afford it. The front door looked almost directly toward Vail's house in the hollow past the tree line, though the cabin was hidden from view below the road.

John had even been one of the witnesses at the inquest into Vail's death, and said he didn't see anything the night of the fire. That was hard to believe, now that Weaver looked back on it. He'd been so busy trying to prove Mack either guilty or innocent, that he didn't give enough attention to the murdered man's closest neighbor.

When Weaver started asking questions about the "other side" of the Marsden family, he found that John had married in 1881, bringing his wife, Millie, into his mother's house. But Millie kicked John out shortly after the wedding, and very shortly after the Vail fire. Then he moved in with his brother Allen and his wife, over in Crystal City. Before long, Allen's wife had had enough of John. They were getting ready to move over to Sulphur Springs, and she made it clear that there wouldn't be a place for him in their new house. So John was again looking for a home.

By that time there was also another woman living in Louisa's house. Her daughter Bessie, the wife of Thomas Henon Moss, known as Tommy, had left him to move back in with her mother and Millie. So where did John find a home? In the old cabin in Moss Hollow where his brother-in-law Tommy lived alone after Bessie left him. They were quite a pair. John, of medium height and less than average build, and Tommy, a tall drink of water. John frowning and scheming, nondescript and clean-shaven. Tommy smiling, with one of those hopelessly friendly faces, sporting curly hair and a flaring mustache, always clean and looking a little dressed up. John had no manners. Tommy had a few too many. Two married men whose wives wouldn't have them. Men without a source of income. They were trouble for sure.

Louisa Marsden's front door looked almost directly toward Vail's cabin, which was in a hollow behind the trees at the center of this photo.

The Mosses were one of the founding families of Jefferson County, and Weaver knew a whole herd of them, certainly too many to keep track of who was kin to whom. They were fine folks, but like all families, sometimes there are branches of the tree that take a different shape. Tommy Moss was one of those branches.

The more Weaver thought about it, the better he liked the idea of John Marsden as a suspect. Now he had two angles to work in the case, two sides to play against one another. Maybe it wasn't Mack, but John and Allen Marsden who were guilty of the recent crime spree. Or maybe Mack had crossed the boundaries of family fidelity and recruited his bastard cousins into his gang. Maybe one side was hog thieves and the other side money thieves, arsonists, and murderers. And whether John and Allen were guilty of any crimes or not, they might be rough enough customers that they wouldn't be afraid to testify against Mack.

Then there was Tommy Moss. Was he involved? Weaver reached in his desk and pulled out his list of Vail's debtors. There he was, Thomas H. Moss, owing $20. Could that little debt have been reason enough to murder Vail? Then Weaver smiled, thinking that if he played his cards right, the estranged wives might be willing to tell all sorts of tales against their husbands.

Weaver's visit to Louisa Marsden's house only told him that Millie and Bessie were fed up with their husbands, but not why. The visit to Moss's cabin told him only that Thomas and John were no housekeepers.

Tommy had not a penny to pay the debt to Vail's estate, so Weaver marked him down as a loss. He didn't even bother chasing over to Sulphur Springs, where Allen and Elizabeth had moved. But at least now all those people, the "other Marsdens," knew he was looking at them. That's how things stood in the frozen winter of 1882.

Everything was in slow motion. Snows came and turned to slush, along with one ice storm that lasted six days. The men chopped wood while the women trudged to the smokehouse with a hatchet to chop chunks off the pork sides. Fires burned and soups simmered constantly. Everything went into the soup, from pork bones to dandelion greens, dried peas and corn, the end of the barley, and the last shriveled up carrot. Children would bundle up to feed the animals, then come in and snuggle under quilts. It was the cozy time of year when some of the best family memories were made. But it was hard, and it sure got old.

Chapter Eleven
A Big Mistake

Finally, spring arrived, and people got out and got busy. Farmers planted crops and brooded their baby chicks, wives opened their houses and aired out the linens, and the roads began to fill with craftsmen taking their wares to market. There were baskets, woven from last year's willows and reeds. Barrels, benches, and chairs that had been fashioned during the dark months in cold, gray barns. Tools that were formed in the welcome warmth of the forging fire.

When they could find a couple of dry days in a row between the chilly rains, families would turn over the garden. They'd pull weeds and with a little luck find a few overlooked potatoes that spent the winter underground. Then, with prayers for divine help, they'd plant the first seeds of turnips and spinach. On the windowsills they started trays of cabbage seedlings to be set out in a few weeks. Farmers relaxed a little, seeing the pregnant sows, cows, and mares, and the winter-born piglets, calves, and foals that had survived winter's sting. It was the time of hope, new life, and taking deep breaths.

Saturday night there was a social over in Moss Hollow. Thomas and Eliza Moss had hosted the gathering for years, and even after Thomas passed, one or another of the Mosses continued the tradition.

People came from throughout Sandy Valley to hear Thomas's grandsons play. Thomas Hart Benton Moss, called Bent, was a state fiddling champion. Bent was a former constable and sheriff, and one of the most colorful characters anyone knew. When he found out he couldn't

Thomas and Eliza Smirl Moss, friends or relatives of most of the major characters in this story. Courtesy of Nancy Moss Hollingsworth.

register to vote in Missouri because he refused to take the state's oath of allegiance to the Union, he went all the way to Arkansas to register to vote for president in 1864. Unlike most of the men, Bent wore his hair flowing over his collar. More than an affectation, the hair covered a disfiguring wound to his ear. When children saw him they loved to run up and say, "Show us your ear," which brought on his story about how the ear was bitten off in a fight with Jesse James. Then with a swoop of his hand he displayed the malformed appendage, making the little ones scream and run away, pursued by their own gales of laughter.

Bent and his family lived a quiet, citified life above the jewelry store where he clerked in Sulphur Springs. But he was supremely happy when he could get back out to Moss Hollow, smell the hay in the barn and the clover in the field. At the socials, he'd make the music ring with his brothers Frank and George Washington Moss on guitar, fiddle, dulcimer, banjo, or mandolin. Whatever was handy, they could play it. The yard would be packed with wagons, buggies, and horses either hobbled or tied. Men gathered in their groups and women in theirs. There would be a bowl of apple cider or blackberry punch, along with cake, pie, and ginger snaps. One of the men was bound to have a bottle of corn in his back pocket, which he was more than glad to share, out of sight of the Hensleys of course.

The music was a sweet change from the draining workweek. These were women who had a fire in the stove, with bacon and eggs in the skillet, long before the sun peered over the eastern hills. When they finished sweeping and washing, there was sewing, canning, and always the next meal to prepare. Their reward was a loving family who sat down with familiar smiles to savor biscuits with cinnamon apple butter. For the men, every day was a stew of sweat, drudgery, and danger, mingled with equal parts patience, worry, and hope.

Then at last, when a social came around, they could put on homemade calico dresses and clean overalls, leave the demands of home and work behind, and catch up on the latest news. What sweet relief it was, to have a little time to relax together, see people they rarely saw, and touch the blessed reassurance that life was being well lived in their little corner of the world. "Look how big you're getting," the children would endure for the millionth time, and "You remember me, don't you?" For the men, it was crops, livestock, and tools. For the women, recipes, what was ripe in the garden, and who was pregnant again.

Sweet melodies like "Aura Lee" and "I'll Take You Home Again, Kathleen," would mingle with the more danceable "Grandfather's Clock" and the foot-stomping "Turkey in the Straw" and "Buffalo Gals." They would scoot back the furniture and roll up the rugs so there was plenty of room to dance. It was considered best to omit "Dixie" and "Battle Hymn of the Republic," even if someone requested them. It had taken a long time to heal the divisions, back when the Mosses and Hensleys both furnished sons to both sides of the Civil

War. Even in those bloody years, they reluctantly continued to attend Sandy Baptist together, satisfying their different loyalties by sitting on opposite sides of the aisle. Now, this was a new era, they were working for something different, and they shared an unspoken agreement to move on.

Of course spring also meant the gang of bandits was on the move again. Four Chester White hogs disappeared from the farm of C. Thomas Horine, and then five from another farm.

With accusations flying and none of the gang in jail, paranoia spread anew, as if it had never been interrupted by the winter freeze. If people weren't afraid to tell what they knew, they were afraid of telling the wrong person. If they weren't afraid for themselves, they were afraid for their loved ones. Dorsey Hensley decided he knew too much, so it was a good time to take off for the gold fields of Faulk County, Dakota. When he returned to Missouri, it would be to another county. Even the *Post-Dispatch* up in St. Louis was saying that people who had livestock stolen were afraid to press for a conviction, "lest the gang destroy their homes and property."

One person who wasn't afraid to talk to anybody about anything was Claibourn Thomas Moss, a short man with a genuine smile and arms like tree trunks, the one who shared a shop with fellow blacksmith Fritz Koch. Claibourn, a much older half brother to Tommy Moss, had been down a rough road, leaving him possessed of a tough hide, but with a genteel manner that endeared him to his kinfolk and friends. After his first wife died, he married his second cousin, Bertha Hensley, and within a few years she'd given birth to two daughters. Unfortunately, though, the delivery of the second child took Bertha's life in 1880, leaving Claibourn with two infant girls and a broken spirit.

Claibourn was a carpenter, farmer, and blacksmith. He seemed to be clever enough to figure out how to do anything. Unfortunately, that left him a jack of many trades, but master of none. With wood and nails or hammer and steel, he could work miracles. They said he could make

The Sandy blacksmith shop of Claibourn Thomas Moss and Fritz Koch. This photo shows it restored after the arsonist's attack.

a wagon wheel with a butter knife and a chunk of hickory firewood, yet the great wheel of life seemed to conspire against him. As much as he loved his daughters and wanted to give them the upbringing they deserved, Claibourn simply didn't have the resources of time or knowledge to be a proper father to them. The bonds of the Hensley family once again proved strong. Bertha's parents, Pauline and William Hutson Hensley, though aged fifty-seven and sixty, with their own children grown, kindly took Claibourn's two little girls into their home.

Every man in the area came into the blacksmith shop Claibourn shared with Fritz Koch at one time or another. They didn't even need a reason. It was a place for business, as well as for socializing and catching up on the news. It was both a stage for bragging and an alcove for whispered conversations. A man with such a business hears things, including things about who stole which hogs. Claibourn was livid about the arson fires, first Leander, then Fleming, then the trunk being dragged out of William's house. His girls were living in that house! "Everybody says Mack's behind the trouble," he said. "But I tell you it's

John Marsden. And the minute they get him in jail, I'll testify to everything I know."

Three years before, when Bertha died, Claibourn sold the farm in Moss Hollow and never owned property again. There was nothing to hold him in the hollow, and he wanted to be nearer his girls in the Hensley home. He wanted to be near the bridge, his blacksmithing shop, and his cousin Clay, who was married to Priscilla Marsden. First he boarded in the home of the Nichols family, who rented from Leander Hensley. Then, to be sure nobody got tired of him, he moved from one family member's home to another over the years. So Claibourn had no home of his own, but he did have a blacksmith shop. That's how the shop came to be John Marsden's target.

It didn't take long for Claibourn's promise to testify to make its way to John Marsden's ears. John wasn't the kind of man who could stand up and hash out problems face to face. He was an undercover man, a back door man, the kind who does his defiling work, then scurries away like a rat along a riverfront drainpipe. No, he couldn't stand up to Samuel or any of them. But he knew how to keep the mouths of his accusers closed, one way or another. In his twisted logic, he planned an attack that would keep Claibourn's mouth shut, and would continue to keep Mack and Allie quiet. The message was, "If you say anything about where I got the hogs, bad things are going to happen to your side of the family." And one cool night in the middle of March he delivered his message with a can of coal oil and a match.

It was late Sunday, March 15, 1883, long after everybody had passed by the shop, headed home after evening services at Sandy Baptist, and long after good folks were in bed. Claibourn and Koch had not worked that Lord's Day, as was the custom, so there had been no fire in the forge, and no lanterns lit. That's how they knew without a doubt that it was arson when the charred ruins were discovered the next morning. Nobody even saw the blaze. It just burned itself out, leaving the shop a complete loss. Poor Koch was caught in the Marsden-Hensley family crossfire. He and Claibourn had no insurance, and besides losing the building and a stock of wagon parts, all their tools were in the shop. Oak handles were burned out, and all the hammers, saws, axes, chisels, and other steel tools had lost their temper. The loss was devastating, the attempt at intimidation was obvious, and tempers exploded.

After every other fire, John made sure rumors were abroad in the community that it was Mack's work. It was easy to spread that gossip. A word to the right people was all it took, and they were off talking about how Mack was behind the deadly scare tactics. But there was no way to hang the Claibourn Moss fire on Mack. Mack had no reason to set that fire, and besides, Claibourn was one of Samuel's dearest old friends. No, John Marsden went too far into the Marsden backyard, and from that time on, it was clear to everyone that Mack was not the one who was out in the darkness with a can of coal oil.

Two weeks later, on a clear, warm night the last week of March, in one brazen raid, eleven fine, mixed-breed white hogs disappeared from the farm of William Plass, who lived south of Antonia. That was a big bunch of hogs and it was a long way to drive them to a buyer. At last, the gang might have made the mistake that would hang them.

It was unfortunate timing for Prosecutor James Green, who was looking forward to marrying attractive nineteen-year-old Essie Tetley on March 28. He paced, mumbled to himself, and had repeated conversations with Weaver, but always had to get back to Essie and the wedding plans. Troubling as the latest robberies were to James, Essie didn't want to hear about it. She was a young bride, and like any young bride, had one thing on her mind, a beautiful, picture-perfect wedding. James had to smile, say, "Yes, dear," and let the local justices take care of anything that came up while he was on his honeymoon. The thefts were on Weaver's plate.

Chapter Twelve
Eleven Fine White Hogs

William Plass was a stout, hardheaded, and red-faced German, self-sufficient, resourceful, and not about to let any grass grow under his feet waiting for Weaver, Green, or anybody else to find out who stole his hogs. Eleven hogs and a couple of men make a lot of tracks, so Plass followed them through the woods and saw that they headed up the Lemay Ferry Road north. Once he knew their direction, he went back home, saddled his horse, and rode quickly into the town of Carondelet, muttering in German all the way. All he had to do was start asking, and sure enough, a personal friend who had bought many of his hogs before, meat processor Jacob Hoffman, said yes, he bought a bunch of prime white hogs off Mack Marsden that very day. He picked up the spindle on the counter and thumbed through the tickets impaled there until he found the right one. Eleven white hogs for $125 to Matthew Marsden. Hoffman pulled it out of the stack and waved it above his head like a banner as the two men walked around to the pens. Walking quickly between the pens, casting his gaze right and left, Plass stopped suddenly, pointing and talking loudly in German, as happy as he was angry to see his hogs safe and sound.

The two men went to the local constable together and reported what had happened. The sympathetic constable couldn't arrest Mack in Jefferson County, he explained. "Now, if he comes back to St. Louis County…." "Don't worry," said Hoffman, "he'll be back. He's a stock trader who comes up the road regularly, and we'll fetch you the next time he shows up." Plass slept soundly at home that night, woke up excited, and went to Hillsboro to swear out a warrant so Mack could be brought to Hillsboro as soon as he was caught.

They didn't have to wait long. A few days later, Mack brought the wagon to Carondelet to wait for Big Allie, who was driving a herd of hogs up to market. Mack tied Coal in front of Jacob Hoffman's packing plant, yawned, and stretched himself before sidling over to the boardwalk. As usual, he and Allie would probably stop at one of their haunts, a combination hotel, livery, and tavern. After all, it was over twenty miles to home, and St. Louis beer was always cold. Of course staying the night was always an option. They could pay ten cents for a cot and stable the horse, all right there. He eased into one of the chairs, tipped it back against the wall, pushed his hat over his eyes, and settled in for a little snooze.

A half hour later his nap was interrupted by his name being spoken as a question, "Matthew Marsden?" Peeking out from under his hat, Mack saw the constable no more than two strides away, a big badge on his coat pocket and a double-action pistol in his hand, inches from Mack's chest.

Hoffman had seen him drive into town, and kept an eye on him while an employee ran to fetch the cop. "That's him," Hoffman chattered. "He's the one who sold me Plass's hogs." "I'll handle this, Jacob," the constable said nervously, eager to play his part in this important case. After all, Mack's reputation had grown as the report about the Plass pigs circulated. Now this constable, who had never done anything more exciting than evict a squatter from a shanty, had a real desperado in his sights.

Mack looked absolutely surprised when the lawman asked him about the white hogs. Of course, Mack said, I sold those hogs to Hoffman. But I didn't steal them. I bought them fair and square off another man. "Well, if you've got a bill of sale for them, you should be in the clear," the officer advised. Mack didn't respond. Who was it, the accusers wanted to know. Who did you buy them from? Mack wouldn't answer that question, saying he didn't want to be guilty of getting another man in trouble. Even more important than his loyalty was the fact that he living with John Marsden's threats in his head for over a year, and didn't want to speak his name.

Mack explained to the constable that he was away from home, and of course he didn't have the bill for last week's sale. The constable shook his head, said he had no choice but to book him on the warrant, and Mack would have his chance to produce the bill of sale later. Then he escorted Mack off to the Carondelet calaboose at gunpoint.

The hapless Big Allie had no way of knowing what was happening to Mack. He and Mack's uncle, Jesse Gabriel Johnston, had bypassed Hoffman's place earlier in the day with their little herd of four hogs, hoping to get a little more money for them closer to St. Louis. Then when they returned to the meeting place, Hoffman's, and found the wagon but no Mack, they inquired and found out about the arrest. It was a long drive home, carrying the disturbing news to the family.

Meanwhile Sheriff Weaver had been dealing with the news that another bunch of four hogs had been stolen from farmer Horine. He was just recovering from the pain of kicking his desk when the news came of Mack's arrest in Carondelet. He threw up his hands. There he was, starting to consider John Marsden as a hog thief, and Mack goes and gets himself arrested for stealing hogs. Maybe they're both guilty, he thought. Or maybe neither is.

Rather than fetch Mack from Carondelet himself, he played one of his hold cards, Constable Tom Frazier. He was the thirty-three-year-old son of Rev. Sullivan Frazier, one of the pastors who pioneered Sandy Baptist Church with the Hensleys and other families. The reverend and Richard Marsden married sisters from the Shelton family, and "Sull" was one of Samuel Marsden's best friends. Their sons Tom and Mack grew up together in church, in school, and in the Sandy Creek shallows, so the sheriff thought Deputy Tom might learn some-

Rev. Sullivan Frazier, a founder of Sandy Baptist Church whose sons were among Sheriff Weaver's most trusted deputies.

thing from Mack. More than that, it demonstrated Weaver's faith in Mack. If Weaver thought Mack was a dangerous man, he'd have gone himself.

Tom and his brother Lawson saddled up and rode to Victoria, where they hopped the train for Carondelet. They started out excited and purposeful, but during the train ride they had plenty of time to think about what could go wrong. There were people who wanted Mack out of the way. If Weaver's theory about Yerger's murder was right, Mack's enemies would stop at nothing to rub him out, and a couple of amateur deputies better not be standing in the way.

At the St. Louis jail they signed Mack out, changed one set of handcuffs and leg irons for another, and went straight back to the depot. When they boarded, the sun was just dipping below the horizon under a violet sky, skidded with clouds. The young deputies knew the train was getting them to Victoria an hour after sundown, and their imaginations were beginning to take a toll on them. Having Mack seated beside them on the train was bad enough, and they had no intention of travel-

Top: Victoria train depot. Bottom: The Victoria Hotel and the livery, with the railroad tracks running between them.

Cornelius Marsden, son of Richard and Elizabeth Shelton Marsden. Richard owned the hack line, and Cornelius drove four trips daily from Hillsboro to the Victoria depot.

ing three miles up to Hillsboro in the dark. So the three of them got off the train, looked into the night in every direction, and seeing nothing but inky blackness, walked across the street to the Victoria hotel. A panther's eerie scream came from a ridge far to the south, and Lawson noted how he hadn't heard one in a long time. Mack commented that it was all the people moving in. The panthers had to move out. Then the only sound was the dragging of chains as Mack shuffled his manacled feet between his guards. They got a room, and Tom and Lawson took turns sitting awake in the chair, while the other slept beside their chained friend and prisoner.

When the welcome dawn appeared, Cornelius Marsden pulled up in the hack. Richard Marsden owned the hack line, and his son, Mack's cousin, operated the business, making four round trips daily from the train station to the county seat. The men exchanged greetings, happy to see each other, but aware of their grim circumstances. The prisoner and his escorts climbed aboard, but nobody else at the depot was willing to

The Jefferson County Jail at Hillsboro, with the sheriff's office and quarters upstairs, and the cells below.

ride with the infamous Mack. The other waiting passengers said they would just wait for the hack's next trip.

After all that, the ride was uneventful. Mack got safely locked up in the Hillsboro jail, and it wasn't long before Samuel rode into town. Leading the black Fox Trotter, he went straight around the courthouse to the jail, mortified and with no shadow of doubt that his son was innocent. As he approached the stout brick building, he thought about how he knew all the county leaders who planned and built this jail. The courthouse too. That was when his Mack was sixteen, and Samuel never dreamed that his boy would be locked up there.

The six cells were on the first floor, with the sheriff's office and quarters above. There was a single steel door to the jail area, and the windows were all hidden inside a twelve-foot-high brick wall. Samuel climbed the weathered stairs to Weaver's office, coldly stated that he'd come to get his son, and together they walked back down to Mack's cell. Weaver unlocked the steel door, but let Samuel go in alone and hear his son's story about buying the hogs. You got a bill of sale, didn't you, the father asked, confident in his son's business experience. Raising one eyebrow, Mack adamantly reassured his father. Of course he got a bill of sale. He made a deal for the hogs with a down payment, and the rest to be settled after he sold them. It should have been quick and easy, and after all, he got the hogs from someone he knew. Samuel shook his head. He knew it.

"It was John Marsden, wasn't it?" he asked. Mack nodded.

Samuel thought for a moment, then said it would be smart to leave John's name out of it for now. Samuel was afraid of what that bunch would do in retaliation. Mack agreed that for the time being, it was smart not naming John. He just wanted to go about his business. In any case, Mack could produce the bill of sale with John's signature if he needed it to clear himself. But for now, they would let the law solve its own cases. Samuel put up Mack's $1,000 bond, and he walked free.

Once again, Mack's brazen behavior was one of his best defenses. On the way out of the jail, Samuel asked Weaver if he really thought a man would steal that big bunch of white hogs, sell them at the nearest town, then go back there a couple of days later and wait to be arrested. The man you want is the one who sold him the hogs. Weaver studied his shoe tops. He knew Samuel was right. And I know you think he was involved with the Vail killing, Sam went on. He walked down the road from his house to Vail's, then back home, speaking to neighbors. Any fool could see that he wasn't walking home from killing someone. Weaver nodded and had to admit that Samuel made a good point.

Chapter Thirteen
Every Man for Himself

Walking out to their horses, Mack smiled and asked his father if he was kin to everybody in the county. "That's what Weaver asked me," he said, with a hint of a smile. "Everybody tells him they're kin to me, and most of them say it's by both blood and marriage." He was sorry for the trouble he was causing his father and hoped the conversation would lighten the burden just a little.

Samuel was glad to share the humor with him and confirmed that yes, the bloodlines of Marsden, Moss, Hensley, King, Johnston, and Thomas were a spiderweb that seemed to get more dense as years went by. "And your family will stick by you through thick and thin," Samuel stated flatly. "Of course there are exceptions to that rule," he said, raising an eyebrow. Mack understood the warning carried by that remark.

They had to push past the reporter outside the jail, fairly salivating to cover Mack's arrest, which reminded Samuel that he wanted a word with the editor of the newspaper. He had been there before to declare his son's innocence and tell them he didn't like the way they wrote about Mack. The paper was right around the corner from Main Street as they turned to go home, and it was worth stopping in to remind them again that they should leave Mack's name out of all this trouble. The two men reined up at the office of *The Democrat* and Samuel went in while Mack waited outside.

Newspapers of that era had a public service chip on their shoulder, and spoke freely on behalf of whatever the editor considered the best

Main Street, with the newspaper office on the Hillsboro-Victoria Road over the hill.

interest of the community. Cases were frequently tried in the press long before they came to trial. Candidates for office were lifted on newsprint shoulders. Reputations were made and decimated in the space of a paragraph. With that crusading approach, Mack's name had been associated freely with the Vail murder. When Samuel came in the first time to complain, owner, publisher, and editor R. W. McMullin was sensitive to the old man's plea and promised to treat Mack more fairly. But he was an establishment man who somehow managed to enhance his status by talking out of both sides of his mouth, both in person and in his newspaper. McMullin was one of those men who felt himself entitled, partly because his father was one of the earlier settlers in that area in 1805. R. W. thought everybody's business was his business, which, to some extent, is true for every journalist. But McMullin's newspaper became a natural extension of that belief and his unbounded ego. He was a Mason, and a former county clerk, who had enlisted in the Union army. Though health problems cut his military career short at three months, he was proud to say he was a veteran.

R. W. McMullin, publisher and editor of The Democrat.

The publisher greeted Samuel warmly, but he knew it wasn't going to be a happy visit. Samuel stated his case and left with McMullin's promise to be fair, but that didn't keep Mack's name out of the paper. In fact, the very next edition of *The Democrat* would offer this about whispered accusations in the neighborhood:

> They would take you to one side, and after extorting a promise of secrecy, whisper in your ear accounts of how crimes had been traced to Mack Marsden's door.

It would say Mack was "suspicioned" of Vail's murder, then Yerger's. It would go on to say others had been associated with various crimes, "but Mack is always spoken of as the leader." Then, presumably in deference to Samuel's protests:

> We do not pretend to know who the guilty party is; our only interest in the matter is that of the general public, to have the guilty party punished.... Marsden has never been convicted of any of the crimes of which he is accused, and at all times as-

> serts his ability to prove his innocence. His father and uncle, his bondsmen, are old citizens of the county, and men against whose good character there has never been as much as a whisper, so far as we know.

On the way home, Mack and Samuel had time to think about the situation. When Mack said it looked like Tommy Moss was in on it too, Samuel dropped his gaze to the road passing below them. He loved the Moss family so much, and they'd been so good to them. He again begged his son to keep quiet. "Please don't testify against them."

Meanwhile, farmer Horine, whose hogs were stolen the week before, hearing that Plass recovered his hogs, headed up Lemay Ferry Road in the hope of finding his own. They weren't at the same place where Plass found his, so Horine kept going. At last, at a south St. Louis butcher, he identified two of his hogs still alive in a pen. There were four of them, he told the butcher, who clearly remembered buying the herd of nine, including these two and two more just like them from a local man, Landsdoy. "We don't get many like this," he said.

Landsdoy did everything by the letter of the law. When he heard about the Plass hogs showing up at Hoffman's, he reported to the police that he bought nine from another Jefferson County man, a big man named Allie Hensley. That just happened to be the same day Mack was arrested while waiting for Big Allie, but of course at that time, the law wasn't looking for Allie.

Landsdoy kept the hogs a few more days, checked with the police, and found that nobody showed up to report them stolen. Relieved, he sold them to the butcher. Fortunately for Horine, he came looking for his hogs just in time to identify the remaining two. Better late than never. Irate and hungry to see the thieves punished, Horine hurried down to Hillsboro, knocked on Weaver's door, and reported that Allie Hensley had sold his stolen hogs in St. Louis.

"Allie sold them," Weaver echoed. "Allie." Then to himself, "And Mack was arrested, sitting there with his wagon."

That's when Weaver saw how they worked it. He stood up, pumped Horine's hand, and thanked him. It was the first time anybody had seen the sheriff smile in months. It all made sense now. The gang was using Mack and Allie as their stock traders. Mack and Big Allie never stole the hogs, but bought them from someone who did, then sold them up the road.

Weaver was getting more excited. Drovers worked on foot, and usually someone brought a horse or wagon for the return trip. So either Mack or Allie would drive the hogs to market, and then the other one would bring him home in the wagon. The operation started with just the two of them. Then as the size of the herds increased, they needed another drover. "That's where his Uncle Jesse came in. He helped drive the hogs." By that time Weaver was fairly hollering at Horine.

A few days before, Weaver said, he was talking to farmer Michael Clover, who seemed to know more than he was telling. "Look," Weaver told him, "you have nothing to fear. If you tell me what you know, we'll have them in jail before sundown." Reluctantly, Clover revealed that he had seen Mack with Jesse, out in Bechler's field, near Plass's farm, the night the hogs were stolen. Of course at the time Clover didn't know Plass's hogs were going to be stolen. But now that he knew, he reckoned it was Mack and Jesse who stole them.

No, Weaver explained to Horine. They weren't there to steal them. Mack was there to buy them from the ones who did the stealing. Jesse was just there as a drover.

"It all fits. You see?" he asked Horine. "That was eleven hogs, and Mack needed Jesse to help him drive that many to market. And the next week, it was nine more, including yours, and Big Allie drove them, again with Jesse's help."

Horine was trying to keep up.

So Mack was a stock trader, just as he claimed, and he dealt in plenty of legal sales. But now Weaver also knew Mack was trading in stolen livestock. Horine nodded, trying to take it all in. There's a gang of rustlers, and they've been dealing the stock off to Mack as quick as they could. Thinking out loud, the sheriff said, "The night they stole the Plass hogs, they had Mack and Jesse waiting over by Bechler's, and sold the hogs to them within the hour."

But Weaver still didn't know who was doing the stealing. By that time, Weaver was wearing a hole in the floor of his office, pacing, waving a pencil at Horine as each revelation came to him. Horine watched in wide-eyed astonishment, wondering what Weaver was going to figure out next, and what he'd do about it.

"It's the others. They're the ones who set the fires, and that's how they kept Mack and Allie quiet. See, Mack's wife is a Hensley," Weaver said, wagging the pencil violently. "Every time they set a fire at a Hensley house, it scared Mack that they'd do even worse. They wouldn't let him quit.

"Of course, he should have come to me," the sheriff continued, looking to Horine for agreement. Horine nodded. "But who can blame him!" Weaver concluded. Horine shrugged. Weaver tapped the pencil on his hand, and Horine wondered what was next. What was next was saying goodbye to Horine and getting Big Allie in jail.

The man Clover saw with Mack, the one who helped drive the hogs to Carondelet, was Jesse Gabriel Johnston. He was Mack's fifty-year-old uncle, a poor farmer, widowed, with five children, the youngest of whom was a teen. He was a friendly, talkative sort, with a ready sense of humor, and anything but a troublemaker. In fact, he was well respected because late in the Civil War he had gone to St. Louis to enlist in the 12th Missouri Volunteer Cavalry, a unit that saw plenty of action, including the bloody Battle of Nashville. He was a courageous man, loyal, and ready to help when needed.

After his wife and his father, County Judge Gabriel Jones Johnston, both died in 1880, things were hard for Jesse. But he continued hunting with his old friends and wearing his familiar weathered stovepipe hat. Most important, he was doing his best to make a home for his five children with no wife to help him. Samuel Marsden had been married to Jesse's sister before she died, and after his own loss, Jesse grew closer to Samuel, who had years of experience at being a widower. Jesse was also fond of Mack. When Mack needed help driving livestock to market, Uncle Jesse was handy, and he was eager to pick up a few extra dollars. Weaver had to shake his head. Jesse's daughter Julia was married to Phillip Moss, Tommy's uncle. Jesse's son Eugene was married to a Hensley. As far as the sheriff knew, Jesse got along with the Mosses, Hensleys, and everybody else just fine. Besides, he was hardly the livestock rustler type.

It was time for Weaver to go see Mack again. He went out to Mack's house, where he could work on him without Samuel or Prosecutor Green, or anyone else around. The clouds in the west made a beautiful sunset and he liked the ride up Lemay Ferry, along the sparkling creek. It was the kind of spring evening that spoke of the frozen past and the warming to come. A time that was good to be outdoors at any hour, when things change so fast it makes people want to watch so they don't miss anything. A time when everything's alive, and winter's sleep is a distant memory.

Weaver's knock brought Mack to the door, and the lawman reassured him that he just wanted to visit. Mack told Emma Jean not to worry, and stepped out. Sitting together on the quiet porch, away from Emma Jean, Lydia, Allie, and the babbling baby, Weaver could afford to indulge his sympathy for Mack. The guy was in over his boot tops with some relentless crooks, and the harder he struggled to free himself, the deeper he sank. The lawman and the suspect were adversaries, but right there on that porch, cloaked in the gathering darkness, they could almost forget the deadly game they played. But not quite. Weaver had work to do.

They lit their pipes. Mack settled into a rocker and the sheriff leaned back against the railing. "Mack," he said, "People don't understand you. You don't say much. You're so serious. People are afraid of you. Should they be?"

Mack cast his eyes up and the hint of a smile turned the corners of his mustache. Just for an instant Weaver saw those sad eyes lighten.

A warm, gentle rain began to fall on the cedar shingles above them. "Mack, I'm no Bible thumper, but my daddy was a preacher." He hesitated to see whether Mack was paying attention, then added, "And one thing I've learned from being a law man…it's never too late to come clean. Just like in the Bible."

He let that settle in while they smoked. Then he started in earnest, suggesting to Mack that he wasn't really afraid of the hog thieves. Was he? No answer. Then he patiently explained that Mack had to help the investigation. It looked like Mack stole those hogs. If it wasn't him, then Weaver had to know where he got them. Maybe the man Mack bought them from had bought them from someone else who stole them. That would be up to him to prove. But if Mack didn't want to stand trial for stealing pigs, he'd have to point the law to someone else.

Mack knew the sheriff was right. He thought, watching the pipe smoke disappear into the yellow light from the window, and at last muttered, "I refused at first."

"So are you saying they forced you to buy them?" Weaver returned.

"Every time I said no, they did something to my wife's family."

"And started rumors that it was all done on your orders," the sheriff added. "That's why the newspaper's after you. Everybody thinks that's all your dirty work."

Weaver looked into the rain, as if somewhere out there he could see a picture of how it all happened. After a minute it came to him and he turned back to the confessor. "You became too much of a problem and they had to get rid of you, didn't they?"

Mack's gaze turned distant. "That's why they fired Claibourn's shop," he said, "Because I said I wouldn't do another deal.

"I wasn't going to buy that last batch, those eleven highbred hogs from Plass. Those were too easy to track down, because there were so many, and they were so special." Looking back, Mack could see exactly what they were doing. "They were setting me up."

Weaver agreed. "They knew that big bunch of purebred hogs would be tracked back to you."

Mack hung his head.

Weaver saw now. "It was John Marsden," he offered. "Am I right?"

Mack nodded.

"Will you testify?"

"Yes," was the sad reply.

He went on to tell Weaver he didn't have near enough money to pay for those eleven prime hogs, so he gave John a nice sixteen-shot Winchester '73 rifle, the one he brought back from Dakota. John had always envied it, so he was a sucker when Mack offered it. As much as it meant to Mack personally, it was only worth about $15. Mack believed the hogs would sell for about $6 a hundredweight, so those two-hundred-pound hogs would yield $130. It was a deal too good to be true.

"Yeah," Weaver agreed, "That's the kind of deal a thief makes to get rid of his loot. Not the kind of deal a man would make if he really owned the hogs."

He thought, then observed, "You couldn't drive that many by yourself. Who helped you? Jesse? I know you were out with him that night." Mack looked over, surprised. How did Weaver know he was out with Jesse?

"And what about Allie," Weaver pushed. "How's he in it?" Mack hesitated. He had no loyalty to John Marsden, but he hated to name Jesse and Allen. Yes, Weaver had it pegged right. Uncle Jesse helped drive the Plass hogs to Carondelet. Big Allie brought the wagon to fetch them back home, as he'd done a hundred times before.

"But you don't want them," Mack insisted. "The man you're after is John Marsden. Believe me, you don't want Uncle Jesse and Allie."

He was right, of course. As far as the sheriff was concerned, Jesse and Allie could wait. Weaver had the break in the case he'd been waiting for, and turned to go.

"I knew he was stealing them," Mack said, as if he really didn't want the sheriff to go. It was a relief to finally be able to tell someone. Weaver turned, listening. "Sure as I'm sitting here I knew it. But we never discussed it," Mack added, as if that would make any difference to the law.

"Mack, when it comes to the law, you can't step a little bit over the line. Once you're over, you're all the way over."

"You don't know what it's been like," the quiet one said. "Emma Jean's been scared to death. She can't understand."

"And you can't tell her," Weaver completed the thought. Nodding his understanding, he tapped the ashes from his pipe, put it in his pocket, and stepped into the rain. He untied his slicker from the saddle, slipped it on, and as he mounted, said simply, "Watch your back."

Chapter Fourteen
"They Want Mack"

All the cards were in Sheriff Weaver's hand now. The next morning he rode out with deputies to arrest John Marsden, but John wasn't at the Moss Hollow cabin he used to share with Tommy Moss. They rode quickly over to Allen Marsden's home in Sulphur Springs, but he wasn't there either. Weaver told Allen that his younger brother needed to turn himself in. He was right, of course, and Allen sent the sheriff off with a promise that he'd see if he could find John.

The tired posse then rode all the way back, about five miles to Louisa's house, and John wasn't there either. In fact, the sheriff was surprised to find Tommy at Louisa's, where Bessie was letting him stay with her now and then. None of the family members knew where John could be found, they said, so the posse stopped by Mack's place to tell him they were going home empty-handed. As long as John wasn't in jail, he was a danger to Mack, and Weaver thought Mack deserved to be warned.

Mack went over and told his father that he'd revealed everything to Weaver, and Samuel's reaction was strong and immediate. They not only wanted John brought to justice, they wanted him brought in quickly, before he could pull any more intimidation raids on the family, and before he could ambush Mack. Samuel and Richard Marsden, some Mosses, and others were determined to raise a reward for John Marsden's arrest. On horses and mules, from farm to farm they went, soliciting pledges until the total bounty was $3,000. Word of the reward spread quickly and soon the county was crawling with men on foot, men on horseback, and men looking in public places, all asking questions, trying to ferret out John Marsden. Where could he hide?

Though none of Vail's money was ever traced, the men who took it left some tracks. The smartest thing they ever did was stash it away for four months, then turn it into real estate. They couldn't risk flashing a lot of money around Sandy, especially since it was widely known that Tommy never had two nickels to rub together. So he and John went over to Crystal City, where nobody knew them. There were so many little home sites being bought and sold there, nobody would notice. So there they each bought twenty acres. Tommy's parcel cost more because it had a little house on it.

Tommy tried to get Bessie Marsden to marry him for a couple of years, and she kept refusing because he was always broke. She said, "I don't need a man to help me starve to death." Then in '81, just a month after the Vail killing, he showed up with enough cash to impress her, along with a promise to buy her a farm before summer. She was convinced, and said, "I do." However, the cash ran out after a couple of months, and he wasn't bringing in enough to keep them fed, so she went back to her mother and sister-in-law Millie. When he bought the little farm in the spring, he took Bessie over to see the place, she swooned appropriately, and she even agreed to sign the remaining $85 loan with him. Yes, she was happy to be a property owner, but that didn't mean she was ready to move in with him and John. So he obediently returned her to Louisa's house.

As for Millie, she never gave a minute's thought to returning to John's arms, so John and Tommy ended up together in Tommy's little Crystal City house. It worked out well, because Sheriff Weaver didn't know about the house, and didn't know to look there for John.

After Weaver's posse visited Allen Marsden, he did exactly what Weaver figured he'd do. He wisely went to John and told him it wouldn't be long before Weaver found him. "You're either going to get arrested

Bessie and Tommy Moss.

or shot," he told his brother. "Besides, maybe I can collect the reward on you and we'll share that."

Of course John thought that was a terrible idea. Still, Allen was right that he couldn't hide forever. "What I need to do is turn state's evidence," John returned. "Mack's trying to slip free by hanging me. I'll confess, but they'll let me off in return for my testimony. All I have to do is hang it all on Mack. The Vail murder, Yerger's murder, everything."

They figured now that Weaver smelled blood, he'd be ready to spring at a chance to convict Mack. Yep, John and Allen agreed it was a pretty good plan. Or at least the best they could do under the circumstances.

On April 4, 1883, *The Decatur Daily Republican* in Illinois reported John's arrest, saying, "About thirty men brought Marsden in, all mounted and well armed." But it wasn't nearly that exciting. It was a Tuesday morning when John Marsden surrendered, accompanied by big brother Allen and his neighbor James Adrin Williams, who came along to enhance their chances of getting the $3,000 reward. They quietly rode into Hillsboro, tied their horses at the jail, and John reported to the sheriff, posturing himself as an accomplice to Mack's evil leadership. They made the sheriff promise not to tell anyone, especially the newspaper, who brought him in. Williams signed a marker for the reward, and he and Allen lit out for home.

Interesting, Weaver thought, John just rode into town as plain as you please. He and Allen carried rifles across their saddles, yes, but it didn't look like they were afraid of Mack or anyone else. In the sheriff's mind, if John wasn't afraid, that meant John was the one everyone else should fear.

Prosecutor Green arrived at the jail ready to question John, and found a sheriff who could hardly wait to tell all he'd learned in the last few days. John was the busiest man in Missouri, Weaver told him. He's figuring all of the angles and playing both ends against the middle.

Green raised an eyebrow. Weaver laid out the whole thing. John stole the livestock and sold it to Mack. Then Mack wanted out, and John wouldn't let him quit. To keep him in it, and keep him quiet, he committed arson against Mack's in-laws.

Green was listening. "Then why does everyone think Mack's the leader?" he asked.

"That was what kept John so busy," Weaver explained. "Every time they made a move, John told people it was Mack's work. And he said Mack would get revenge on anybody who went to the law. John has everybody in the county talking about what a bad man Mack Marsden is," Weaver laughed.

Green was unconvinced. "If all that's true," he said, "why hasn't it gone the other way? Why hasn't Mack been saying John's behind it?"

"First," Weaver said, "because Mack's not that kind of man. It was like pulling teeth to get him to tell me what's been going on. Besides that, because he's afraid for his wife's family."

James F. Green, Jefferson County prosecuting attorney.

He thought a moment and added, "After what happened to Yerger, who can blame him?"

He told Green that sooner or later Mack was going to go to the law. That's why John was scared of him, and that's why he set him up with those purebred hogs. It was too many, and they were too fine. John knew Mack and Big Allie would get caught with them, but they had to take them because of John's threats.

Weaver stood back, proud, and watched to see if all this was sinking in with Green. When there was no response, he added, "All you have to do is make a deal with Mack, let him off easy for his testimony against John."

He didn't react the way Weaver hoped. He didn't say a word. "We've got our man downstairs, James," Weaver prompted.

But Green balked. "They want Mack," he said.

"What?" Weaver blinked. "Who wants Mack? What do you mean?"

"McMullin, Edinger, J. T. Moss, all of them. There's talk of organizing what they call the Protection Society." Weaver's eyes widened. Such a vigilante bunch was the most dangerous thing a lawman could face. "They're not going to settle for John. Not without Mack's head too," Green explained, casting his eyes to the floor.

Weaver couldn't believe what he was hearing. John had done such a perfect job of painting Mack as the devil, nobody was going to believe that Mack was a victim in all this.

They chewed on it a while longer, these two men who'd been side by side trying to clean this thing up for two years. They talked about doing the right thing, and about pleasing the powers that be. They agreed the stealing was one thing, but they still needed to solve the murders too. When there was no more to say about it, they had a deputy bring John up to the office for questioning.

Weaver told John that they needed to know everything. "Who's behind it all? Mack says you sold him Plass's hogs, and you have to stand up to that charge."

John said he was ready to turn state's evidence and tell everything he knew. But he was afraid of Mack. Besides, he'd heard the talk about a vigilante committee forming, and the law had to protect him. Could they get him out of town? Could they get the charges against him dropped? Or get him pardoned? It wasn't just the gang he feared. He was afraid the people of the community would come in there and string him up. That's funny, Weaver thought to himself. But he was right. The people were so worked up, Weaver didn't blame John for being afraid he'd get lynched.

"Look, you don't want to get killed, and I don't want you killed," Weaver said. He confided that he would get John up to the jail in St. Louis where he would be safe. On the other hand, if John bailed out of jail, rather than go to St. Louis, he'd be on his own, and Weaver couldn't keep him out of danger.

John grunted his approval, and said he sure didn't want to be out until Mack and the others were behind bars again. Then he started his story. "It's Mack," he said. "He did everything. All I did was take this bunch of hogs from Plass and sell them to Mack. That's all. He made me steal those hogs. Threatened to kill me if I didn't do what he said." Weaver and Green were listening. "Mack stole everything else," he went on. "Him and Big Allie and Jesse Johnston."

"How much did he pay you for the Plass hogs?" Green led. He wanted to see if John's answer matched the information Mack gave. John said Mack gave him that fine sixteen-shot Winchester rifle he was carrying when he rode in. Weaver picked up the handsome piece and studied it. It was a Winchester Model 1873, just as Mack had said, in 44.40 caliber with a twenty-four-inch barrel. The magazine held fifteen, plus one in the chamber, making sixteen shots.

"Then after he sold the hogs he was supposed to come back and give me another $150 to leave the county," John said. "That was the deal, so when I left town, it would look like I stole the hogs and he'd be in the clear."

The stories were pretty close. Of course, Mack's story didn't include the promise of $150 in exchange for disappearing, but that was a small matter. John signed an affidavit about all he'd said, and when he was locked up again, Weaver turned to Green.

"You know he's lying, and Mack's telling the truth," the sheriff said.

But it made no difference. "You've got to bring Mack in," Green replied flatly. So Weaver sent Deputy Tom Frazier out once again to bring Mack back to jail charged with multiple thefts.

Later that night, John was sitting on his bunk in the first of the six cells when Weaver led Mack past him to the last cell on the other side. As a finishing touch, he let two reporters into the jail. Mack had no interest in talking to the reporters, especially to make accusations against John. Of course his silence worked against him, as usual. John, on the other hand, was thrilled to have the pulpit. Keep it short, Weaver threatened. John nodded and told the reporters, "The last gang of hogs, those taken from William Plass, those are the only ones I helped steal. Mack Marsden gave me a sixteen-shooter Winchester repeating rifle, and they were to give me $150 to leave, but have not done so yet."

Weaver hustled the reporters out the door of the jail, and made doubly sure everything was locked up tight, with both Frazier boys on guard. As he climbed the stairs to his rooms, the sheriff knew he was holding the belly of a rattlesnake. He just hoped he was right about which end was the head.

Chapter Fifteen
The Society Rides

On Friday night, April 6, 1883, 135 men gathered in a barn outside of Hillsboro. They came in wagons and on horseback, some alone, and some in groups of family or neighbors, from all around the northern part of the county. Nearly every livestock owner was there. Nearly every business owner and political figure. This was no spontaneous bunch of drunken riffraff. It was a well-planned collection of some of the leading citizens of the county.

The first part of the meeting didn't last long. The men all knew why they were there, and R. W. McMullin only got through about half his flowery and overindulgent speech before someone shouted, "Let's get on with it," and was echoed by the crowd. They formed the Jefferson County Mutual Protective Society, a euphemism for "vigilante committee."

It had become a common practice throughout the West, where towns sprang up literally overnight, and might not have a real, full-time lawman for years. Western states were supposed to have a U.S. marshal assigned to every district, but those men were generally too far away and too busy to be any immediate help. The frontier citizenry were independent thinkers who expected action. If the law wasn't getting the job done, which was most of the time, the citizens didn't hesitate to take the law into their own hands. The violence they brought with them was a threat to the guilty, but sometimes to the innocent as well. And more than one lawman came to his end when he got in the way of vigilantes.

McMullin had his plants in the audience, men ready to make predetermined motions to get the ball rolling in the right direction. McMullin was elected president and he appointed a committee to write articles for the group. He chose Mayor Edinger of Antonia, James Thomas Moss, and four other friends. Then a recess was taken while the writing was done, which really amounted to discussing articles that McMullin had prepared beforehand.

The entire group reconvened and acted with as much conviction as if it were a legal government body. The statement of purpose, demanding justice, was worded so that any reasonable person could hardly fail to agree, extolling the general fear in the community and a resolve to "stand by and protect" each other.

They adopted five resolutions, the last ensuring that McMullin would wield the gavel for a year. The first said they "deprecate illegal acts." Second, they resolved to help each other recover stolen property and bring criminals to trial and prosecution. Third, they promised to protect each other when serving as witnesses against criminals. The fourth resolution stated that if anyone was injured while asserting their lawful right to prosecute criminals, "the guilty party shall suffer."

Finally, they passed two items of business. The first was a statement that the hog stealing had to end. Second, that every member should go to DeSoto the next day for Mack's hearing. Everyone there, 135 men, signed the document.

The next morning, even the presence of the Society didn't explain the crowd in DeSoto. It was Saturday, and word had been spreading, so they came by horse and by the wagonload, hundreds of curious people from miles around, all to see the notorious Mack Marsden. The crimes ascribed to Marsden and his gang had taken place in the northern part of the county. So around DeSoto, fifteen miles south of the action, the legend, rumors, lies, threats, accusations, and exaggerations had grown to even greater proportions.

The train tracks leading out of Victoria.

Mack was to ride in about midday in the custody of Sheriff Weaver and appear at the office of Justice of the Peace Charles T. Rankin for a preliminary examination on the charge of grand larceny for stealing livestock. He also planned to ask for a change of venue. Public sentiment was so stirred up against him, Mack was going to claim, that he just couldn't get a fair trial in Jefferson County. He and Weaver had ridden from the Hillsboro jail, where Mack had been locked up for the past three weeks. They had a quiet ten-mile ride that morning, through the edge of tiny Victoria, past the hotel and the railroad station. From there the road ran alongside the railroad track, southwest to DeSoto.

DeSoto stretched out in a line facing east toward the brick buildings of the massive railroad maintenance shops, imposing themselves along the banks of Joachim Creek. The tracks and shops were part of the St. Louis, Iron Mountain & Southern line, the product of Justice Rankin's uncle Charles S. Rankin and former governor Thomas C. Fletcher. Well over 150 men found good, steady jobs there, so in just a few years the shops had made DeSoto the largest town in Jefferson County. It was already home to four hotels, a Masonic hall, a healthy complement of saloons, and other businesses along Main Street, which

A view of the DeSoto business district, taken from among the homes on the hill, with the train yard beyond, and the wooded hill opposite.

paralleled the tracks and the wide, rolling creek. To the west, the land rose sharply, sprinkled with houses big and small, giving the whole layout the appearance of an amphitheater, with the crowd watching the performance of the trains that came and went, while tools clanged, machines chugged, and engines belched day and night.

Onto the stage rode the star attraction, Mack Marsden, visible a mile away, cresting the hill beyond the roundhouse at the north end of town. The eager onlookers began to point and talk excitedly. "Look there. There he comes." But Mack and the sheriff weren't alone. No, five mounted men were silhouetted against the cloudless sky. They descended the hill, disappeared behind the shops, then emerged around the corner at the head of the street. It was a straight shot for five minutes, the horses walking easily, in full view of people lining the sidewalks. The crowd's chatter rose, then stilled to an awed silence. It was plain to see that Mack's escorts bristled with the cold steel barrels of

DeSoto, looking west.

rifles and shotguns. Nor did they try to hide the revolvers in their belts as they paraded down the street. The sheriff and the accused thief, on the glistening black Coal, rode side by side, trailed by Mack's father Samuel, brother Buzz, and uncle Richard Marsden.

It was insane, Samuel told Weaver, to take his son all the way to DeSoto without any deputies. There were desperate men out to get him. But Weaver was unconvinced. He said nothing was going to happen to them in broad daylight, and it was more important to leave his deputies guarding John Marsden back at the jail. So the father, brother, and uncle provided the escort themselves. They rode calm and steady, but glances cast left and right let all know that they were on their guard to see that Mack got safely where he was going.

When they came even with the depot they turned right on Easton and continued up the hill to the Rathbun Building. It was one of the oldest in town and provided offices, as well as a hall for town meetings.

The Rathbun Building on Easton Street in DeSoto, home of city meetings and the law office of Justice Charles T. Rankin.

The men tied their horses, entered the Rankin law office, and closed the door without saying a word or acknowledging their audience, leaving the crowd to its gossip. Buzz stood outside like a statue, his back to the law office door, a Springfield rifle cradled in the crook of his arm.

Rankin knew the men only by name, but everyone in the room was familiar with their respective families. Among his friends Rankin counted Cornelius Marsden, who ran the hack line that shuttled people to and from the train station at Victoria. And the Marsdens certainly knew about the record of Rankins in commerce and county government.

Justice Rankin shook hands all around. He wasn't threatened by the show of weapons, and understood the need to protect Mack. He explained the charges and offered to question Mack, saying if Mack could convince him there was a doubt, he might be able to drop the charges, at least until the grand jury heard the evidence. But Mack shook his head, waiving the examination. He knew John Marsden had accused him of the whole string of thefts and that the case against him looked bad. So he'd just as soon step over the justice's questions and get on with the trial, where he knew he could prove his innocence.

He just wanted Rankin to move the trial someplace else. Unfortunately, Mack had the idea, but not the legal wherewithal to make that happen. Rankin explained that such a move is called a change of venue,

Justice of the Peace Charles T. Rankin, who denied Mack's first change of venue request, and presided over the inquest into his murder.

and Mack needed a lawyer to argue for that. He should bring in witnesses, and the state had to have time to bring in witnesses too. Then Rankin could ask them all if they could be impartial jurors, and decide, based on what they answered.

Mack nodded, and could plainly see that he wasn't prepared for all that. He didn't even have a lawyer at that point. The Marsdens weren't people who needed lawyers, and they naïvely thought honesty alone would get them through the current trouble. Mack nodded and said he guessed it was worth asking, anyway. Samuel was mortified, and shook his head at the sorry state of affairs when a man has to have a lawyer when someone else is causing all the trouble. Rankin said what he could do was note in the record that Mack requested a change of venue and it was denied. That might help him if he made the request again later. Mack nodded again.

Then all Mack wanted was to be out on bond. I'm innocent, he said, and I shouldn't have to wait in jail for the trial. Rankin was sympathetic, but the charge called for a sizable bond, he explained. The Marsdens understood, and when his decision was $2,500, Samuel and Richard Marsden readily signed for it. With that, Mack was free to go, and Samuel returned his son's pocket pistol to him.

It had taken only a few minutes. The door opened and the Marsdens emerged silently into the sunlight, walking to their mounts. Mack was leading the way as they mounted and rode calmly, purposefully, back up the street, just the way they came in.

But the Marsdens had ridden blindly into the devil's own trap. The real proof of a conspiracy was in the place chosen for Mack to appear. Why would the court order the sheriff to bring a prisoner like Mack, who was both accused of violence and threatened with violence, on a ten-mile ride through open country, woodlands, hills, and creeks? Several justices, including squires Honey, Goff, and Thomas Williams, lived and worked within blocks of the Hillsboro jail, and any of them could have held the preliminary examination in Hillsboro. Besides, Mack had been in custody for three weeks, so why wait until a Saturday, knowing a huge crowd could gather? Clearly, the trip to DeSoto provided a chance for vigilantes to do what the law couldn't do. Mack was loose and vulnerable, in daylight, with a long ride home accompanied only by a handful of family members.

The posse had been up early, waiting in DeSoto, with pistols under their coats and rifles on their saddles, before Mack ever rode into town. Their plan hinged on what happened after Mack's hearing with Rankin. If he came out of the office still in Weaver's custody, the crowd would just have to watch them ride out and return to the Hillsboro jail. The society didn't want a face-to-face showdown with the sheriff. But they were hoping Mack would post bond and Weaver would stay behind.

Sure enough, Weaver leaned against Rankin's doorway watching Mack ride out with his family. He didn't want anything to happen to him while he was free, but he didn't want to be responsible for protecting him in his jail either. Weaver had heard rumors of the society meet-

The busy Main Street of DeSoto.

ing and the talk of a lynching. Mack sure wasn't snow white in all this, but he didn't deserve to be lynched. And John Marsden and the rest of the gang might be after Mack too, afraid he was going to testify against them. Just do your job, he told himself. Babysitting Mack Marsden ain't your job. Besides, it was the middle of the day, and vigilantes always did their dirtiest work under cover of the night. Weaver never dreamed that Mack was in any danger on the road back home.

When the vigilantes saw the Marsdens turn up Main Street without Weaver, that meant Mack was out on bond, and that's all they had to see. In the time it takes to tell it, hot heads were prevailing and voices were growing louder. Marsden had been the topic of conversation wherever men gathered over a glass of beer for the past week. People wanted to see the so-called desperado punished, as much for the pure excitement as for the sake of justice.

Some of the locals ran home to saddle up or arm themselves. But the leaders of the Society didn't wait for stragglers, or for those who had to argue with worried wives about whether they could go. No, like a pot boiling over, the mob was beyond restraint. Somebody already had a stout rope. The shouting subsided amid the thunder of hoofs, and thirty vigilantes rode out with vengeance in their eyes.

Chapter Sixteen
The Standoff

Mack and his three escorts had ridden out of the DeSoto basin, keeping their horses at an easy walk on the gravel-paved Victoria Road. They were eager to get back to their stomping grounds of Sandy Creek, but it was a long ride, so they weren't pushing it. The first half of the journey to Victoria was a series of three steep hills, and the last half a nice, level sweep along the Joachim Creek bottom. The men had traveled about two miles and were about to crest the second hill, when a casual glance over the shoulder revealed a mob topping the hill behind them. They didn't need words to tell them they'd better get a move on.

Meanwhile, standing on a DeSoto street corner, the tweed-suited reporter from the *St. Louis Globe-Democrat* straightened his necktie and smiled with satisfaction as he watched the crowd turn into a lynch mob. He had written three previous stories about Mack, and kept hoping for his amorphous legal troubles to turn into something big and fact-filled. The hearing with Rankin might not have been worth covering, except that all the way up in St. Louis he heard whispers about the vigilante plan, and he was drawn to the prospect of a sensational headline. Now, the impending noise and danger, the rebellious fervor of vigilante vengeance, with a heated pursuit and violent end to the criminal, were even better than the reporter expected for the day.

Vigilante justice, as much as it was detested by responsible community leaders, has always been the stuff of legends. There's little story in an acquittal, but the retelling of a mob hanging in the name of deserved punishment is the fuel for endless retellings and "I was there" bragging. So the reporter talked to some of the Protective Society members, and they all confirmed that if Mack rode out without the sheriff, he was going to swing that day. The moment the lynch mob rode out after Marsden, the reporter faced a dilemma. He had to either borrow a horse, saddle up, and ride with the vigilantes to witness their result, or run to the telegraph office and file his story. Being a writer, and not a range rider, he opted to go ahead with the story. He frantically scratched his notes, then ran to the telegraph office to put his big story on the wire, and it appeared in print the very next morning.

The Associated Press, organized in the mid-1800s, was already a vital force in American newsgathering by the time of Mack's legal entanglements. Stories spread on the wings of electricity. Newspaper journalism was beginning to taste its power. Reporters understood the value of speed and getting the story first, and knew well how sensationalism could build readership, not to mention the status of the one who did the reporting. It was on such journalism that the reputations of Billy the Kid, Jesse James, Wyatt Earp, and countless others were built. Dime novels, rife with descriptions of the Wild West, fueled the imaginations of plenty of reporters who dreamed of covering such colorful characters, and here, just a few miles south of St. Louis, a story about a good mob lynching was just what was needed. So it's no surprise that the facts were stretched long before Mack Marsden's neck was.

That explains the headline in *The New York Times*, "A Missouri Ruffian Lynched. Mack Marsden, Murderer and Thief, Dealt With by a Mob." Big-city readers must have thrilled at the account that followed of the lawless frontier savagery.

> Mack Marsden was hanged by a party of lynchers near DeSoto yesterday. They waited in a clump of woods until Marsden rode up in full view, and just at that instant five double-barreled shotguns were leveled at him with the command, "Throw up your hands." He needed no second bidding because in less time

> than it takes to tell it the DeSoto crowd galloped up in a way that plainly told a commander was there. Without any bandying of words a rider from the rear leaped from his horse and encircled Marsden's neck with a noose at the end of a long rope. He saw he was surrounded and attempted to parley, pleading innocence of the crimes charged upon him.

The article went on in great detail about the fifty-foot rope and exactly how high his feet were off the ground when he was strung up. It even said the lynch mob made sure he was dead, then rode off toward Sandy Creek.

But it was all a reporter's fancy, and the story was far from over. A very different, but no less exciting, scenario played out that day across the hills of Jefferson County.

Mack and the three men with him had no question about the cloud of dust raised by the dozens of riders closing in on them. The older Marsden men were scared, but resolute. The only question was how cool, fearless Mack would respond. One look in his steel eyes let them know he was mad as a hornet and ready for anything. The first thing to do was to try outrunning the mob and see how serious they were.

The four kicked their mounts up to a canter, and Mack was surely glad to be on his trusted Coal. While Mack was in jail, the family retrieved Coal from the sheriff's stable and took him home. Fortunately, when the trip to DeSoto came up, Samuel brought him along for Mack. Coal was not only sure-footed on such rocky roads, but he was absolutely tireless, and the Fox Trotter's easy gait made a smooth ride.

The Marsdens checked back over their shoulders to see if the crowd was losing heart. But another two miles passed with neither group relenting. They cantered across the wooden bridge and past the Victoria depot and hotel. Beyond it they could see the town, where Victoria residents were happily ignorant of the dangerous chase passing so near.

Suddenly, as if on signal, another dozen heavily armed riders came boiling out of the trees north of the village. They'd been waiting to block Mack and trap him for the pursuers. And in fact they were further proof of the well-planned vigilante conspiracy, because they were part of the news story filed by the reporter who wasn't even there. Somebody had told him the plan, so he reported the plan. What the reporter couldn't know is that the riders waiting in the trees would be surprised by the Marsdens' speed. Failing to block the way, they fell into the pursuing pack, bringing the total number of mounted men to almost fifty.

The Marsdens and the posse rode hard, back the same way Mack had come with the sheriff, up the Hillsboro-Victoria Road. The Marsden men were envisioning what lay ahead, a ride that was not easy under any circumstances, and was sure going to be tough while playing the prey to the predators behind them. The road rose steeply, then fell into one hollow after another. At one point the horses splashed into Cotter Creek, then across a little rise, then down through the creek again, their hooves clattering against the uneven stones. Mack's horsemanship was the equal of his Uncle Richard, and although none of them were accustomed to that kind of riding, they all rose to the need.

After three punishing miles they slowed down, with the Hillsboro cemetery on their right. Most of the way Coal had been in that gliding fox trot that was like a rocking chair for Mack, while the other horses had been alternating between gallop, canter, and trot, which was so hard on riders. Coal and Mack were still strong, but the others were heaving for breath. They checked behind them, again hoping the pursuers had given up on the hard ride. No such luck. They could see the dust and hear the pounding of dozens of horses.

Mack said he'd go on alone. "They're not after you," he told his family. "Coal and I can outdistance them." But the Marsden men's loyalty was stronger than their exhaustion, and they refused to leave his side. Again they kicked up the horses. The road ran outside of town, up the east side, but all those horses racing and the gravel flying behind Hurtgen's blacksmith shop and *The Democrat* newspaper office couldn't escape notice. People looked out too late to see the Marsdens, but in time to see the thundering herd on their heels.

Looking through the bridge, it can be seen that the approach from the south descends Fort Hill and turns to the right.

Then the riders were out into the country again, north up the Lemay Ferry Road. On the left was the creek, and field after field of new, green corn, inviting them to rest, to admire the birth of new spring life and the smell of rich bottom land. But on the right, Fort Hill rose two hundred feet, a sentinel holding them fast, reminding them that there was no retreat in any direction, only a desperate escape northward, ever north. The pounding hooves were unrelenting, as the posse pressed on the Marsdens. A mile fell, then another, then three more, then their home ground and the banks of familiar Sandy Creek were quickly approaching.

The water, deep with spring rains, swirled below the long, red, covered bridge as the Marsden horses clattered across. Just when they passed off the north end, Mack called to his family, and in an instant whirled Coal to face his tormentors.

Mack and his family in the standoff at the bridge. Drawing by Joe Johnston.

The approach to the bridge comes after a little rise, so as the posse, intent on its chase, came over the rise, they were looking slightly down at the roof of the bridge. It wasn't until the ones in front got to the bottom that they could see what waited on the other side. They jerked back hard on their reins, skidding to a stop, but the ones behind them were still riding hard, trying to funnel down into the bridge, resulting in a mass collision. The tangle of excited horses bumped together, snorting and jerking, turning the posse's attention from pursuit to settling their mounts.

Then all of them could look through the bridge and see the reason for the sudden halt. Samuel, Buzz, and Richard had all leveled their long guns. Mack laughed out loud at his nervous adversaries, his voice echoing through the wooden tunnel. Then he glared from beneath his hat and spoke as calmly as if they were chatting about the weather, but loudly enough for all to hear. "You boys have been mighty brave so far. The one who's the bravest, come on across."

There was a tense pause, then four of the leaders glanced at each other, and started over the bridge. The three behind Mack tensed and cocked their weapons. With a smooth sweep of his hand Mack skinned the nickel-plated .32 from his coat pocket and held it at eye level, glistening in the afternoon sun. "Cl-lick, bam! Cl-lick, bam!" The single action revolver cut the air with two shots over the posse leaders' heads, and they stopped dead still. Hard men exchanged hateful gazes, but the only sound was horses panting and leather squeaking under the weight of uneasy riders. Mack had them right where he wanted them. The only way to cross was one or two at a time, and they'd be coming right into those waiting gun barrels. The standoff lasted only a few seconds before all four dozen vigilantes resigned themselves to the fact that they had wasted a long ride. The ones in the back of the group peeled away, and the courage they had as a gang evaporated into individual frustration.

Riders headed out from both ends of the bridge, blood boiling. The four going northbound were relieved, but stern. Sure, up until now, Mack had never faced any proof of his guilt in any of the crimes. But neither had he been able to clearly establish his innocence. Now the law was calling his bluff, and there was nothing good in the cards for him. He faced the charges on the hog stealing. Some people were sure he murdered Vail and Yerger too. He was suspected in other fires, and probably in every other recent crime and more to come. All eyes were on him. Anyone, anywhere could turn on him. He was feared and hated. Every loyalty had to be bought by friendship, kinship, or threat. The men who rode beside him were the only ones he could truly trust.

The lynch mob's pursuit made news all the way to New London, Connecticut, where *The Day* reported it this way: "Mack Marsden's Case, THE TERROR OF SANDY CREEK A TERROR STILL. Faint-hearted Vigilantes put to Flight by a Fusilade – The Desperadoe's Clan Gathering."

There it was in print again, the "desperado" label that he would never again be able to shake.

On the other end of the bridge, the embarrassment was beyond measure. The mob was organized, empowered by community leaders, and rode with the adrenaline of justice in their veins, and still they cowered before the muzzle of Mack's pistol. They felt like fools. And that accounted for an ironic journalistic twist on the day's events. R. W. McMullin, self-righteous organizer of the Protective Society, was doubly embarrassed when he read the *St. Louis Globe-Democrat*'s report that Mack was lynched. He responded with a chest-beating piece in *The Democrat* saying the *Globe-Democrat* ran the lynching story in an effort to goad Jefferson County people to rise up and actually lynch Mack. He further said the St. Louis paper did that because it hated the people to its south and hoped to abuse them for their cruelty after they hanged Marsden. It was senseless.

As if that weren't ridiculous enough, the article allowed that a crowd did gather, but, "all but twenty or thirty" of them were stopped by the sheriff. The riders chased Mack and Allie, it said, which was ludicrous because Hensley was in jail at the time. The story made no mention of Samuel or anyone else with Mack. The facts were mangled, saying the crowd gave up after a few miles, and then the two fugitives went home to get their shotguns and returned to face their pursuers, after which both sides backed down.

McMullin was scrambling to save his own face, as well as the Protective Society's. He said he was sure the mob probably just wanted to scare Mack. Like the father of child who misbehaves in public, McMullin was proud of his carefully crafted Protective Society until they failed their first attempt at vigilante justice.

Chapter Seventeen
Tensions Rise

Unlocking the cell, Sheriff Weaver told John Marsden he was getting him out of town. John started rattling one question after another about where they were going and who was going to protect him on the way. Weaver was busy slipping the handcuffs on and didn't answer. With Mack and Allie free on bond, Weaver was plenty worried about his star witness. He didn't think Mack would try anything, but Mack had plenty of reason to shut John's mouth. And Mack wasn't the only worry. The Protective Society had been worked up enough to try lynching Mack, and since that proved to be too dangerous for them, Weaver figured it was entirely possible that they could turn their anger on John.

There had been no effort to hide the Protective Society. In fact, besides setting up the lynching of Mack Marsden, their first meeting was intended in part to be a bold show, a sort of public relations stunt aimed at putting the hog thieves, murderers, and arsonists on notice. McMullin, being not only the Protective Society's prime organizer, but also a crusading newspaper editor, wrote a detailed report of it in the following issue of *The Democrat*.

In the front-page article McMullin made it clear that the Protective Society was going to help people get past their fear of telling what they knew. If someone reported a crime to the sheriff, he had to launch an investigation, during which the witnesses were vulnerable. Like poor Joseph Yerger had been vulnerable. But the Protective Society was all about action, not investigation. The article said, "In case any member uncovered any evidence of crime and was afraid to divulge it to the proper authorities that the president of the association be designated as the proper person to receive such evidence and place it before the officers." In other words, if a member of the society heard something, he'd tell McMullin, and he'd see that the vigilantes did what was needed. Tucked away in the newspaper report was a chilling threat: "There will, probably, be other organizations soon, of not as public a character." Publishing all that made it clear that the society's work had the blessing of not only those who participated, but also those who turned their eyes away and let McMullin's upstanding bullies do their work.

Weaver didn't like it one bit, but he understood how they felt. They wanted someone to blame, and they wanted someone punished. But Weaver wasn't going to let John hang at the end of a lynch rope, and he wasn't going to let Mack Marsden ambush him. Or vice versa. No, to put an end to it all, John and Mack had to face each other in court. Anything less, and the case would be argued until the end of time.

With his Winchester tucked under his arm, Weaver handed John Marsden his hat and they stepped out of the jail into an unseasonably warm night. Still, being out in the fresh air was better than the unmoving, unchanging jail air. John looked up and down the street. Sure, he had Weaver's protection, but a man in handcuffs and leg irons just can't feel any too safe. Tom Frazier was on the seat of the wagon just beyond the glow of the gas streetlight behind the jail.

"I can't ride like this," John protested, holding out his handcuffs. Weaver told him that's the only way he'd ride, then rolled him up into the wagon bed beside Lawson Frazier, cradling his shotgun. Weaver climbed up beside Tom and they started for the Victoria depot. Rather than take the usual way, east up Main Street, they went west, to the spring, then swung south, making a wide circle to hit the road leading south outside of town.

It was only three miles to DeSoto, but that was more than enough for the lawmen. Riding at night was never safe under the best of circumstances, and it was even worse on this trip, a quarter-moon night, with men and horses all on edge. Tom let the horses pick their way along the road, hoping there wasn't a stumble, hoping neither of them spooked. The men listened, but heard only hooves and wheels clattering on the rocky dirt. They peered into the dark but saw only shapes.

Ambushers could have been waiting anywhere along the route, from the trees along the ridge to the banks of Cotter Creek. Still, the trip had to be made, and it was safer than doing it in the daylight. As they approached DeSoto they had to cross the bottomland, where the road ran through a wheat field. There was no cover at all. But it had advantages too, because in the open they could see that nobody was near. Besides, it was good to have the depot in sight with its lanterns shining below the gingerbread roof.

At last they got to the depot, and after a wait that seemed like an eternity, they heard the train whistle from around the bend. Once Weaver and Tom got their prisoner aboard, they all breathed easy again, and Lawson drove the wagon back to Hillsboro. In a couple of hours, John was deposited in the St. Louis jail, and the men grabbed a little welcome sleep. Weaver and Tom returned home on two different trains, so as not to attract attention. No one was to know where John Marsden went.

The next couple of weeks of April 1883 saw relative quiet in the Sandy Valley. No stolen hogs. No suspicious fires. No burglaries. Weaver knew it was because the leader of the gang was out of action. He even told Prosecutor Green that everything was quiet because John Marsden was in jail. That was the proof of which man was behind it all.

But Weaver couldn't convince Green. His response was that they needed to talk to Mack again, so they brought him in to Green's office near the courthouse for questioning. He wasn't under arrest, but they needed to get him to the office where both men could grill him. This time there was no coffee, no friendly visiting.

As Mack's story unfolded, the lawmen could see how Mack had carefully set things up to protect the "good" side of the Marsden family, while the "bad" side, John's side, took all the chances. Mack looked from Weaver to Green and said he had a bill of sale for every transaction he ever made. Every one, he emphasized. That's one thing Uncle Richard taught him—he always got a bill of sale.

But you knew you were dealing in stolen livestock, Green accused.

"Well," Mack mumbled, "as long as I didn't ask, I didn't know for sure."

Green rolled his eyes, and Weaver chuckled. He thought to himself that if circumstances were different, he and Mack could have been friends.

"All right," Weaver said, "now let's talk about the murders." Under such questioning, a lot of men would have been staring at the scuffed oak floors and fiddling with their hatband. But not Mack. He was one of those rocks who looked a man in the eye. No wavering. No hint of a lie. No backing down. Always the same, steady voice. The unflinching gray eyes.

"Look, Sheriff," Mack said, "all those things you've asked me about, the fires, the murders, anybody could have done those. John and Tommy Moss knew I was going over to Vail's that night. I said so over at the store, 'cause I made a good profit on those two steers. I bought them with Vail's loan, and I was glad to pay him back. I was braggin' about it. Those boys and some others heard that over at the store. They could have waited 'til after I left Vail's place and just gone right in and jumped him." It was more words than anyone had heard Mack speak at one sitting.

"And the fires? Tell Mr. Green about the arson fires," Weaver urged.

"You know those were done to keep me and Allie quiet. And to keep us from quitting." He explained to Green the series of events, how every time he'd refuse a deal, there'd be another fire at a Hensley house, followed by threats from John that he'd do worse if Mack didn't do as he was told.

"Tell Mr. Green what you told me about the patched five dollar bills," Weaver said. Weaver's predecessor Jones was sure the marked money was part of the loot Mack stole from Vail. So was Green. But Mack repeated for Green what he'd already told Weaver: that he got the patched-up bills from John in a hog deal.

"I paid him, and those bills were in the change I got back from him," Mack said, looking Green squarely in the eye. Weaver believed him, and kept watching for Green to show the same response. But it wasn't forthcoming. Green was a dog on a scent.

"If all that's true, why didn't you come to the sheriff right at the start?" Green asked, still doubting.

Mack was defiant. "I wanted to. Thought about it. But Emma Jean, she was scared, and...well, I just figured I'd be able to end it myself."

There was still no proof of whose hand stole the hogs, set the fires, and pulled the triggers, and even the motives for some of it were unclear. But they were all tied together somehow. Weaver and Green knew it was all done by John or Mack or somebody associated with them. And as Weaver and Green watched Mack walk confidently out of the lawyer's office, they had to admit that to some extent, solving each individual crime wasn't as important as busting the gang. It would all boil down to proving who was telling the truth and who wasn't.

Green turned to the papers on his desk and said simply, "He's lyin'."

Weaver had no big political ambitions. He was a simple man trying to do his job. And at his age, in his forties, he was enjoying living in town. He thought maybe after his term as sheriff he could move into some sort of less dangerous civil service. Then if he lived long enough, maybe he'd go back to the country and put some new calluses on his hands.

Green, on the other hand, was a man in his thirties, just married and starting a family. He was building a reputation and hoping for a long, lucrative career. His relationships with Mayor Edinger, the judges, and the man who appointed Anton Yerger to his judgeship, Governor Thomas Crittenden, might all be important to his future. But not as long as Jefferson County was under the cloud of an outlaw gang. Breaking the gang was vital to Green's career. In the end, getting the truth was not as important to him as getting a conviction. How far would he go to make that happen? It was a question Samuel Marsden had already asked himself often, and many would ask later.

Chapter Eighteen
"Somebody's Lying"

Green was unsatisfied with the interview of Mack. Sure, they got Mack's story, but there was still no evidence, no witness to any of the crimes. It was all too flimsy. So the next day they were on the train to St. Louis, where John still sat in jail.

Green took the lead, telling John, "I was glad to hear you say Mack stole the hogs. That's fine. But we need to know who killed Anson Vail and Joseph Yerger. If you'll help us, it'll go easier for you on the hog stealing."

John looked from the sheriff to the prosecutor and back. "I could help you," John offered.

"You better," Green told him. "Mack's going to hang it all on you. You know, he's denying that he stole any livestock. Somebody's lying."

"All right," John said. He paused, taking a long look over the cliff from which he was jumping. "Mack killed Vail. He killed Yerger too."

"Slow down," Green told him. "For now, just tell us what you know about Vail. And we need details. I need something to build a case on."

"He strangled him," John went on. "Then set fire to the cabin so you'd think Vail burned up accidentally. He robbed him too, and bragged about it."

Green asked, "Do you know anything about some marked money that Vail had?"

John got his thoughts together, and then said that one time when they were with Mack he pulled out some bills and said they were the last of the money he took from Vail.

"How'd he recognize that was Vail's money?" Green asked.

"Well, they were torn pretty bad and fixed with packing tape," John said, looking hopeful that he was saying what the other two wanted to hear.

Green and Weaver looked at each other. John knew everything. Certainly too much for an innocent man. Weaver could feel the tension growing between himself and Green, as he watched Green using John to hang Mack. It was wrong, and Weaver knew it. But the way Green played it, he didn't know how to stop it. He was no lawyer.

The attorney pressed, asking if John would testify to all that. Yes, John said he'd testify, but of course he wanted something in return. He wanted the hog stealing charges dropped. We can't do that, Green said. John was going to have to stand for the hog stealing. But in return for Mack's conviction in the Vail murder, they'd try to get him a reduced sentence in the stealing. Maybe a month or two in jail. That was the best John could expect, and he took it. But, Green reminded John, they needed conviction. It had to be a conviction.

Finally, Weaver thought, Green had done it, found a man to take the murdered Joseph Yerger's place as the star witness against Mack Marsden in the murder of Anson Vail. At one time that's what Weaver wanted, but not at the expense of the truth. Now that he knew how John controlled the gang, that he was willing to continue his lies on the witness stand, and that Green was ready to let him do it, Weaver felt like his insides were tied up in knots. It was just wrong.

But Weaver had a job to do, and he moved quickly to get Mack back in jail. For the third time, it was the accused man's boyhood friend, Tom Frazier, who was sent to bring him in. And again, it was peaceful. No handcuffs. No posse. It was simply a stoic Mack Marsden riding in once more to face his accusers. In reporting the arrest, the newspaper would again use its backhanded way of convicting Mack, saying, "It is not our duty to prejudice the mind of the public," but since Mack was back in jail, people in the neighborhood had "slept more soundly."

Acting on John's accusations, it wasn't long until Big Allie and Uncle Jesse joined Mack in jail. Before Weaver and Green left St. Louis they got John to reveal that his accomplice was Tommy Moss, so they arrested him too. Then Weaver figured it was safe to bring John back to Hillsboro, and soon Weaver had them all tucked into his jail, where he could press for more answers. Allie wouldn't say a word. He never said anything. But Jesse might be willing to talk, Weaver thought.

Yes, Jesse said, just last week he went to Mack and warned, "I heard they're working up a case against you that you murdered Vail." Mack replied in a near whisper. For those who didn't know him, that voice might have sounded reserved, possibly shy. But those closest to him knew that quiet speech exhibited his hottest anger. He scowled at Jesse and said, "That's some of John Marsden's lies. If I did that, then he killed Yerger."

What he meant was that he didn't know who murdered either man, but he could sound very convincing if he had to. If John hung one murder on him, then he would accuse John of the other. But that still didn't tell Weaver for sure who was guilty, and he was sure Jesse knew nothing about it.

Leaving the cell, the words echoed in Weaver's mind, "then he killed Yerger." Weaver knew John was stealing livestock and setting the arson fires, and it was certainly possible that he committed the horrible Yerger arson and murder. But why on earth would John do that?

Then suddenly, he saw. Mack had received the patched money from John in one of their hog deals, just as he said. So John knew if Yerger testified that Mack came into the store with Vail's money, Mack would be forced to save himself by telling where he got it. Yes, if Yerger fingered Mack, Mack would finger John, and the whole gang would fall one by one. For the first time Weaver saw that Mack had nothing to fear from Yerger, but John had everything to lose if Yerger testified. That was enough reason for John to shut Yerger's mouth. John could have done exactly what the newspaper accused Mack of doing.

It was as if Mack and John were two figures walking toward Weaver out of a dense fog, and he was seeing them clearly for the first time. Mack was bold, the smart one, and the quiet one. John was the weasel, the impetuous one. Mack had a terrible temper when cornered. John had one, cornered or not.

The law had both men in jail, and that was pretty good. Yet for as much progress as they'd made, Weaver and Green were still looking at an incomplete picture. They had no way to prove who killed Vail or Yerger. The two sides accusing each other didn't make a tight case for the prosecutor in any of the crimes. The only thing they could count on was John's confession to stealing hogs. When it all boiled down, keeping quiet was a bigger mistake for Mack than buying stolen hogs.

At last it was all brought to the grand jury to sort out, and they in turn decided to let the court sort it out. Mack, Big Allie, Uncle Jesse, and John Marsden were all indicted for grand larceny, stealing hogs. Mack alone was indicted for murder in the Vail slaying.

Samuel Marsden and his brother Richard went down to the sheriff's office and posted bond for Mack in the murder charge. They followed the deputy downstairs and through the steel door because they wanted to speak to Allie and let him know he'd soon be out too. As they passed John Marsden's cell, John angrily chided them for not posting his bond as well, reminding them sarcastically that he was a Marsden too. Samuel ignored him, but Uncle Richard, ever the gentleman, stopped to shake hands and wish John well. John's response was sudden and violent. His fist flew between the bars, smack into the older man's jaw. Richard staggered against the opposite cell door, but quickly righted himself. By the time the deputy heard the exchange and reacted, it was over. Richard refused to press any more charges against John, but rather glared at the red-faced convict, and walked stoically from the barred corridor. When Weaver heard the story it told him once again what a temper John Marsden had.

Allie's bond was reduced to $1,000 by a sympathetic justice, but the Hensleys wouldn't help him. While Samuel had both feet in Mack's troubles, Leander Hensley and his brood stayed out of Allen's mess, and stuck to their farming and their church. They treated him like the embarrassment he was. So his mother's brother, W. F. Williams, posted the bail.

Jesse wasn't about to cough up a bunch of money for bail. All he did was drive some pigs to market for his nephew. He asked to be examined by a justice of the peace, and protested his innocence. Though he was loyal to Mack, nobody could really say he was involved in any of the crimes, so he was released.

John Marsden had his supporters too, or at least some backers who thought Mack was guilty. John's bond for stealing the Plass hogs, the same crime for which Mack paid a $2,500 bond, was only $700. The people who stepped up to pay appeared on the surface to be an odd assortment with little to draw them together. But they had family ties. E. F. Donnell was a wealthy and powerful man whose daughter was married to one of John Marsden's cousins, so he was happy to put up John's bail. For Donnell, it was a power play in the interest of family, as well as ridding "his" county of Mack. E. F.'s second cousin James Eli Williams bailed out Tommy Moss.

Even more powerful than blood was the bravado of an increasingly bold circle of justice-minded men, all members of the Protective Society. They were friends with Green, as well as his fellow lodge members of the Ancient Order of United Workers. At their lodge meetings they discussed the case with Green and all agreed that Mack was guilty. If he was free on bond, they thought, then John should be free. Besides, they joked through their cigars, if all the outlaws were out of jail, maybe they would just wipe each other out.

Weaver was a member of the lodge too, but since the Protective Society formed, he stayed away because of exactly that kind of talk. He figured things had only gotten hotter among the accused men, and they were anything but safe from each other. But there was only so much he could do to protect them, and he was more than relieved to get them all bailed out of his jail.

Chapter Nineteen
The Meeting in the Yard

Well, it was certainly a new day for John Marsden. He had pointed the finger of blame at "cousin" Mack, and now everybody was out on bail. No more hiding in the St. Louis slammer for John.

True to his character, Mack took the lead. He'd thought it out, and it wasn't too late to do the right thing. In fact, he could probably convince John to tell the truth, take his punishment, and get the rest of them off pretty easy with a chance to start fresh.

John and Tommy Moss had a special camaraderie, living on the little farm in Crystal City. In fact, if it weren't for all of the legal trouble, they'd have been enjoying living like bachelors, while their wives lived with John's mother, Louisa. But their brand of brotherhood was cloaked in secrets that allowed for no pleasure at all. The little house was a place of fear and distrust, where every step was an effort to cover the last.

It didn't take Mack long to find John and Tommy. Then one cool, early spring night, he and Allie climbed up in the wagon and drove over to Crystal. It was late when Mack turned into the edge of a field, stopped, and tied Coal to a tree. He and Allie approached the cabin, their footsteps silent in the dirt, but swishing against the dry leaves of last year's plowed-under corn stalks. They watched carefully to be sure they weren't walking into the sights of someone's rifle, but there was no ambush waiting that night. On the contrary, the two men in the house played cards and sipped glasses of whiskey, trying to still their troubled thoughts.

When Mack called out from the yard, they almost jumped out of their skins, scattering cards in their haste to blow out the lamp. They grabbed their revolvers from the table, where they had been placed for just such a moment. Mack hollered that there was nothing to fear, he just wanted to talk. Tommy cocked his pistol, slipped to the door, and opened it a crack, making sure to stay out of sight. Tommy liked to fancy himself a pistolero, even though everyone knew he couldn't hit a barn with a banjo.

Mack walked over to the edge of the porch and greeted them in a disarmingly casual way. He simply invited them to step outside. Of course they protested, but Mack reassured them. "We all need to have a talk," he muttered. And he wanted to do it outside so there were no surprises, nobody listening, no hidden weapons, and nobody walking in on them. Tommy opened the door enough to see if Mack had a weapon. The moonlight revealed that Mack wore no coat that could conceal a pistol, and he and Allie held up their hands to show they were empty. It was clear that they didn't believe John and Tommy would shoot them, even if those two were armed. Mack told them to relax and said they should just stroll out in the yard a bit and have a little talk. And leave your pistols on the table, he commanded. They looked at each other as if to ask, "How'd he know we had pistols in our hands?"

Tree frogs sang and a whippoorwill called as the men sauntered side by side, acting more relaxed than they felt, stopping near a section of old cedar rail fence. The scene was so pastoral, an onlooker would never guess the antagonism that boiled between them. Here they were, John and Tommy on one side, Mack and Allie on the other.

All four men knew what had been going on in the valley, who did what, and who said what. And they all had a pretty good idea of what they had to tell the law in order to save their own hides. The question was, were they going to tell the story in the best way for all of them, or was each one going to tell the version that would help himself, and let the rest be damned?

Once they started talking, Mack's congenial tone changed. It was down to the licklog, he said. The law had them in a corner. He wanted an end to it all. Right then. He had to know if John and Tommy were going to tell the truth and protect him and Allie.

At first, they both laughed nervously and exchanged looks, as if to say Mack was out of his mind. But Mack said they couldn't threaten him anymore, because keeping quiet only got him in more trouble.

He said he already told his story to the sheriff. If John and Tommy didn't say they stole the hogs, Mack would have to swear to it in court. Mack begged the two not to make him testify against them. But it was in their hands. He would if he had to.

Several ideas were proposed, various blends of truth and lies, with different ones taking the blame for various pieces of the crimes. Mack reminded John that he'd already pleaded guilty, so he should just go down for all the livestock stealing. No sense in dragging all of us into it, Mack insisted.

But John was listening with different ears than the rest. He thought he was protected because he had turned state's evidence. They don't know, he thought to himself, that I hold all the cards. The way he figured it, by testifying against Mack, he'd get a short sentence, maybe even get off completely, and same for Tommy, while Mack and Allie went to prison for long stretches.

When John refused to take the full blame, Mack said he should just move away. Then nobody would go to prison. Everyone would know John was guilty, and that would end it for all of them. Mack pulled out his pocket book, and said, "I'll give you the cash to go away on. I know you told Weaver I already promised that, but I'll really do it." John shook his head. He still wasn't willing to be the only one to take a fall.

John changed the topic, saying he was concerned about Mack facing the charge of murdering Vail. "They forced me to accuse you, Mack," John said. "I didn't want to do it." In truth, John's unspoken fear was that if Mack was acquitted, the law would keep looking for Vail's murderer, maybe stopping at John's door. He suggested they find someone else the law could hang for that. He favored casting the blame on someone totally outside the group, perhaps a stranger. Maybe a Negro, one of them suggested. They even talked about the possibility of accusing the stranger, then killing him before a trial could reveal the truth.

But Mack was against all that. He was unafraid of being charged with that murder because he knew there was no evidence against him. He didn't need to get into some complicated scheme to prove his innocence, and he wasn't going to agree to murder.

Mack was getting worked up. "Who has suffered here?" he asked, leaning up into John's face until their noses almost touched. "My wife's family. You haven't. If you and I tell different stories, I'm the one they'll believe."

John had a retort, to which Mack said, "When they find me innocent on Vail, they'll come for you next." In the middle of it all, voices were raised, fingers were pointed, and John and Mack were in each other's faces. John pushed Mack. Mack grabbed him up by the shirt front, his toes dragging against the grass, and growled in that low, back-in-the-throat voice, a stone cold threat: "If you swear in court that I murdered Vail, then you better prepare your coffin."

Tommy convinced them to calm down, but at that point there was no conciliation to be found. They continued to talk about doing anything to stay out of jail. They talked about drawing the line at murder. They discussed telling some lies, but not other lies. Though some ideas sounded good as they were tossed out, they all fell apart when discussed to their logical conclusion. Into the night they talked, but in the end they could find no common ground.

They were desperate men in desperate times. The meeting in the yard ended with distrust, with accusations, with threats both loud and low, and without agreement. At last it was clear, there would be no story on which they could all agree, so it was Mack and Big Allie against John and Tommy. They were all going to be tried for stealing livestock.

Mack was going to be tried for murder. One side walked back to the cabin, one side to the wagon. They weren't all going to win, and they could certainly all lose.

Chapter Twenty
Dirty Dealing

A couple nights later Tommy was over at Louisa Marsden's house visiting Bessie. He'd been coming around and being overly nice to them and Millie. Bessie let him stay the night with her once in a while, and it was one of those nights.

Louisa and Millie were both sewing. Tommy and Bessie sat on the front step and watched the sun go down behind Brady's hill. It had been dark for a half hour when Millie came to the open door and said, "Tommy, we heard a noise out back."

The fear that came over his face was far beyond what would normally be expected in such a situation. "What kind of noise?" he asked, his eyes narrowing. Millie shrugged. "A kind of…like someone scooting something across the floor."

Tommy hurried them both back in, closed and locked the door, and blew out the lamps. Then he fetched his pistol from the bedroom. Timidly, he peered under a rear window shade. Then another. The way he was moving was really scaring the women. When he was satisfied that he couldn't see anybody on the porch, he slowly opened the back door just a crack and peered into the night.

The women sat in the parlor, looking at each other. They all agreed the noise was probably a coon. But Tommy kept slipping from door to window to door to window until they told him they were going to bed. He told Bessie he'd join her in a little while, but he never did. He sat up the whole night through, with no lamp lighted in the house, the pistol in his grip.

The next morning, after coffee and cornbread, Tommy said he needed to head back to Crystal. But there was a look in his eye Bessie had never seen before. He was wearing the pistol thrust into his belt, pulled it when he went to the barn for his horse, and that's the way he rode out. He was spooked.

The women soon settled back into their chores for the day. Again that evening, just after they turned in, they heard something moving on the back porch. They were too scared to get up and check on it, but rather huddled under their blankets. After a while they drifted off, but about 11:00 p.m., Louisa was awakened by a crackling noise and found the house filling with smoke. An arsonist had applied his deadly fuel to only the north side, creating a slow blaze that was expected to awaken the occupants of the house without trapping them. It was a humane twist on a deadly game. All three women escaped unharmed into the warm April night, dragging their mattresses and bedding with them. They had a good well, but not enough help or buckets to put out such an inferno, so they could only stand helpless as they watched the house being consumed.

The arsonist might have been Mack, turning John and Tommy's own weapon against them. Maybe the fire was a signed letter from Mack saying, "Tell the truth or your women are in danger." And that's exactly what many people concluded. But that's not who did it.

One thing Mack said during the meeting in the yard stuck in John's mind. "Who has suffered?" John could see the way it looked, with the Hensleys being hit, and nothing bad ever happening to any of his people. That was easy to fix.

He was surprised to find Tommy there at Louisa's house the first night, so he waited. The next night it was easy. Just a little coal oil, and when he was sure the blaze was started, a handful of stones clattering against his mother's window was enough to wake her and get the women out. What a twisted mind he had, justifying a crime against his own mother and sister in the name of saving his own hide. Watching from the brush, once they were safely out, he told himself it was perfect. He ran north along the sand bluff, carrying in his chest the coldest of hearts.

When the news came in to *The Democrat*, McMullin was thrilled at the opportunity to flex his vigilante muscles. He gathered a few Protective Society members and went out to investigate. They followed the tracks away from the house along the sand bluff, but that was the extent of their detective work. Like the sheriff, they figured it was one more chapter in the outlaws' ongoing war of intimidation, a war that someone was going to have to lose sooner or later.

That was the same week *The Democrat* published an odd article based on a long letter to the newspaper from Michael Clover, the farmer who told Weaver he'd seen Jesse Johnston and Mack out together the night Plass's hogs were stolen. Now that Mack was out on bail, he knew Clover had figured in Weaver's case against him, and Clover wasn't about to stick his neck out any farther in the interest of justice. He wrote a lengthy diatribe to *The Democrat* about how he'd been misquoted and misunderstood, and he had never seen Jesse and Mack together in Bechler's field or anyplace else, ever.

Clover was just one example of the kind of nervous jerking that was going on around the case. Weaver read Clover's retraction in the paper and wondered if he could hold the case together. If Clover was backing down as a witness, who was next?

With no stealing and no selling going on, and legal bills mounting, the gang was getting desperate. Tommy, as always, tried to find ways to pick up a buck here, a buck there. When his distant cousin Fess Donnell told him he'd seen the fugitive ex-sheriff Thomas J. Jones working in a blacksmith shop in Crystal, Tommy's eyes brightened. There was a meal ticket! Even though Jones had been out of office and on the run for a year, somebody might pay a reward for his hide. Come on, he told Fess, let's arrest Jones.

First they went to the men Jones had borrowed from, and got them to promise a total of $150 if Jones was brought in. Inspired by the

Martin Linn Clardy, leader of Mack's defense team in the hog stealing trial.

promise of a reward, Tommy and Fess, with pistols in hand, appeared suddenly in the door of the blacksmith shop and arrested the terrified man. When he protested, they decided to ask around about him, and found out he was not Jones at all, but the son of a Methodist preacher in another town.

The very next day about noon, Tommy went out to the barn to saddle his horse. When he opened the door he was thrown to the ground, and two cold Colt revolvers were pressed up against his nose. Peering down the barrels he saw Jones's brother and brother-in-law. They made it clear to Tommy that he better drop his crusade to arrest the former sheriff. And that was the end of Tommy's career as a bounty hunter.

The excitement ran high in early May when Hillsboro found itself playing host to Congressman Martin Linn Clardy, known to many as Major M. L. Clardy, CSA. His appearance was one of the shrewd Mack Marsden's best public relations moves, as the major arrived in town with no little fanfare to join attorneys J. D. Perkins and Sam Byrns on

The Commercial Hotel, across from the courthouse, site of Clardy's headquarters.

Mack's defense team. It was in the paper and it was the talk of the town. When the major descended from the hack that brought him up from the Victoria train station, he looked grand in his gray suit, black tie, and gold watch chain. And yet, there was nothing haughty about his red cheeks and the warm smile under his exuberant mustache. Hillsboro provided plenty of good wishes and hands to shake. He was trim and looked fit to lead the troops once more against the Yankee interlopers.

Clardy was a native of Farmington, just thirty miles to the south. He had commanded a brave Missouri cavalry battalion that participated in the famous Confederate general Sterling Price's raid into Missouri late in the Civil War. It mattered little that he was on the losing side. So were at least half of his neighbors. Among the common people, the laborers, and the Democrats, former Confederate officers approached sainthood. Furthermore, by that time Clardy was practicing law in his hometown,

Judge John Wesley Emerson, who filled in for Judge John Thomas at the change of venue hearing.

which was known for its lead mines, and it's through that industry that the Marsdens were led to him. The major was that rare breed of man who found it easy to befriend both miners and mine owners, and that's how he came to be elected to Congress in 1878. He set up headquarters in the Commercial Hotel, across the street from the courthouse. When *The Democrat* reported that Clardy was backing Mack, it undoubtedly helped his case in the minds of many a prospective juror.

But prospective jurors weren't making decisions yet. One of the most intriguing turns in the case came about on June 9, 1883, when the defense team requested a change of venue before Judge John Wesley Emerson. The judge was a veteran of the Union army, who had been appointed colonel of the 68th Enrolled Missouri Militia, a unit that was soon disbanded. His desire to serve the Union cause remained so strong that he gave up any thought of being an officer and enlisted as a private in the 47th Missouri Volunteer Infantry, where he rose to the rank of major. He won fame pursuing the retreating General John Bell Hood after the disastrous Battle of Nashville, and was widely known as a hard fighter.

Though the Marsdens didn't serve in the war, there were Hensleys on both sides. Emma Jean's uncles Alfred and Fleming Asaf Hensley grew up in a slave-owning family, joined the Confederate army, were captured, and suffered horribly as prisoners of war in the Union prisons of Alton, Illinois, and Fort Delaware. Only Alfred survived. Both Marsdens and Hensleys were Democrats to the core, surely the antithesis of Emerson and his ilk. It was such leanings among the cast of characters at the trial that lead to rumors of a continuing Civil War feud. That wasn't precisely true, but there's no doubt that twenty-five-year-old politics colored the legal proceedings.

That was first evident at Mack's request for a change of venue. On this side, common laborer Mack, from a mining and farming family, with his attorney, a Confederate officer and champion of the common man. On the other side, the Union officer and future business executive presiding, with a concerned Republican leadership looking over his shoulder. Newly elected governor Thomas Theodore Crittenden was a Democrat, but Jefferson County Republicans saw eye to eye with him in his tough stand on crime.

To determine whether Mack could get a fair trial in Jefferson County, Mack and the prosecutor were each allowed to bring three witnesses from each of the county's six townships. But Mack's side brought none. After failing to get a change of venue before Justice Rankin back in April, Mack might have been expected to come loaded for bear this time. Instead, Mack's attorneys Clardy and Perkins thought public sentiment was so stirred up against Mack that instead of bringing witnesses, they could turn the prosecution's own witnesses to admit their bias. It would be apparent to any judge that a fair trial for Mack was impossible.

Prosecutor Green had collected about forty prospective jurors for the hearing. Almost to the man, the witnesses said they believed Mack was guilty of Vail's murder. Mack's attorneys were beaming. That alone would be enough for most judges to approve the venue change. But instead, Emerson went on to ask two more questions: Should the guilty

Entrance to the Jefferson County Courthouse.

be punished, and could the courts determine who was guilty? Again, to the man, the witnesses said their primary concern was that the correct guilty party or parties be punished and that they were sure the evidence would reveal who was truly guilty. Apparently that's what the judge wanted to hear, because he summarily denied the change of venue request, setting jury selection for the very next day, and the trial for July 9 in Hillsboro. Mack's defense team complained to each other that he must have had his mind made up before he even walked into the courtroom.

A frustrated Mack emerged into the sunlight with Gabe Johnston at his side. Mack's older brother Buzz was a few steps behind and saw the pair turn toward the wagon tied out front, then stop and look across the street. Someone had shouted to them, and Gabe hollered back, something Buzz couldn't make out. Then Gabe and Mack started across the street with long, determined strides.

When he got outside Buzz could see that John Marsden and Tommy Moss were coming from the other side of the street. The four men met in the middle, and Mack immediately grabbed John's shirt and suspenders in both hands. As they struggled they turned, and Buzz saw Mack's face contorted with icy hatred. John pushed back against Mack's shoulders and spit sprayed from their mouths along with one threat after another.

Gabe and Tommy were a few feet away, locked in a sort of standing, arm's-length wrestling match that was about to explode into blows at any moment. Buzz rushed into the road, grabbing Mack, about the same time Allen Marsden appeared and grabbed his brother John. The big brothers pulled hard, shouting at the two fighters until they had them beyond punching range. Buzz pulled Mack around to look in his eyes and reminded him emphatically that he didn't need any more trouble. Allen told John the same. Gabe and Tommy fell down, losing their grip on each other, and other men stepped over quickly to keep them apart.

With hateful glares and curses, the two groups parted. Not a punch was landed, but the confrontation showed everybody in town exactly how bad the blood between them had become.

Judge Thomas was to conduct the Vail trial, but he was sick, and Emerson filled in for him at the venue hearing. When Thomas recovered in time for the trial, the defense thought they might get another hearing on the venue change. However, Thomas denied that request too. No doubt he felt the pressure of a community that was eager for a trial and hoped for a conviction when he read McMullin's pompous article in *The Democrat* that said, "The prisoner's right to a change of venue has been once fully investigated, and ought to be settled by the decision of the court already considered." There was no escaping the impact of the Protective Society on every aspect of the case, and each passing day seemed to turn more people against Mack.

The decision to hold his trial in Jefferson County amid the growing climate of distrust and accusations, and where everyone thought they already knew the details of the case, was a decided miscarriage of justice, and one of the reasons that for generations to come, the Marsden family legends would contend, "There was dirty dealing at the trial."

Chapter Twenty-One
Who Killed Vail?

Over on the Victoria Road, at the north end of the cemetery, stood an imposing, brooding tree known as the gallows oak. It had been a long time since its massive and sprawling gray branches were used for an execution, either at the hands of a sheriff with a legal writ, or by a wild and drunken vigilante mob, but it had a grim history of serving ably for both purposes. It was still strong, quiet, and patient, there on the corner, and it would be ready if Mack Marsden was the next to swing.

The day was hot and sticky as only eastern Missouri can be in the middle of July. The courthouse crowd was packed into the benches and sweltering, as still more people kept coming. Although the tall windows stretching up the white walls were open, they provided little relief. If any breeze meandered around the simmering hills northwest of town, it was bound to run out of breath before it could get down Main Street. There was a constant and graceful waving in the room as everyone fanned themselves, the men using their hats, and the women with wooden-handled fans from the church bearing full-color pictures of Jesus knocking at the door. In spite of the attorneys' attempts to maintain dignity, their suit coats came off and collars were unbuttoned long before noon.

The trial started on Monday, with Judge John L. Thomas presiding. He knew practically everybody in the room from his days as an attorney, handling everything from land disputes to Fleming Hensley's request for a Revolutionary War pension. He quickly moved to the

Top: The courtroom of the Jefferson County Courthouse, the setting for both murder trials. Left: Judge John L. Thomas, who presided at both murder trials.

prosecution's case, which focused on establishing that Mack Marsden was at Anson Vail's house the night of the murder. The coroner reported Mack's testimony from the inquest. He said Mack claimed that Vail was fine when he left his cabin that evening after repaying the $90. Prosecutor Green called to the stand Mack's neighbors and relatives, and some others who lived closer to Vail, and they all said the same thing: They either saw Mack go to or leave Vail's cabin.

Part of the purpose in all that testimony was to fix the time of the visit relative to the discovery of the fire, and thereby establish the time of the murder. Green hoped to squeeze the murder as close as possible to Mack's time at the cabin. Trouble was, life in Sandy revolved around the sun, not the clock. Everyone who testified quoted the time relative to sundown, dusk, dark, or "almost dark."

Late that cool Sunday afternoon Mack and his little brother Clarence had climbed the rise west of his house to the bald above, scattering a herd of six deer, including one beautiful buck, which Clarence pretended to shoot as he ran. They stopped at the home of his sister Priscilla and her husband, Clay Moss.

Mack and Clarence climbed this rise to the bald above on their way to the home of Priscilla and Clay Moss.

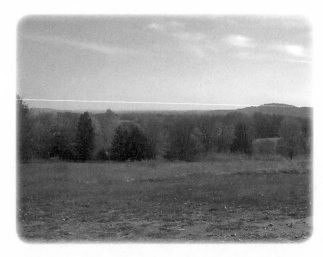

From their farm atop the ridge Clay and Priscilla had a commanding view of the valley.

There were other Claibourn Mosses, but this was the one who preferred to be called Clay. He was a hardworking farmer who loved his wife, his children, and his church. When he and Priscilla married, he bought the broad bald from his uncle Mark R. Moss. From that farm atop the ridge they had a commanding view of the valley. Clay was happy to take up farming over there near her Marsdens, and they also kept close ties to his folks back in Moss Hollow.

Clay smiled and waved when he saw Mack and Clarence coming across the field. They visited for about twenty minutes, then Clay and Clarence had to leave for evening services at Sandy Baptist.

Their walk to church was the trial's only testimony involving clock time. They had to cover three miles to get there for services at "about seven," meaning they left home no later than 6:30. Probably closer to 6:15. Mack left at the same time, which placed Mack's arrival at Vail's, only a mile away, no later than 6:45. Probably closer to 6:30.

Vail's neighbors, Brady and the Meyers brothers, testified that the dogs barked around six, and they got to the fire about seven. That's the sort of scene-setting that must take place at any such criminal trial. Mack was where he said he was, when he said he was. But that didn't mean he killed Vail.

Next, the prosecution trotted up its star witness, the small and furtive John Marsden. He was twitchy and too eager to talk. His eyes flitted around the room, answering questions while 'Squire Green frowned and did his best to calm him down and help him focus. John was followed on the stand by his well-dressed brother-in-law, Thomas Henon Moss. Even when everyone else in the packed courtroom was melting, Tommy looked terrific.

Mack glowered as both men said that one time after Vail's death, when they were with Mack, he pulled out some greenbacks and some unusual, patched bills fell from his wallet. He quickly stuffed them back in, saying, "Get back in there, Old Vail. That's the last of Vail's."

And that was that. Green was less than satisfied, but there was no place to pursue that line of questioning. Those were the patched bills Joseph Yerger was going to testify about. The trouble with John and Tommy giving this testimony, instead of Yerger, was that Yerger had seen the bills in Vail's pocketbook first. John and Moss had not. So there was no way for Green to establish in court that the bills had ever actually been in Vail's possession. Of course, it was not very good testimony anyway. There was any number of ways Mack could have come into possession of those patched bills, including getting them in change from John, as he had told Weaver. Did he truly make the comment about "the last of Old Vail's"? In the end, it meant nothing.

John and Tommy also told the court about the meeting in the yard with Mack and Allie after they were all bailed out of jail. Rather than describing Mack's plea that they tell the truth, they gave a convoluted account of how Mack came to them with a plan. How he wanted John to take the hog stealing blame and move away. Of course, Weaver thought as he listened, if John really did steal the hogs, it was perfectly logical to suggest that he run away, since he'd already confessed. It wasn't legal, but it was logical, and it did nothing to help the case against Mack.

John and Tommy testified that it was Mack's idea to blame a Negro for killing Vail, then kill the accused man before he could be tried. Both witnesses claimed dove-like purity in their refusal to help Mack lie. They even said Mack boasted that plenty of other people would lie for him, and told Tommy to "prepare your coffin" if he wouldn't cooperate. They quoted Mack as saying, "Damn a man who would not swear a lie to save his brother-in-law! See what I have done and they never could prove it on me—see how I got old Vail; when I had him he was kicking and hollering, and a big roll of money fell and I had to let go of Vail to save it from rolling into the fire." Mack closed his eyes and fumed.

In an attempt to prove that Mack premeditated Vail's murder, the prosecution called Michael Clover. At the time of the murder he'd been working for Vail in his fields every day, and staying with Vail. One day as Mack was passing on the road he stopped to chat, and asked Clover if he went home on Saturday and Sunday. He said yes, he did, and the prosecution hoped that was enough to imply to the jury that Mack intended to kill Vail on the weekend while Clover was away. But Clover made the question about weekends sound like mere idle conversation. And the defense calmly suggested that maybe Mack asked out of concern that Clover went home and kept up his own place once in a while.

Then the defense truly took charge under Clardy's command. They brought forth several people who saw and spoke with Mack the evening of the murder. They painted a picture of a businessman, happy to have completed a profitable deal. He was a family man, not agitated or nervous, hardly the portrait of a desperate murderer and arsonist. Emma Jean and her sweet sister Lydia both said they all ate supper that evening after he returned from Vail's.

Joseph King brought his empty coal oil can over to the Marsden home that night to borrow some lamp oil. He was married to Mack's baby sister Carrie, and his father was married to Mack's big sister, Sis. It was another one of those kinship stories that made folks in the courtroom shake their heads and smile. Joseph and Carrie were just setting up housekeeping in a little rented house on Marsden Lane, and they seemed to always be out of something. So of course it wasn't uncommon for them to turn to Mack and Emma Jean for coal oil, sugar, or whatever they needed. That night Joseph visited for quite a while, returning home at bedtime, and noticed nothing out of the ordinary about Mack.

Then the defense called Henry Koerner and Frank Boehne, who had gone to Vail's home one time with Sam Morris so he could obtain a loan. On the road Morris had talked about how easy it would be to kill Vail and take his money, because he lived alone, hidden in his valley. Frances Marion Johnston, who ran the little store in Sandy for a while, said that on one occasion several of the men were standing around talking tough like men do, and John Marsden said he didn't think it would be any more harm to kill Vail "than to choke a possum." The "choke" imagery was important, because that was the general opinion of how Vail was killed. And Charles Maupin said he and John were drunk one night when John said he didn't know how they could "make a raise," meaning get some money, unless they "tapped old man Vail." Mack concealed a smile, remembering that he was kin to everybody in the county. Johnston and Maupin were both his uncles.

John Marsden's wife, Millie, the one who kicked him out of his own mother's house, proved to be one of the best witnesses for the defense. She reported that one time Tommy Moss's wife, Bessie, said she could kill Vail herself. And another time she heard Tommy talking about how they ought to take care of Mack. He said that he and John could fix up a tale that would put Mack in the penitentiary for a long time. Then a shiver of fear ran through the simmering courtroom with her next statement. She reported that Tommy's brother Jimmy said he'd kill Mack Marsden himself if someone would give him enough money to move away. And to that, Bessie Marsden Moss cracked, "Well, why didn't you give him the money?" Though no one knew at the time, it was a chill foreshadowing of the evil that was brewing in the neighborhood.

That was the first time Jimmy Moss's name had come up in any of the dealings. But it wouldn't be the last.

Finally, they introduced the list of Vail's debtors, all familiar names, dating back several years. John Marsden was among those with unpaid loans. Mack was not.

All of that was to establish in the minds of the jury that there were plenty of people, including John Marsden, who thought seriously enough about killing Vail to talk openly about it, and that some of them harbored thoughts of getting rid of Mack too. It was a defense strategy that worked.

The case was given to the jury the second evening, and the last thing they heard was a splendid appeal for acquittal from the eloquent congressman, Major Clardy. The next morning the jury came in with its verdict for acquittal. That verdict is different from "not guilty" and means that there is not sufficient evidence to judge whether the accused is guilty or not. But as far as Mack was concerned, it was all the same. He was a free man and would never be tried for Vail's murder again.

Samuel Marsden solemnly shook hands with the lawyers and well-wishers. While they enjoyed kind words and pats on the back, many more in the crowd muttered angrily about the outcome. Mack knew the packed courtroom was no place to linger. Through the crowd he caught sight of Emma Jean's homemade blue flowered dress, and pressed toward her. She reached for him and he grabbed her hand, putting on a little smile just for her. Mack guided her through the milling people, into the sunshine, and down the street to where his wagon was tied. They were among the first on the gravel road back home.

In an odd series of events that morning, Judge Thomas had come to the bench and court was convened, but the jury wasn't quite ready to come in when he called them. While the judge was in conversation with the bailiff, Prosecutor Green quietly slid his chair back from the table and left the courtroom for an urgent trip to the outhouse. When he returned several minutes later the verdict had been read. The next issue of the *St. Louis Republican* raised a concern that the judge had read the verdict when one of the key attorneys was not present. Thomas was infuriated that the paper would imply he had created such a scenario on purpose, and made a fast trip to Green's office to apologize in person. When he read the newspaper, Thomas emphasized, that was the first clue he had that Green had missed the verdict. That was his mistake, because he was supposed to call roll of the principal parties in the trial before receiving the verdict from the jury. But Green realized the mistake was partly his for leaving the courtroom at such a time, and beyond a little embarrassment was not worried about it at all. Hands were shaken, smiles exchanged, and the men went together to the office of *The Democrat* to ask that their version of the story set the record straight. There was no impropriety intended, and Green's absence, of course, had no impact on the outcome of the trial.

However, there was something else that did affect the outcome. Green wanted the jury to be instructed that they could find Mack guilty of either first- or second-degree murder, but the judge refused to give them the second-degree option. The definition of first-degree murder, as defined in the Revised Missouri Statutes, Section 1232, read, "Every murder which shall be committed by means of poison, or by laying in wait or by any other kind of willful and deliberate killing or which shall be committed in the perpetration or attempt to perpetrate any arson, rape, robbery, burglary, or any other felony shall be deemed murder in the first degree." Second-degree murder generally means that it was done on the spur of the moment, or in a fit of rage, or perhaps in a fight, but not intending to kill the victim.

That was a part of Green's plan that backfired on him. The city fathers, the Protective Society, and Green himself all agreed that Mack needed to hang. They wanted to make sure the jury didn't convict him of second-degree murder, which carried a sentence of prison time. Governor Crittenden had proven to be very soft on men convicted of second-degree murder, pardoning many of them, and the Society didn't want him to turn Mack loose. So certain people talked to Judge Thomas, stated their case, and left him under a lot of pressure to disallow the second-degree option. Nobody truly thought the jury would consider

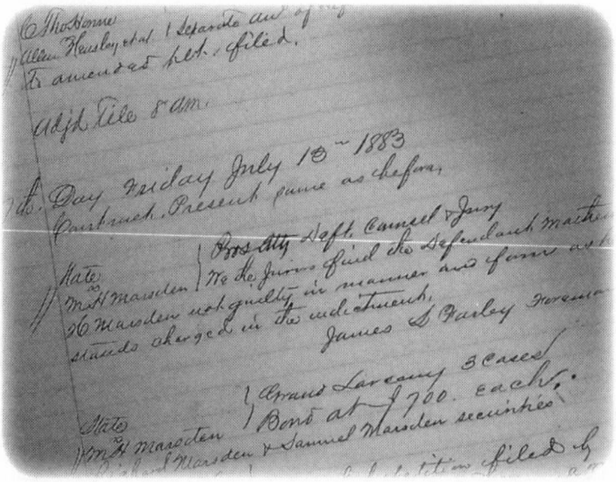

The court record of Mack's acquittal of Vail's murder. Below it can be seen his bond for stealing livestock, posted by Richard and Samuel. Above it is the arraignment of Allen Hensley for stealing Horine's hogs.

acquittal. In fact, Thomas was later quoted in the press as saying he was very surprised at the verdict.

Mack's neck was still in the hangman's noose up until that Friday morning, with the jury divided eight for acquittal and four for conviction. Those four jurors believed beyond a doubt that Mack killed Vail, but thought he went to Vail's cabin intending to pay back the $90. Then when he found himself alone with Vail, with a chance to get his roll of cash, he took it, and he had to kill the old man. The murder was a crime of opportunity, not planned in advance, which would have been second-degree murder. Once it was explained to them again that second-degree murder wasn't an option, they changed their vote for acquittal. In startling revelations to reporters after the trial they said all twelve might have all agreed on a second-degree murder conviction if they had had that option.

In fact, no, there was no proof that the killing was premeditated. There was not even proof that Vail had been robbed. Although there was probably arson, that wasn't proved either. In fact, since the coroner couldn't be sure how Vail died, it wasn't even proved that he was murdered.

Mack headed the green and yellow wagon up the gravel road with Emma Jean holding tightly to his arm, tears of sweet relief on her cheeks. He said not a word, but drove home exhausted after a trial with no eyewitnesses to the crime, a trial rife with hearsay, devoid of material evidence—a trial that never should have been held.

Chapter Twenty-Two
Boiling the Soup

It was mid-August. Mack had been found innocent of Vail's murder, and Sheriff Weaver and Prosecutor Green saw the futility of finding someone else to take the blame for killing Vail. If Mack couldn't be convicted of it, nobody could. So they turned their attention once again to Yerger's killing. Could they make a case against Mack, or John, or any of the gang in that one? The pressure was still on from the Protective Society and everybody else.

Weaver continued making his rounds, visiting with folks. That sort of investigation fit well with Weaver's easygoing manner. He had a knack for engaging folks in common conversation so they felt like they were just chewing the fat with a neighbor, rather than being questioned. That's how he got most of his best information.

Then one morning he was called out to Delo Rogers's place, where the barn had burned. Rogers declared he wasn't even in the barn that day. It just started burning in the middle of the night. It was clear to him and Weaver both that it was arson. "It was the gang, wasn't it?" Weaver observed. "You know something you want to tell me?" Delo said nothing. That was the whole point of the fire, to keep him, or someone close to him, from telling what he knew. Well, Weaver had better things to do than stare at the remains of Delo's barn. Disgusted, he said he'd look into it as he made his rounds.

Weaver and Green were already planning to question Jesse Johnston again, so when they got to his home Weaver asked if he knew anything about who set fire to Delo's barn. Whether he truly knew or not, Jesse opined that it was John Marsden who did that. Okay, Weaver thought, that was something to use in keeping the gang stirred up, so he and Green moseyed over to see John Marsden, and told him what Jesse said.

Well, Marsden hit the roof. By that time he hated Jesse and distrusted him just as much as he did Mack and Allie. And to think now Jesse would accuse him of burning Delo's barn!

Weaver truly didn't know who did it, and didn't much care about Delo's barn. At that point he simply wanted to keep boiling the soup down. He still figured if he kept working on these men they'd hang each other one way or another.

Green told John he was going to see this kind of trouble continue until Mack was out of the way. Or vice versa. John paced the floor, wrung his hands, and protested that he had already helped the law, and Weaver and Green promised him protection. Yes, Green reminded him, but that was in return for a conviction. They didn't get the conviction, so now John was on his own.

John had admitted stealing only the Plass hogs, but Weaver cautioned him that Mack was going to say he did all of the stealing, and the arson as well. Green asked John, now that he'd sworn that Mack killed Vail, what would he do if Mack swore John killed Yerger? For once, John Marsden was at a loss for words. The two lawmen left, and Weaver worried about the dark and dangerous fire Green was feeding. One of these desperate men was going to do something to protect himself.

The more John thought about Jesse's barn-burning accusation, the madder he got. Finally he went into Hillsboro, to the office of Justice Honey, and swore out a complaint against Jesse for criminal slander. If he had filed civil slander charges, that would have made life easier for the sheriff. Criminal slander meant Jesse had to be arrested. The suit was just so much rooster crowing, and the sheriff hated to waste time on it. And yet, just like his incessant questioning, he was curious to see where it would lead.

Tom Frazier was then constable of Central Township, so Weaver sent him to bring Jesse in. But Frazier came back alone. It seems that when he got out to the house he arrested Jesse just fine. But Jesse said it wasn't really necessary to take him to jail, and promised he'd come in for his hearing. That was enough for the constable. He couldn't very well argue with a man almost his father's age, whom he'd known his whole life. But Weaver said it wouldn't do. The slander was a criminal charge, and Jesse had to be taken into custody. Then if he posted bail, that was fine, but you have to put him in jail, the sheriff explained.

Jesse wasn't at church that Sunday. So after services, Frazier again went to Jesse's place to bring him in, but Jesse wasn't there. Jesse sure had a nice piece of flat land in the heart of the valley, Frazier observed, scanning the tree lines separating that spread from the neighboring parcels. Right over there was the huge farm where Jesse grew up, the place belonging to his father, the judge. But ponder the landscape was all the constable could do, as he waited all afternoon until sundown, and still no Jesse. He had to keep waiting. Weaver would wring his neck if he came back without the suspect again.

Finally, as twilight hung gray above the trees, Jesse came walking up a trail out of the woods in his familiar top hat, carrying his double-barreled shotgun. Seeing the weapon, Frazier pulled his pistol, then stayed out of sight and let Johnston walk all the way up to the house before getting the drop on him. The constable calmly ordered him not to take another step. He took the shotgun from Jesse's hand and explained that they had to do it by the letter of the law. He asked what Jesse was doing out with the gun. "Hunting deer," was the reply. That was an odd thing to be doing on an August afternoon, especially with a shotgun, Frazier prodded, unloading the gun. Of course it was possible Jesse was telling the truth. Buckshot could be used for deer, but the hunter had to be within about thirty yards of the target, so most men preferred a rifle. Jesse just shrugged his shoulders, which only increased Frazier's curiosity.

Frazier retrieved his horse from the shed, and Jesse said his was tied in the adjoining field. They started that way, and just as they reached the rows of brown cornstalks, Jesse bolted into the gathering twilight, holding onto his bouncing hat. He had to cover only a few yards before he disappeared into the field, shrouded in darkness. Frazier fired a shot into the air, kicked the dirt, and called a curse after the suspect that he was glad his daddy didn't hear. There was nothing he could do but ride into Hillsboro Monday morning and report to the sheriff that he "almost" got his man.

Weaver was as mad as Frazier was embarrassed, letting an old man run away from him. But more than that, he was curious about the shotgun. And why did he run away?

Then looking at it from Jesse's viewpoint, he understood. Jesse was running away from something bigger than the slander charge.

He figured John Marsden had him in his rifle sights, along with Mack and Big Allie. So even walking home from Sunday dinner with the Marsdens, Jesse figured he needed his shotgun. And he ran because he figured the law was being controlled by the Protective Society. He'd already been arrested once, and now he couldn't trust anybody. Not even the Frazier boys.

Boy, Weaver thought, people sure are getting twitchy.

After the constable left, Weaver thought about these men Jesse feared. He thought about Jimmy Moss, who was mentioned at the trial. He didn't know how Jimmy fit in with the gang's business, or if he was in it at all. But Tommy and Jimmy Moss had a lot in common with John and Allen Marsden. All four men were entering their twenties. The Marsden boys' father, George, had rarely been home, and died before they were teens. Tommy and Jimmy's father, Mark R. Moss, was along in years when they were born, and died when they were but toddlers. As far as male influences go, none of the four had much to go on.

Emily Moss and her sons Tommy and Jimmy were taken in by Napolean Williams and his wife.

Mark was sheriff when he was forty, but was forced out of office because of his gambling addiction, and his first wife died soon after. He remarried and had more children, but was never the same robust leader who was elected to be the county's top lawman. Tommy and Jimmy were the youngest boys in that second family.

Even their older brothers failed to provide any direction for them. The firstborn son, named Mark after their father, was known as "Devil Mark." His first wife, it was said, went mad and put a shovel full of hot coals in his bed while he slept. Given his nickname, maybe she had reason to roast him. Andrew, a son by Mark R.'s second marriage, died in an accident when the boys were teens.

Their mother, Emily, moved with them to Illinois and back, and by the time Tommy and Jimmy were teenagers, she was struggling to keep them and their little sister Cora fed. She also knew how much her wild boys needed a man to keep them in line. They were taken into the home of Napolean Bonapart Williams, a distant relative, a lifelong farmer, former sheriff, and perennial constable. His sister was the wife of Rev. Sull Frazier and one of his cousins was married to Rev. Joel Hensley, and so Emily and her boys were welcomed into the arms of Sandy Baptist Church.

It was a good arrangement for all. The Williamses' children were grown and gone, except for one daughter. Emily could be a welcome help to the women, and Napolean looked forward to having the boys' help on the farm. But weeks went by with one disappointment after another from the two uncaring teens. When Napolean went to the barn after breakfast, the horse was not hitched to the plow as he had asked. The axes that needed new handles never got them. The piglets weren't weaned. Unfortunately, the boys' hard knocks had hardened their hearts to family and shared chores, so they didn't turn out to be the willing workers for which Napolean had hoped. He was a fine man, and might have had a positive influence on the boys, had he not appeared so late in their lives, when their course was already set.

Allen Marsden had been Mack's neighbor when they moved to Crystal City together. Although he was bolder than his younger brother John, he was also more careful, and just plain smart. That's why he remained a part-timer with the gang, moving on the periphery. After all, Allen was married to a strong-willed wife and had a couple young sons. That's why they lived away from the others, in Crystal City, then Sulphur Springs. They were particularly glad to be there on the other side of the county after Vail's murder. That was also when John Marsden's and Tommy Moss's wives decided they didn't want to live with their husbands. It was clear that 1881 was the year that a whole group of people had decided John Marsden was too dangerous to be near.

Chapter Twenty-Three

"Don't Shoot, Boys!"

The hog stealing trial was a month away, with Mack, John, and Allen Marsden, Tommy Moss, and Big Allie Hensley all facing charges of grand larceny in the theft of the Plass hogs. They'd all pleaded innocent. Mack was still madder than an old wet hen at the men's refusal to collaborate on a story that pinned the blame where it belonged. So here they were, all caught in John's trap, John hanging it on Mack and Big Allie, and Mack with no choice but to name John, Allen, and Tommy as the thieves.

The prosecution's list of witnesses read like a census of the Sandy Valley. Everybody knew something. Even Mack's own Uncle Richard. And Dorsey Hensley, Delo Rogers, and John Gillman. Gillman was on Vail's list of debtors and his sister was married to Allen Marsden. The prosecution had heard that he might know all kinds of things. The prosecution was going to put them all on the stand. Of course who would tell the truth, the whole truth, and nothing else, was yet to be seen.

Samuel Marsden still begged Mack not to testify against the thieves. "They're dangerous men," he said. "You've seen what they did to keep others quiet, and they'll do the same to you."

"No," Mack told him, "they're afraid of me. They wouldn't dare try anything against me."

"Not face to face," Samuel agreed. "That's not the kind of men they are. They're the kind who'll ambush you." He paused. "Or your family. Look what they've already done to the Hensleys."

Mack's younger brother Samuel J. Marsden.

"That's exactly why I've got to testify, to protect all of us," was the answer. "I've been a coward and look what it got me," Mack declared. He said he was determined to put them away, clear his own name, and end it all.

He lifted his bat to his shoulder and said, "But right now I've got a game to play."

"Good," Samuel smiled. "Go have some fun and forget all that."

Mack walked out to the wagon, where Gabe, Big Allie, and little brothers Samuel and Clarence waited. They scolded him for being slow and Gabe started pulling his wagon out of the yard, making Mack run to throw his bat in, grab the hind gate, and hurl himself in. They were all excited about the rematch of the Sandy versus Hillsboro game. Mack missed the first one, so they were glad to have him back in the lineup. There were no uniforms, but they wore red neckerchiefs and each one had his own handmade bat. Gabe was the catcher, the only one with a glove, and he had a fine mask made by blacksmith Moss.

When they pulled into the field at the edge of town their teammates were already there, and the Hillsboro boys in their blue neckerchiefs had some feed sacks filled with dirt and laid out for bases. After handshakes and back slaps, the Sandy team was ready for their first at-bat. They looked over to see the Hillsboro team huddled in a circle, and then a lone player walked over. He sheepishly reported that they didn't know Mack was on the team, and now that they knew, several of their players refused to play against him.

Now Mack had heard everything. He couldn't even play baseball without hearing about how hated he was. Gabe, ever the defender, spoke up, as the men shouldered together, pushing Mack to the back. They were here to play as a team, and it wasn't up to Hillsboro to decide who was on their team, Gabe told them.

The Hillsboro spokesman looked over the group and asked, "Mack, what do you say?"

"He says he's playing, if you little babies aren't afraid to lose a game today," Gabe answered before Mack could open his mouth. Gabe looked up and down the line and let it soak in. Every man's jaw was set. They were standing up for their own.

The Hillsboro huddle continued, and two men walked away. Then with a little more protesting and a little convincing, nine agreed to play. But they may have been sorry. After the controversy the Sandy squad played like men on fire.

While the Hillsboro men scolded each other and cussed their luck, the Sandy nine smiled, had fun, and pushed each other to play better. They started Mack as pitcher, and the opposing batters were obviously unnerved when they saw him hurling the ball their way. Sandy's offensive strategy was to get men on base, then bring up Big Allie's big bat. At the end, they all walked wearily away, and Sandy had won by a blistering score of 59 to 23.

While Mack was reclaiming his life, standing up for his family and his name, John Marsden was pressing down hard to undo it all. He sat in the dark that night, working up a sinister plan that was at once complex, and yet simple enough to work. Monday morning he and Tommy went over and got brother Allen, and the three of them went to a saloon on the Sulphur Springs riverfront where they could talk.

John said with the noose tightening around them, the only sure way to get in the clear was to kill Mack. Trouble was, everybody knew John and Mack hated each other so if they got Mack out of the way, the blame would surely fall on him, John. What this little gang of Marsdens and a Moss had to do was get rid of Mack, but make sure John had a solid alibi.

John was calling upon the oldest of bonds, blood loyalty, to work his own salvation. He would get his family to help him do his dirty dealing on Mack, while making sure he was in the clear. Allen didn't like it one bit and stood up, kicking his chair, clattering against the wall. He knew everything they were saying was right, but he cursed John for a devil and a dirty dog for dragging him into his dirty business. Tommy studied his beer. John looked up at his older brother and reassured him that he didn't even have to be at the scene when they got rid of Mack. If he'd just do what John said, he'd be totally in the clear.

Allen knew none of them could say no to the plan. They had to help John because he was true kin, and Mack was of that other side of the Marsdens. That thought had a calming effect on Allen. All that old pain of being shunned began to come up, and that helped justify the awful things they had to do.

Allen sat down again, still red in the face, but ready to listen to the plan. "Look," John said, "I've already confessed to stealing the Plass hogs, so that's that. As for the rest of us, who can testify against us?"

"Mack," Tommy answered.

"And Big Allie," John added. "They both have to go. That'll be the end of it all."

They all exchanged looks, hoping the eyes would confirm a commitment to their common black-hearted cause.

"Besides, John said, "the Protective Society is behind us. They've told me directly that this is what they want. We'll be heroes around here."

Heroes. That sounded good to Tommy. Allen raised an eyebrow.

Only one thing was missing. They needed a shotgun. These men weren't long-distance rifle marksmen. They were going to have one chance, and only one chance at Mack. They had to get close, and they dared not face the cool Mack Marsden without a shotgun, the most lethal weapon on the frontier at short range. As the pellets emerged from the barrel and spread into an ever-widening circle, they made sure something got hit. And tiny as they were, they might do little damage, or any one of them could be fatal. Buckshot, the size of peas, had the best chance of inflicting lethal wounds. A shooter didn't have to be a particularly good shot, just bold enough to face his target when he fired. Even at a distance up to a hundred feet, a shotgun could speak death, with a couple of dozen shot packed into an area from a man's head to his waist.

John had that excellent Winchester rifle Mack gave him. Allen and Tommy had only rifles. But Tommy's little brother Jimmy was a turkey hunter who owned a fine shotgun. Jimmy, the one mentioned at the Vail murder trial, the one quoted as saying he'd kill Mack if paid to do it. It was perfect. Part of the other men's defense would be that none of them owned a shotgun. And since Jimmy had never been in the gang, he would never be suspected.

They asked Tommy if he could get Jimmy. "Don't worry," he assured the Marsden boys, "Jimmy would love to take a shot at Mack Marsden." And Tommy went off to recruit his brother to their cause.

With the plan in place, John, Tommy, and Allen began to spend their days keeping an eye on Mack, waiting for the right time and place. Time was running out, with the trial fast approaching in September. Finally, the last Tuesday afternoon in August, they took their horses and followed Mack and Big Allie all the way into St. Louis in a search for some new meat processors. Hoffman and the others wouldn't buy from them anymore. Mack had a business to run, and he needed new customers. So they made some calls a little farther up the river into St. Louis, and by the end of the day he was satisfied that they had lined up plenty of good places to sell.

It was getting late when the men shadowing them watched Mack and Allie stop the green and yellow rig at their usual tavern. They led Coal to the livery, then went in and sat down for a meal and a beer. The spies knew Mack and Big Allie would pay a couple dollars for a cot and spend the night before heading home. It was the perfect opportunity they'd been waiting for.

The gravel road was easy to see, even in the dark, as they rode to the home of Jimmy Moss, just outside Sulphur Springs. He had already agreed to the plan, but had no way of knowing when the trap would be set. The late visitors woke him and told him it was time to act. John put on a pot of coffee and stayed there with him while Tommy and Allen went on to Allen's home, arriving there before midnight. John had them in pairs because that made sure nobody backed out.

Allen told his wife they were going hunting early the next morning, then he and Tommy sat at the kitchen table eating beans, greens, and cornbread, washing it down with corn liquor, and talking deep into the night about the prey they'd be stalking in a few hours. Allen had tried hard to stay out of it, and now here he found himself pressed back into service. He went to sleep that night troubled, but hopeful that tomorrow's action would end it all.

The next day, Wednesday, August 28, after coffee and side meat, Tommy Moss and Allen Marsden set out with their loaded rifles around 6:00 in the morning. At the edge of town they met John Marsden, along with Jimmy Moss, who was nervous as a frog in a skillet and carrying the shotgun loaded with buckshot. It was a Parker Brothers side-by-side twelve-gauge lifter model with pistol grip stock, exposed, engraved hammers, and twist barrels. But there was no time to admire the fine weapon. In less than a minute they parted company.

Allen mounted the horse Jimmy brought for him and rode for DeSoto, where nobody knew the Marsden brothers well enough to tell them apart. There he would entrench himself at Strickland's Saloon on Main Street, drink and play cards, and make sure lots of people took note of his presence. He would introduce himself loudly and often, not as himself, but as John Marsden.

The real John, with Tommy and Jimmy, followed Glaize Creek northwest on foot. Horses would have been too easy to see, too slow in the trees, and they left tracks. A wagon would have required them to stick to the roads. Old-fashioned foot power was the stealthiest way to get to their destination, and the fastest way back. It allowed them to walk on the road for speed and ease, and if necessary, to move into the trees and keep moving, unseen.

They walked along the Antonia–Sulphur Springs Road, which followed the creek, but about halfway the men cut off on the barely used Dry Fork Road. It was wide enough for people and horses, but narrow and difficult for wagon traffic, as it wound over one little ridge after another. Up and down they hiked, always ascending the 250-foot grade up Frisco Hill. Arriving at the junction with LeMay Ferry Road, they walked a little ways to the exact spot they wanted. There they could see and hear anyone approaching from either direction, and the bushes on the north side offered a comfortable and complete hiding place.

It was approaching noon when Mack drove his wagon toward Antonia, Big Allie at his side. Though it was a typically sticky August morning, Mack still had his coat on. It was the easiest place to carry his engraved Smith & Wesson .32, and those days he made sure it was always in easy reach. As for Allie, he'd always refused to carry a gun, figuring if he had one, it would just give somebody an excuse to shoot him. Besides, everybody was so afraid of Mack, Allie felt safe with him.

They'd been ascending the last incline before starting down into Antonia. As they approached the last curve before the grade leveled out, the weary Coal strained against his traces, and the wagon crawled along slower and slower. The road ran around the shoulder of the hill, which at that point descended on the left into a steep-sided, mile-long hollow, one of many leading out to Glaize Creek. On the right the hill rose sharply. There, years before, a huge downed tree had lodged itself, building a wall of dirt behind it and giving root to thick brush. Beyond it was a clear gap in the bushes, and that's exactly where Big Allie was looking as his face was naturally turned slightly toward Mack, intent on what he was saying. He was the first to see three armed men stand up in the gap and step quickly into the road.

Because of their nerves, they'd stepped out a little sooner than they intended, and Mack's quick instincts had instantly stopped the slow-moving wagon, leaving them several yards away. Tommy and John held their rifles at chest level, while Jimmy came out in the middle with the shotgun, drawing a bead on the two men in the wagon. Mack recognized them immediately, and as his hand eased gently toward the pistol in his coat, he called, "For God's sake, don't shoot, boys!" just as the first shot rang out. He was hit in the head and chest with several pellets, any one of which could have been fatal, and the force sent him up and out onto the shoulder of the road. Jimmy took one step forward, lifting the scattergun up high to clear the horse, and his second shot followed instantly, slamming into Hensley. The startled animal lurched and ran down the road, knocking the gunmen aside, leaving them to watch the wagon bounce away carrying a living witness to their merciless assault.

The assassins had no way of knowing they'd left a man alive. No one would have thought that, seeing Hensley propelled over the seat to flop limply into the bed. Thinking they'd killed them both, they bounded down the hill, running and walking through the woods, the quickest, most direct route back to Sulphur Springs. This time they stayed off the road, breaking through the underbrush, which was just beginning to die back under the strain of August heat and drought, and taking advantage of game trails when they found them headed in the right direction. It was bloody hot. Limbs of overhanging oaks and seedling poplars swatted at their heads. Bushes grabbed their legs and arms. But the assassins barely noticed, plunging onward away from their deed, and toward their alibi.

It was a welcome sight when they saw Glaize Creek glistening through the trees. They fell to their knees, plunged their burning faces into the water, and drank deeply. But they couldn't linger. Jimmy split off for his house to clean up and put the shotgun away, and the other two followed the creek to Allen's house. There they freshened up, changed shirts, quickly ate some lunch, then got into Allen's wagon. After swinging by Jimmy's house to pick him up, they headed for DeSoto. When they got there, John stayed outside while Tommy and Jimmy strode into Strickland's saloon. Allen looked up from his poker game and froze. What did he see in their faces? There was an instant of recognition as knowing looks shot between them. Tom hollered a hearty, "John," which told Allen the deed was done. There was a catch in his chest, but he couldn't allow himself to feel anything at that point. This was survival. "Tom," he hollered back, then excused himself from the game.

That's where the tricky part came in. They quietly slipped out the door, to where John waited in the alley. He and Allen traded shirts and hats. They were exactly the same size and build, both clean shaven, and they looked almost exactly alike. Allen fussed with his clothes and could hardly stand to look at the other men. Quickly, he shook hands all around, mounted the horse that brought him, and started riding for home, relieved that his part in the murderous adventure was over.

Then when John went back into the saloon, he was simply taking his brother's place. Those who had met Allen as John, now saw John as John, in the same shirt and hat, and across the dark room, he was taken as the same man. So as far as the other customers were concerned, he'd been there all day. He, Tommy, and Jimmy found a table to themselves, and opened a fresh bottle of comfort. The talk was deadly serious, but they were so relieved, little smiles played on their lips. Their plan had worked.

Except for one thing: Big Allie was left alive.

Chapter Twenty-Four
Deathbed Testimony

Ten minutes after the shootings, Coal trotted into the streets of Antonia with the mortally wounded Allie sprawled across the wagon bed. At about the same time, Mack's body was discovered by Bill Fine, the mail carrier.

All through the evening there was a deathwatch at Allie's bedside, and Sheriff Weaver was there when the dying man talked. Though riddled with buckshot in his chest and stomach, he was able to whisper the identities of the attackers. It was the same thing he'd already told others as he lay bleeding on the streets of Antonia. Dr. Hull, Buzz Marsden, and Gabe Johnston all heard Allie name the shooters to Weaver as he lay in John Gillman's bed. It was John Marsden, Tommy Moss, and Jimmy Moss.

Armed with that, Weaver went to one of the justices for warrants, dispatched deputies, and sent telegrams to all the surrounding towns, warning the local law to be on the lookout for the suspects. That very night, a DeSoto town marshal named Beal arrested all three men, still sitting at the same table in Strickland's saloon, and early the next morning they were all tucked away in the Hillsboro jail.

When they were arrested, John calmly told Beale he had an alibi, and he repeated it again to Weaver. "Frisco Hill? Ha. That's fifteen miles away." All day he'd been drinking and playing cards right there in DeSoto, and he was sure a hundred men would be happy to testify to that effect. Weaver locked him up anyway, at least until he could check out the card-playing story.

Buzz Marsden stayed at Gillman's house with Allie, in case he talked any more, and others came and went during the day. Later, with the three men in jail, Weaver returned to the dying Allie, and told him about John's alibi. He was in DeSoto all day.

"Allie," he said, "you're not going to make it. You're gut shot, bleeding inside, and the doctors say there's nothing they can do to save you. You've got to tell it straight, Allie, because I know you don't want to die with a lie on your lips."

Allie thought a moment, gathered his strength, then whispered that he might be wrong, and if the third man wasn't John, "It might have been Allen Marsden." What he hadn't accounted for was the fact that the men had the guns at their shoulders. That, with their hats casting black shadows in the midday sun, obscured their faces. He recognized Jimmy, and there was no mistaking the tall, slender Tommy, with his big ears. Allie had instantly assumed the face he couldn't see was that of John Marsden, just because he and Tommy were always together. Besides, John was the only one Mack and Allie really thought could do such a thing. Allie was sure of Tommy and Jimmy Moss, and yes, if the other one wasn't John, it must have been Allen Marsden. "John and Allen look so much alike," he whispered.

Weaver didn't know what to think. He'd seen more than a few men die, and deathbed testimony was as good as it gets. Even the worst liar tells the truth when he's going to meet his maker. So Allie surely was trying to tell it straight.

On Friday the coroner, Dr. Brewster, went out to Samuel Marsden's home and conducted an inquest. The only material evidence was a few large shot taken from Marsden's body, and the only testimony was by Sheriff Weaver, farmer Meng, mailman Fine, and farmer Beckleg, all men who saw Marsden only after he was dead. The verdict of the inquest was simply that Mack Marsden came to his death through the hands of one or more "unknown" assassins. The finality of that was a crushing outcome for Samuel Marsden.

As if in belligerent testimony to his bigger-than-life size, Big Allie clung to life all that day, but finally passed away Friday night. So Brewster held a second inquest, and this time, unlike Mack's inquest, Allie's deathbed accusations could be brought into evidence. The official verdict was that Allen Hensley was killed by "Thomas and Jimmy Moss and either John or Allen Marsden."

McMullin and his *Democrat* fearlessly sang an even bolder tune with the edition that reported the murders of Mack and Allie. It said right out that the Yerger killing had been "laid at [Mack's] door." And it said the paper had been "abused" by his family for simply reporting the facts of various crimes. The *St. Louis Globe-Democrat* took a similar tone, bolding proclaiming that Allie's death "had rid Jefferson County of one of the most thoroughly equipped terrors of the state." It went on to observe that the killing was the work of vigilantes, and nobody was going to say anything against them. The *Post-Dispatch* said Mack's death brought "a feeling of thankfulness in the breasts of the respectable citizens...." And it was all detailed under the headline, "A Desperado's Doom," branding Mack with that label forever.

The victims' families buried Mack Marsden and Allen Hensley, attended by only a handful of people. Mack's death record said he was buried in the family cemetery, beside his mother, Mary, and away from public scrutiny. Big Allie was interred at Sandy Baptist Church, nestled amid generations of his kin, but without a stone. It wasn't because they never had money to spare for a stone. Plenty of the Hensleys had nice stones.

That's the way things stood through the weekend. By Monday morning Weaver had checked out John Marsden's story about being in DeSoto the day of the murders, and it seemed to be true. Every bartender, barfly, and barmaid in DeSoto said yes, John Marsden was in there, loud, friendly, and having a good time all day last Thursday. And yes, the Moss boys had joined him early in the afternoon. Weaver had little choice but to release John, go arrest his brother Allen, and throw him in with Tommy and Jimmy.

At that point, John's brilliant scheme to change clothes was working beautifully for him. But it was backfiring in a deadly way on his brother and the Mosses.

Justices of the Peace Rankin and D. G. Goff came up from DeSoto to give the accused murderers a hearing. There were justices in each township. But the justice in Rock Township, where the murders happened, was George Edinger, brother-in-law to the murdered Joseph Yerger. He had a vested interest in the case, probably thought Mack killed Yerger, and would have loved to shake hands with Mack's killers. Big Allie's father, Leander, and his uncle Thomas Williams were the justices in Central Township, where the murdered men lived. And the justice in Joachim, where the accused men lived, was a Moss. So Prosecutor Green wisely brought the two justices from the southern township of Valle, because they would be perceived as impartial. Goff truly was. But Rankin was steeped in the case and, after all, was the one to whom Mack was brought in DeSoto for the hearing that set up his pursuit by the lynch mob.

A sizable crowd gathered in the Hillsboro courthouse for the hearing on Monday, Sept 3. *The St. Louis Post-Dispatch* knew the conspiracy ran deep and jumped on board. The paper cheered for the political powers that brought about Mack's death, saying there was "a feeling of thankfulness in the breasts of the respectable citizens who have lived in that district for three years in dread of incurring his displeasure."

The newspaper had already decided the accused men were guilty, but justified, saying, "If it develops that the suspected men prove their innocence, it will have but one plausible theory, viz.: that he [Mack] was taken for the county's good and that the citizens know more about the same than they are willing to tell."

For the state's case, Green did little more than produce the witnesses who heard the dying Hensley name his assailants. They all agreed that he had named John, Thomas, and Jimmy, and later replaced John with Allen. Then Thomas, Jimmy, and Allen testified that it was an unfortunate coincidence that they had been out together hunting that morning from Sulphur Springs. They said two of them carried rifles, and one a small shotgun loaded with squirrel shot. It couldn't have been the big gun used in the killings, they implied. Several witness said the men were seen in Sulphur Springs about noon. The time of the shootings was fixed at about 11:00 a.m., and it was agreed by all that nobody could have made it all that distance over such rough country from Frisco Hill to Sulphur Springs in less than two hours.

The prosecution clearly established that the two sides were at each other's throats, Mack and Big Allie on one side, and John, Tommy, and Allen on the other. With the threats that had been made on both sides, it was no secret that the death of the two men left the other three breathing easy. And yet, the accused men were entirely charitable toward Big Allie, saying he "must be mistaken" about what he saw. No accusations that he was out to get them. They were just playing the innocents. It was an act that played well in the court and with the press, which said Allie "had always been accounted a determined bad man" who had "the worst of motives." But nobody had ever before talked about the meek, hulking man that way, and it was by far the most attention any newspaper had ever paid to Allie.

John and the others let the lawyers and newspapers vilify Hensley. They just shook their heads sympathetically and suggested that in the excitement Hensley didn't really know who shot him. The defense actually used the fact that the men hated each other as to why Hensley named John, Tommy, and Jimmy. If someone were going to shoot him, they're the ones he would suspect.

Of course the hole in that argument was that Jimmy Moss had never before been mentioned in any of the gang's activities or accusations. Why, with all the cousins and other kinfolk running around the county, would Allie name young Jimmy, unless he really saw him? However, nobody raised those questions at the hearing.

In the end, the judges observed that there was no evidence beyond Hensley's uncertain eyewitness account. Though their feelings were left unspoken, Rankin and plenty of others felt a service had been rendered to the county by whoever fired the fatal shots. As the *Post-Dispatch* described the scene, "Outside of the natural curiosity there is no great desire to ascertain who the public benefactors are or avenge the death." So in the end, the defendants were released, acquitted of the charges for lack of evidence.

The courthouse cleared amid hand-shaking and joking, as Marsdens fumed. How could the law so easily dismiss the killing of my son, a man repeatedly accused, arrested, and investigated, and never found guilty, Samuel Marsden wondered. It was obviously collusion, crooked business up and down the line. A wink here, a promise there, a whispered plan behind a closed office door. Samuel swore he would not let it rest. If it took the rest of his life, he'd clear the name of Mack Marsden.

While his heart was breaking, he had plenty of supporters in the neighborhood who were ready for a more brutal approach. Men talked and women encouraged. The shotgun ambush had taken away any allegiance to civility, and there was nothing to stop them from lynching the same ones the court turned loose.

After the hearing, Sheriff Weaver stopped John Marsden and suggested that if he wanted to live long enough to see his hog stealing trial, he should check himself back into the Hillsboro jail. John saw the wisdom in Weaver's advice and stuck to him tighter than a judge's hatband.

Meanwhile, a man from the Protective Society took Allen aside and told him it was all turning out wrong. Because Big Allie lived long enough to name the shooters, some members of the Society were saying the group should do what the law couldn't. Some of the same men who once wanted Mack's head now wanted Allen's, John's, Tommy's, and Jimmy's. Even worse, as he knew, the people on Mack's side, who hated the Society, were after them too.

So that evening following the hearing, Allen and Elizabeth Marsden, Tommy Moss, and Jimmy and Jane Moss packed their clothes. They had to get out, and they weren't telling anyone where they were going. The day before, they had delivered to their relatives some things they couldn't take with them. Some fine dishes and silver. Pickling crocks. A good saw, mining tools, and a mule. A spinning wheel and a baby crib. Those could be used by someone in the family. The livestock had been quickly sold for a fraction of its worth. The rest of their possessions were abandoned as they sat, in cabins and sheds and on porches.

John and Tommy had to walk away from their land on the outskirts of Crystal City, bought with Anson Vail's money. It was the best-kept secret in Sandy history, and they abandoned the thing for which they risked so much.

It took until well after noon Tuesday to fit their personal items into bags and trunks, load it all into Allen's wagon, and then drive over to the Pevely train station. They were all going to make their getaway on the St. Louis, Iron Mountain & Southern train headed south, leaving out of Pevely's Riverside Station at 8:14 p.m. .

The approaching travelers saw the old station sitting like an island, a half mile beyond the eastern edge of the tiny town, floating in an ocean of grass and scrub willows on the sandy bank of the mighty

A train from St. Louis pulls into Riverside Depot.

The Pevely train station, where the group made their getaway, was east of town on the banks of the Mississippi, and aptly named Riverside Depot. Courtesy of Timothy W. and Jacob C. Jones.

Mississippi. With a weary sigh, Allen pulled the wagon up and set the brake. He and Jimmy stacked the bags on the platform, Tommy climbed slowly down, stretched his lanky frame, brushed the wrinkles out of his shirt, and walked to the window to buy their tickets. The stationmaster pulled long strips of paper and stamped them repeatedly in all the right places. Thomas smiled and shook his head. Only an agent could understand that system. They exchanged money for tickets, and then the whole group settled down for a long wait on the platform.

The men dearly wanted to walk into Pevely for a cold beer, but it was just too risky. They weren't going to go anywhere without their guns, which were bound to attract attention, and the fewer people knew where they were and what they were doing, the better. So Allen, Tommy, and Jimmy sat on a bench, long guns in their laps, casting glances over their shoulders as the afternoon sun played longer and longer shadows across the tracks. The view offered nothing but the trees along the river. There were no other travelers boarding the train there that night. It seemed like a safe place, where no one knew them. And yet who could blame them for being nervous? There was plenty of suspicion, plenty of circumstantial evidence, and plenty of whispered threats. Those boys had every reason to fear for their lives.

There was a somber flurry of activity when John Gillman rode his horse over to pick up the wagon and team. He handed Allen the price they had agreed on, then tied his horse on the back, bid them all good luck, and headed home. And the little group felt even more alone.

That night the train pulled south out of Pevely with some anxious, silent passengers. They were starting over, but leaving so much behind. Elizabeth's thoughts were on her family. The men couldn't get their minds off of Mack's friends and relatives, some of whom were probably out looking for them at that very time. By morning the talk around Sandy would be, "It's a good thing they lit out, because if not, somebody would have lynched 'em."

Chapter Twenty-Five
"Let's Go, Mother"

John enjoyed the safety of the Hillsboro jail for the next two weeks. He'd already pleaded guilty to grand larceny for hog stealing, so when the trial came around, he threw himself on the mercy of the court, pleading pitifully that he was under the influence of the evil Mack Marsden, and Mack forced him to steal the pigs. But it did no good. There were five other men tried for completely unrelated charges of grand larceny that day. They were all convicted, and the judge had no choice but to give them all the same treatment, two years in the state pen.

That was Thursday, September 19. Early the next morning Weaver set out with John Marsden and the other five thieves, plus a man convicted of assault, accompanied by guards Jesse Waggener, Jesse Clark, and Lawson Frazier. They were headed to Jefferson City and the Missouri State Penitentiary, known as "the Walls," for its gray stone fences that stretched completely around the grounds. Weaver had no desire to keep that big bunch in his jail. They were expensive and a lot of trouble. Most important, he didn't want to be responsible for protecting John Marsden one minute longer than he had to.

One odd thing, Weaver thought, was the change in Marsden's demeanor. He used to whine incessantly about how he helped the law, and the law had to help him. But lately, since he'd been cleared of murdering Mack and Allie, the prisoner had grown uncommonly quiet, brows knitted with a furtive look that was at once morose and nervous. Of course as long as he was quiet, it suited Weaver just fine.

Top: Missouri State Penitentiary in a view that shows how it earned its nickname, "the Walls." Left: John Marsden passed through these gates of the prison, where he served only a fraction of his two-year sentence for grand larceny.

The fact is, John Marsden was quiet because he was mulling over the dark and deadly deal he'd made. To fully understand the cunning of John and his co-conspirators, it's necessary to consider the case of a more notorious fellow Missourian, Jesse James. Both cases had direct ties to the crime-busting, pardon-granting governor of the state, Thomas Theodore Crittenden.

He campaigned on an anti-crime platform, proclaiming in his inaugural address, "Missouri cannot be the home and abiding place of lawlessness of any character." Though Jesse James certainly wasn't the only criminal in the state, Crittenden's promise to bring him and his brother Frank to justice helped him win the election. Jesse had once been a beloved folk hero, his family victimized by Civil War brutality and cruel detectives. But after twenty-five years, his continued robber-

Missouri governor Thomas Theodore Crittenden. Courtesy of the Missouri History Museum.

ies, sprinkled with increasingly meaningless murders, wore thin on the people of Missouri. They were finished with gunfights and ready for better schools, telephones, police departments, and imported fruit.

Bob Ford became the people's avenger, but in the process became forever known as "the dirty little coward who shot Mr. Howard and laid poor Jesse in his grave." Bob and his brother Charlie had never proved themselves loyal or capable of being members of Jesse's gang but kept hanging around, asking to be included. As it became harder for Jesse to recruit good men, he took Bob and Charlie on minor escapades. Still, they longed to become completely trusted, rough and ready bad men, and Jesse didn't realize the depth of their frustration. That, plus a nice railroad-funded reward of $10,000, was what the law relied upon in persuading Bob to turn against Jesse, the one man other gang members feared. Bob met with Gov. Crittenden, who agreed to pardon him and Charlie for any gang activities if he would take care of Jesse once and for all, and then leave the state.

About the same time, with Mack Marsden making the newspapers in not only St. Louis but also Sacramento, St. Paul, and all the way to

New York, Crittenden felt that he had to get involved with his case too. In fact, Crittenden made a practice of fighting crime with variations of the pardon-granting strategy he used on Bob Ford.

He pardoned Frank James and other gang members of various offenses. Crittenden was so deep in the gang's business, Frank surrendered to him personally, and when Frank died, Crittenden's son served as pallbearer. One of the gang, Tucker Bassham, was pardoned in exchange for his testimony against fellow gang member Bill Ryan in the Blue Cut train robbery. In all, the governor paid out $20,000 in reward money for the capture and conviction of members of the James gang but refused to divulge who got the money.

It wasn't just the James gang. When a new state law making gambling houses illegal resulted in eight prominent St. Louis citizens being sentenced to six months in jail, the governor pardoned them all summarily. Though the move was widely criticized, his critics didn't know that a couple of those men were helping with entrapments to solve more serious crimes. Besides, since the gambling house law was a new one, Crittenden rationalized that they deserved some mercy, and the fact that they were Crittenden campaign contributors didn't hurt their case either.

In that era, pardons were more common than in later years, and yet Crittenden must rank among the most pardoning of executives. During his four years in office he loosed the bonds of over 350 convicted felons, including dozens of murderers. He averaged almost one release every three working days. As shocking as the number of pardons was the degree to which he reduced sentences. For rape, he thought a couple of years was enough to serve, whether the sentence was five years or twenty. Murderers sentenced to life or hanging were routinely released in as little as three years.

In his 1883 address to the legislature, Crittenden claimed that he had pardoned fifty-four felons in the last two years. In fact, he was only counting the violent crimes, omitting others like grand larceny, arson, and armed robbery. He seemed to have a soft spot for those convicted of second-degree murder, whom he said don't belong in the "criminal class." Addressing the general assembly in 1884, he explained, "Such persons are often the victims of misfortune, rather than criminals, who, under the influence of sudden passion, being assaulted or in a heated personal encounter, killed their fellow man, and in whose hearts no vindictive, no malicious, no criminal feeling had existed prior to the act, but who were driven to it by a mischance that might befall any man in society."

Crittenden's poor judgment of character sometimes came back to haunt him. One Charles F. Stevens, better known as "Omaha" Charlie Stevens, of Maryville, Missouri, was convicted of second-degree murder and sent to prison for ten years. Omaha Charlie knew the governor had a young daughter, and mailed her entertaining wooden toys he made in his cell. The girl became infatuated with the attentive distant prisoner she'd never met, and when she became terminally ill with diphtheria, the gifts from Charlie became her only joy. At last, her dying wish was that her daddy the governor would pardon him. Of course Crittenden obliged.

Soon after his release in the first week of December 1884, Omaha Charlie got drunk at Hilgert's saloon in Maryville, just a little north of St. Joseph. He shot and killed Hubert Kremey and was promptly arrested. The governor was then doubly embarrassed and furious. Of course there was no guarantee Omaha Charlie would be convicted, and even if he was, Crittenden didn't want to face any suggestions that his deceased daughter would want a second pardon. To be absolutely sure Omaha Charlie's criminal career was over, it was generally agreed that a lynching would be a fitting end.

Lynching was beyond Crittenden's normal crime-fighting procedures. But it was certainly worth a try on Charlie, sitting in a small-town jail with a willing sheriff. State agents recruited men who could raise a good crowd against the accused. Around 1:00 a.m. a mob of about fifty arrived at the jail, some wearing hoods or neckerchiefs over their faces. Sheriff John Anderson feigned a struggle, but the mob prevailed, leaving Omaha Charlie dangling from the East Fourth Street railroad bridge, and the governor breathing a sigh of relief. The mob that hung Charlie was never tied to Crittenden, but he was personally tied to the case, and he certainly was a man capable of such swift dealing.

The parallels of the Jesse James and Mack Marsden cases, including the extent of Crittenden's involvement, are astonishing. Though the Fords told people they were Jesse's cousins, they really weren't related. Similarly, John and Allen claimed to be Marsdens, but Mack's side of the family never claimed them. Both stories involved brothers and other family members, key gang insiders versus those on the fringes, threats and mistrust within the gang, intimidation of witnesses, and behind it all, a feared leader, accused of multiple murders and thefts, but never convicted of any crime.

Bob Ford's assassination plot used his brother Charlie, just as John Marsden's plan used his brother Allen and the Mosses. Jesse had Frank in his shadow, while Mack had Big Allie. In the end, both gangs were the victims of excess. Jesse's downfall was trying a raid too far away in Minnesota. The Marsden downfall was a theft of too many expensive hogs. Yet in a broader view, they were also both victims of changing times. Jesse and Mack were about the same age, and died within a year of each other, marking the end of an era that Missouri society would no longer abide.

Bob Ford had a face-to-face meeting with the governor, though John Marsden never did. Nonetheless, a deadly similar deal was struck for John through an intermediary. The first contact may have been through Anton Yerger, whom Crittenden had started on his career as a judge when he appointed him to associate justice of the county court in 1867. In his anguish over his brother's murder, he certainly might have called the governor's attention to the problems in Sandy. However, Anton passed away a year before Mack's fate was decided.

Certainly Samuel Byrns, the Moss boys' attorney and cousin, who put up bail for Tommy, could have arranged it with a letter or a visit. He was not only an attorney, but also a former state representative and senator who wielded considerable power in the Democratic Party. And Prosecutor Green may have played a role, with his desire to ascend to the bench, and the influence of his uncle, a former U.S. senator. It could have been McMullin, Rankin, Donnell, or a number of others. It was never revealed who sat down in the governor's office to talk about using John Marsden to eliminate Mack Marsden, but the terms were simple: in exchange for getting rid of Mack, John would serve a minimum sentence for the hog stealing, to which he had already confessed, then leave Missouri for good.

The law couldn't let John off without jail time. That's what Crittenden had done for Bob Ford, keeping him out of jail by pardoning him within hours of his conviction for Jesse's murder. The governor's collusion was too obvious, and he was criticized roundly for it. He wouldn't repeat that mistake. Instead, John was told to go to prison and await his pardon there.

All things considered, John's options were limited, and it was a deal he couldn't turn down. He demanded a cash reward like the one Bob Ford collected, but that was not to be. There was a vague promise of enough money to leave the state. But his true reward was in a shortened prison term. Without the deal, he and Tommy Moss were looking at a long stretch in prison for stealing livestock. Plus, they'd still be suspects in various arsons, as well as the murders of Vail and Joseph Yerger. If he eliminated Mack, all those crimes would disappear with him.

They all agreed not to speak a word of the deal. In fact, when Bob Ford's agreement with Crittenden was brought to light in the press, it was actually Crittenden who wanted it revealed, so he would get proper credit for ending Jesse's criminal career. But he learned his lesson on that, because many people thought Crittenden had gone too far, participating in murder. That's when he insisted that the deal had never been "dead or alive," but for Ford to help in Jesse's capture. So when Mack's case came up, the governor didn't need any more publicity of that sort. That's why John Marsden's deal remained even more secretive—and the terms even more vague.

Just as Bob Ford was left to figure out how to kill Jesse, John made his own plan to get Mack. In fact, John's plan was better than Ford's, because he had an alibi, while Ford thought killing Jesse would make him rich and famous. On the other hand, Big Allie's deathbed testimony identifying the shooters certainly wasn't part of John's plan. That's when the Protective Society lived up to its part of the bargain and made sure John and his accomplices were acquitted at their hearing on the charge of murder. After all, they did not want to see John get on the witness stand and say the governor told him to do it.

Within two weeks of the time John was hauled off to the pen, a petition was circulating to request a pardon from Crittenden. All they had to do to get a signature was explain that the pardon would require John to leave the state. Nobody wanted him back in Jefferson County, so people signed enthusiastically. But the petition was a mere formality, as the die was already cast. All that was left was for John to serve a few months for stealing hogs, and then April 1, 1884, he was pardoned, just as promised.

The Democrat reported his release from the pen this way:

> Upon petition of citizens of this county, Gov. Crittenden has pardoned John Marsden, convicted by his own confession of hogstealing. The people of this county know John's character, and if he intends to lead a different life in the future, he should go where he is unknown and make the right start. We do not believe that he is wanted here, even by those who petitioned for his release.

On his way out of the state, he stopped for one more visit to Jefferson County. That April night Louisa Chandler Owens Marsden sat rocking on the front porch of the home where she lived with her daugh-

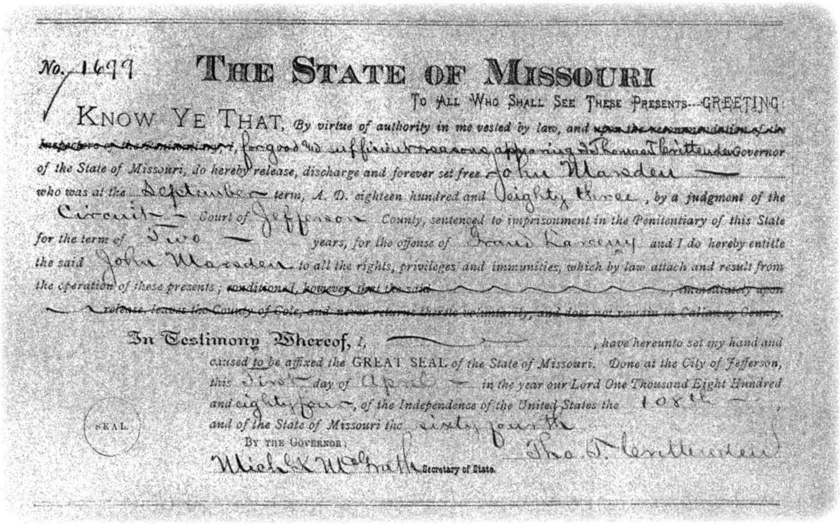

No. 1699 **THE STATE OF MISSOURI**

To All Who Shall See These Presents---GREETING:

KNOW YE THAT, *By virtue of authority in me vested by law, and* ~~upon the recommendation of the inspectors of the penitentiary~~, for good and sufficient reasons appearing to Thomas T. Crittenden Governor *of the State of Missouri, do hereby release, discharge and forever set free* John Marsden — *who was at the* September *term, A. D. eighteen hundred and* eighty three, *by a judgment of the* Circuit *Court of* Jefferson *County, sentenced to imprisonment in the Penitentiary of this State for the term of* Two *years, for the offense of* Grand Larceny *and I do hereby entitle the said* John Marsden *to all the rights, privileges and immunities, which by law attach and result from the operation of these presents;* ~~conditional, however, that the said ..., immediately upon release, leaves the County of Cole, and never returns thereto voluntarily, and does not remain in Callaway County.~~

In Testimony Whereof, *I,* [illegible] *, have hereunto set my hand and caused to be affixed the* GREAT SEAL *of the State of Missouri. Done at the City of Jefferson, this* First *day of* April *in the year our Lord One Thousand Eight Hundred and* eighty four, *of the Independence of the United States the* 108th, *and of the State of Missouri the* sixty fourth.

SEAL

By the Governor:

Mich'l K. McGrath Secretary of State. Tho. T. Crittenden

Governor Crittenden's pardon of John Marsden, dated four months after John's arrival at the state penitentiary.

ter and son-in-law, the Laffoons. Just at twilight, she heard the steady creak and grind of wagon wheels coming out of the trees at the road. As the rig slowed near the house a figure alighted and walked toward her with a familiar gait and a wave. She embraced her son John and they talked into the night. James Laffoon, the son-in-law who was driving the wagon, turned the horses loose to graze, then went on inside while Louisa brought out coffee. There was no butter or preserves, but she brought warm biscuits, and a little bacon grease made them delicious. And in all that, not a smile passed between them.

She whispered to John where Allen, Tommy, and Jimmy had settled with their wives and children in Arkansas. It was best to protect the Laffoons from that knowledge, and they were happy to be kept ignorant. It was nerve-wracking enough providing transportation for John.

The Laffoons lived a quarter mile north of Louisa's old house, and she moved in with them after the house burned. Bessie had no place else to go, so she also was welcomed by the Laffoons. John's wife, Millie, returned to her parents' after the fire. Back in November, when

Sam Byrns, attorney and legislator, who defended Mack in the murder of Vail, and later the men accused of Mack's murder.

John knew he'd be in prison for a few months, he signed a power of attorney for lawyer Samuel Byrns to sell his land over in Crystal City. Byrns was engaged to Tommy's cousin Melissa. As John put the document in the prison mail, he knew Byrns could be trusted to keep it all quiet, and Byrns did that by buying the Crystal City parcel himself. Tommy and Bessie defaulted on their loan, so the Crystal City house went to a sheriff's sale. But Byrns made sure that was also kept quiet, and bought that place too. Louisa also gave a power of attorney to Byrns, so he could sell her place to the Laffoons at a bargain price. It was all very hush-hush.

Deep in the night John and his mother dozed in their chairs, though it couldn't be said that they truly slept. Then as the eastern sky lightened he nudged her arm and said, "Let's go, Mother." They needed to get over to the Riverside Depot at Pevely before people were up and about. Laffoon had the wagon ready, and he was already helping Bessie climb up. All things considered, she thought it best to quit being so stubborn and go to Tommy. She sat on her carpet bag in the wagon bed and nestled under a quilt.

It was at once heartwarming and horribly sad. Louisa loved her sons so much that she would give up the last ties to her home for over three decades, the only thing she ever owned. Willing to leave her daughters with their families. Trusting that her boys would care for her as she cared for them. So with his own faithful mother caught up in his tangle of deceit and shadows, John loaded her meager belongings, and they rode away without speaking, and without looking back.

Chapter Twenty-Six
A New Sheriff in Town

That past February, while John was in prison, a grand jury was scheduled and Delo Rogers was called to testify. Shortly before the grand jury met, he and Elizabeth took a trip to St. Louis and returned home to a big shock. Bundled against the cold, they huddled on the wagon seat, scarcely watching the road. Then as they pulled into the farm they could see people, horses, and wagons in the yard of their home, which lay in smoldering ruins, and beyond that a pile of blackened timbers that had been the tall and spacious barn. Happily, they saw Delo's mother and brother John among the figures. They had barely escaped the fire with their lives.

Everything in the house was gone, including John's trunk and his hard-earned savings of $50. With Delo and Elizabeth gone the previous night, no one working in the barn, and no lanterns in use, the fire was obviously arson, the second time in six months that Delo had been the victim of such a horrid crime. Inside the barn had been Delo's reaper and the summer's yield of hay. They carried only $200 worth of insurance, and the reaper alone was worth $400.

Of course it terrified the Rogerses as much as it disheartened them. The case many thought closed was actually nowhere near an end, and people were saying the gang was still at work, even after Mack was dead. In a way they were right.

Delo was called to appear before the grand jury because he knew not only about the hog stealing, but also exactly who killed Mack and

Allie, and how they did it. That's the trouble with a gang. You can swear them to secrecy, you can threaten them, you can be sure they all know that survival depends on keeping it quiet, and still, the more people involved, the greater the chance one of them will talk. One might think enough time passed, and it'd be safe to talk. One might get to drinking or bragging. Or as in the case of what Delo heard, one might decide it wouldn't hurt to tell just one trusted person. Everybody wants to have someone to talk to.

John Gillman lived on the place just east of Samuel Marsden, and it was in Gillman's bed that Allie died back in August. That was a rare stroke of irony because Gillman's sister Elizabeth was married to Allen Marsden. Allen, in his personal anguish, foolishly revealed to his brother-in-law how he was up to his neck in John Marsden's murders of Mack and Big Allie. Posing as John. Trading shirts. The whole thing. Then he whispered a threat that Gillman could never tell any of what he just heard, but that threat would prove to be too little to seal John Gillman's big mouth.

He was a John Marsden man, or at least wanted to be. He was more of a pest. Just like the Fords sidled up to Jesse James, when the Sandy Valley gang was in its heyday Gillman tried to wiggle himself into whatever John and Allen Marsden and Tommy Moss were doing. He didn't know what that was, but he was pretty sure it was more exciting and more lucrative than his regular farming and occasional blacksmithing. Any time he saw Allen or John he asked questions about their last job and their next job. He wanted to help. John always told him to shut up.

Once he found out from his brother-in-law Allen how the murders were carried out, he couldn't hold it in. To prove he was part of John's gang, he had to tell somebody, and that somebody was his other brother-in-law, Delo. Gillman was married to Delo's sister Elizabeth.

Now, Delo had always been too busy making a living to get involved in all the intrigue. He knew about the gang's violence and threats of violence, and he was not about to put his family and property at risk. It's not that he was a coward. He was just practical. When Gillman babbled about what the gang was up to, Delo kept quiet and tended to his farming. He tried to tell Gillman to stop his criminal fantasies and focus on making an honest living, but that only led to arguments. When the gang stole a couple of Delo's hogs, Gillman told him exactly who did it. And still, the quiet Delo let it pass.

Finally in August, when Gillman told Delo what he knew about the Frisco Hill murders, everything changed. Murder was too much, and Delo didn't like knowing his sister was married to such a man. He told Elizabeth her husband was crazy, and she needed to take the children and get away from him, which only drove the wedge deeper between Delo and John Gillman.

Samuel Marsden and some others were relentless in their efforts to get the gang tracked down, arrested, and punished for their crimes. They had discovered what Delo knew, and if he testified before the grand jury, that might loosen other tongues, and that might be enough to hang the murderers. Gillman thought he could be a hero in the eyes of John and Allen Marsden if he could stop Delo's testimony. In his twisted mind, Gillman thought it was up to him to carry the gang's torch, literally. So he set fire to his own brother-in-law's home.

With that cowardly act, the simmering Rogers-Gillman family feud erupted on the Sandy Valley scene. The fire must have worked as intended, because Delo somehow avoided testifying at the August grand jury.

But then in February, there was another grand jury coming up, and again Delo was called to testify. His home and barn were destroyed by the second arson fire, and then he knew for sure. With all of the gang gone from the county and John in prison, the arsonist had to be Gillman. Delo knew it.

Six months later, Gillman was working in his yard with two of his children playing nearby, when a rifle cracked from somewhere in the trees, and a bullet whistled past his head and slammed into the barn behind him. Three days after that, his blacksmith shop was burned by an arsonist. That was enough for Gillman. He knew it was the work of Delo or someone else in the Rogers family, and they could have killed him with that rifle shot if they'd wanted to. The shot and the fire told him he wasn't quite the bad man he thought he was. He sold his place the very next day, moved to St. Louis, and left Elizabeth to sell their personal things before joining him. He wasn't hanging around Sandy one more minute.

Elizabeth couldn't bring herself to leave the marriage as her brother counseled, but instead followed Gillman. When she arrived in St. Louis with the children, Gillman got them settled and took a job. But he wasn't quite finished with the family feud. As he made his rounds of the big city taverns he chanced to meet one George P. Herzinger, a private detective. Of course the fact that he was a private eye, and the fact that Gillman met him in a bar, probably meant that he wasn't a very good law man.

Nonetheless, meeting him gave Gillman an idea. Gillman told him all about the murder of Joseph Yerger, the horrible fire, how the Yerger family barely escaped, and how the storekeeper was shot from hiding. Then he told Herzinger his brother-in-law Delo did it.

Delo had confessed to him, Gillman said, and went on to give the detective details about the case that nobody else knew. The investigation by Sheriff Weaver had concluded that Yerger's murderer fired from the closest possible spot, directly across the street from the kitchen door. But, Gillman said, Delo confided to him that he actually fired from about thirty yards west of that spot, and a careful check would find buckshot in the icehouse. That building was saved from the fire, and still stood just east of the rebuilt store and residence. Nobody could know that but the shooter, Gillman asserted. That's how he knew Delo was the one.

Gillman assured the detective that Sheriff Weaver, Mayor Edinger, and the Protective Society would hail him as a hero if he would just go down there and bring Delo to justice. Show them the buckshot in the icehouse wall and tell them Delo is the one who confessed it to me. Here was a chance for Herzinger to pick up a few dollars on what he thought might be a fairly easy case among the hill folks, and to make some politically influential friends in the process.

Herzinger didn't waste any time in Jefferson County researching the case. He just wanted to go do what he was hired to do, collect his investigator's fee from Gillman, and get back to his cold St. Louis beer. The accuser had even told him whom to recruit as a deputy, Bent Moss, and it was a role Bent was more than happy to fulfill. On August 29, 1884, the two men made the surprising and dramatic arrest of Fidelo Rogers. Hardly a bad man or even a public figure, his sudden apprehension made the local newspaper, and left his neighbors asking, "Why Delo?"

Of course Herzinger had no material evidence, and made the arrest strictly on Gillman's affidavit. Making the case look even worse, Delo had everyone's sympathy because his property had been burned twice. Yet amazingly, on September 15, the grand jury indicted Rogers. Friends and neighbors managed to post his $5,000 bail, which took ten days and required contributions from his uncle, father-in-law, and several others. But the judge, doubting the merits of the case, pushed it down the docket to the following year.

When January rolled around, Gillman couldn't be found anywhere. Not even Herzinger could locate him. Prosecutor James Green didn't think Rogers was guilty, and couldn't prosecute the case without Gillman's testimony, so the judge threw the case out. Thereafter, Delo's squabble with Gillman was laid to rest.

But for the law, a new light was cast on Gillman. The one thing he told Herzinger that rang true was the position of the shooter. Weaver's investigation had failed to find the buckshot in the icehouse, so when Herzinger revealed that, everyone knew that Gillman clearly had some inside information on the case that nobody else had. If he honestly knew Delo was the killer and wanted to bring him to justice, he would have shown up for the trial. Since he wasn't there, Weaver and Green could only conclude that Gillman was motivated simply by a campaign to shut Delo's mouth. He was involved in the burning of Delo's house and barn, and when that wasn't enough, he tried to pin Yerger's murder on him. Weaver and Green could see that Gillman was protecting someone else. He could only have known about the icehouse buckshot if he knew the shooter's exact position. He could only know that if the shooter told him, or even more chilling, if Gillman were there when the fatal blast was fired. Was Gillman himself the trigger man? And if so, why?

While all that was going on, Samuel Marsden aged rapidly. Though he had always been a stern, hardworking man, he grew stoic, and was perpetually sad. His life was consumed with making sure his son's murder wasn't forgotten. Those who knew him well could see that his passion for proving a case against the murderers was taking a toll, and yet was keeping him alive. He couldn't die as long as justice was undone.

Three grand juries were convened over a year and a half, and each time there was some new evidence or some new testimony related to the Mack Marsden murder case. Sometimes it lay under a rock overturned by Samuel. Sometimes the stone was lifted by Mack's brother Buzz or some other friend of the family. Samuel made sure everyone had it on their minds.

Then, to Samuel's delight, two things happened that broke the case wide open. First, Delo Rogers got out from under John Gillman's intimidation and was ready to testify. Second, a new sheriff came to town.

Weaver was finished with the whole business, and certainly tired of politicians telling him how to enforce the law. As far as he was concerned, the case was closed with the death of Mack Marsden. He really didn't care where "the other Marsdens" had gone, and he cared even less whether they came back for a trial. In 1884 he stepped into a nice office job as county clerk and turned over the jail keys to newly elected Sheriff Henry Hurtgen.

Everybody knew Henry as the blacksmith at the end of Main Street in Hillsboro. He was a public-spirited sort who favored making creative and useful items over shaping horseshoes. He had won considerable fame by creating the delicately beautiful but formidable iron fence around the Hillsboro cemetery. An energetic man with relentless deter-

Right: Sheriff Henry Hurtgen, creative blacksmith and relentless hero, who tracked the accused killers all the way to Arkansas, pictured holding his Bible. Courtesy of Peggy and Charles McMullin. Below: Henry Hurtgen created the iron fence around the Hillsboro cemetery.

The Hillsboro Brass Band, ca. 1880, included Henry Hurtgen, seated fourth from the left, and J. T. Moss, center with the shiny top hat. On his left is Cornelius Marsden, and the shortest one standing is prosecuting attorney James F. Green.

mination, as sheriff he quickly earned a reputation for chasing down those who ran from their legal responsibilities. One Thomas Dugan, for example, had accumulated a string of minor offenses, the greatest of which was misdirecting a train by throwing a railroad switch during a rail workers' strike. When he disappeared, many lawmen would have been glad to see him go. But not Hurtgen. He chased him down and brought him back to face the charge.

Hurtgen didn't know or care about any deals that were made in past years. He was on the level with everybody he met, and at one time even played in the Hillsboro Brass Band with James Green, J. T. Moss, several of the McMullins, and Cornelius Marsden. After he became sheriff, he intended to do right by all of them, just the way he treated everyone. At last, under his determined hands, at a fourth grand jury, in September of 1884, indictments were returned against Allen Marsden, Tommy Moss, and Jimmy Moss for murder.

There was only one problem: Nobody in Jefferson County knew where they were. The night they left, they weren't sure where they were going themselves. They just stopped running when they got across the line into Arkansas. Tommy, Jimmy and Jane, and Allen and Elizabeth with their two sons, had all settled in Pocahontas, Arkansas. John and mother Louisa brought Bessie and joined them in the spring. Jimmy and Jane had a baby there in 1885.

All Hurtgen needed was a lead on which direction the fugitives went, and he would be off after them. Since the mail was sorted by hand, a friendly postmaster could be the sheriff's best friend. Sure enough, pretty soon addresses on letters to and from the Laffoons told Hurtgen the wanted men were just over the border in Arkansas. Of course they assumed their acquittals, pardons, and dropped charges had cleared the slate, and they'd be safe from the Missouri law forever. But they didn't figure on their names coming up before every grand jury, and they didn't account for the relentless Hurtgen.

The trip to Randolph County, Arkansas, was about 175 miles each way. It was December and cold, so the sheriff was glad to have a train about halfway, then for the rest of the trip hired a wagon to haul his quarry back home. The three wanted men were familiar with Hurtgen the smithy, but had no idea he was sheriff. Tommy was the easy one to locate, because the local folks all noticed when the tall dandy moved to the area. A little questioning led Hurtgen to him first. Unfortunately though, while he was talking to Tommy, Bessie slipped out and got word to John, Allen, and Jimmy, and they ran. The entire trip took Hurtgen five days, and he had to be satisfied with one prisoner. Tommy Moss had to be satisfied with Christmas alone in the Hillsboro jail.

When Hurtgen returned home with Moss, he left behind a cooperative sheriff of Randolph County, Arkansas, who surely didn't want two Missouri murderers living in his backyard. He gave Hurtgen his word that he'd keep an eye out, and he did more than that. He watched the wives, because he knew Allen and Jimmy would slip back to them sooner or later. It was the first week of May 1886 when the sheriff and his deputies surprised the two fugitives at a boardinghouse just fifteen miles down the road in Black Rock. A couple days later the sheriff rolled into the Victoria depot, unloaded Allen and Jimmy in chains, and helped them climb into Sheriff Hurtgen's wagon. Hurtgen took them up to the Hillsboro jail, where Tommy Moss had already languished for six months.

Chapter Twenty-Seven
At Last, the Trial

Judge John Thomas was a native of Iron County who moved to Jefferson County in his late twenties, was elected to the legislature, and then elected circuit court judge. He's the one who presided at the Vail murder trial. There had been some criticism of the way that trial ended quickly in Mack's favor. But at the upcoming trial for Mack's accused killers, there would be no hint that the judge had a prejudice for Mack. No behavior that would suggest he was representing a faction bent on exacting revenge on the accused men. In fact, if anything, the court leaned the way it should, putting the burden of proof on the prosecution, presuming the three men were innocent.

The newspaper made a great deal of the careful jury selection. A hundred men were called, forty were selected as competent, and the attorneys hand-picked their twelve. But after all that careful selection process, the jury included E. F. Donnell, who had bailed John Marsden out of jail, and his second cousin, James Eli Williams, who had bailed out Tommy Moss. All that the defense needed to block a conviction for murder was one dissenting juror, and this jury was stacked with at least two proven supporters of the defendants. In fact, Donnell turned out to be the foreman.

The trial began as expected on June 9, 1886, with comfortable morning temperatures that soared as the sun rose higher in the clear Missouri sky. As usual, the tall courthouse windows were open, and as usual, it didn't help much. It was another crime everybody was in-

The Jefferson County Courthouse at Hillsboro.

terested in, and the more people poured into the room, the hotter and steamier it got. Still, a little sweat couldn't stop that crowd from getting to the bottom of what happened on Frisco Hill three years before. They were cheerful, talkative, waving, moving to sit with their friends, and it took a few minutes for Judge Thomas to bring order to the busy room. There among the spectators sat John Marsden, watching his three compatriots argue for their lives. In fact, his greatest worry may not have been that they'd be convicted, but that somewhere in the proceedings his own role in the murders would be revealed. He had just as much at stake in the proceedings as the men on trial.

Over the years of trouble, many loyalties had been forged, and some reversed. One of the most interesting among them was Sam Byrns, attorney and former state representative and senator. He had been one of the attorneys who defended Mack in the killing of Vail. But now, three years later, he was married to Melissa Moss, who was twenty years younger, and the daughter of Byrns's powerful Democratic friend J. T. Moss. It was an advantageous marriage in many ways, so to most eyes in the courtroom, it wasn't surprising to find Byrns had changed his coat to join the defense team for Mack's accused killers.

Once the preliminaries were out of the way, the testimony started with the crime scene being recalled by those who found Mack's body and the dying Hensley. Then three men, Napolean Bonapart Williams, Lewis Adams, and Richard Moss, testified about the crime scene. They were friends, and each qualified in his own way as an expert. Napolean was known as a former constable and deputy. Richard Moss was respected as a farmer, hunter, and outdoorsman.

Adams was a veteran of fierce Civil War fighting, including struggles against Southern guerrillas, having served three years for the Union in the 5th Missouri State Militia Cavalry. He was an exceptional marksman. One of his special feats was to point a .44 revolver up over his shoulder and hit a target some twenty or thirty feet behind him while sighting in a mirror. Everyone called him "Doc," because he provided veterinary services to the Sandy farm animals, and to people too, when he had the chance. He was reputed to have healed more than one child's broken bone with his homemade ointment.

Doc Adams was a man who could be counted on, ready to pitch in wherever needed. A man of loyalty who loved his mother's branch of the Moss family, and his neighbors, the Hensleys. He lived in a log house and kept a small blacksmith shop next to Sandy Baptist Church, where he was the caretaker.

It was in Napolean's home that Tommy and Jimmy lived as adolescents, so he certainly had an opinion of them. Richard was an uncle to Tommy and Jimmy. Doc was their second cousin. However, Doc disliked them, and he didn't care much for Mack either. But he loved Samuel and his Uncle Claibourn Moss, whose shop was burned.

Lewis "Doc" Adams.

So all three men had relationships with the defendants, but there was no bias in their testimony. They simply scouted the location to find where the assassins had trampled the grass and left footprints behind the great fallen log on the uphill side of the road. The testimony confirmed that it was a good place to hide and gave a view of anyone approaching. They said there was an opening in the brush from which the assassins probably strode into the road and leveled their guns. Finally, the three investigators found ample evidence of where buckshot had hit the trees on the side of the road beyond the Mack Marsden wagon. Everything they found substantiated the dying Allie Hensley's description of what happened.

Coroner Brewster and Dr. Hull, who sat with the dying Allie, both testified about the dead men's shotgun wounds. And the prosecution presented its key evidence, Hensley's deathbed testimony, naming his killers as John, Tommy, and Jimmy. Several men, including Napolean, were called to say they heard those accusations from Hensley. And some of them testified that Allie, when told that John Marsden had a solid alibi, said he might be mistaken about him, but not the other two men. It was Buzz Marsden who reported that Hensley said to him, "If it wasn't John, then it might have been Allen Marsden." Not that it was Allen for sure, but that it "might have been." That was one of the breaks for which the defense was hoping. If Allie was unsure about whether he saw John or Allen, the attorneys asserted, then he might also have been wrong about seeing Tommy and Jimmy.

The trial was characterized by a parade of witnesses and attorneys getting up and sitting down. It was quite physical, with lots of cross-examination and recalling witnesses. The action really entertained the audience, and from behind his great oaken bench, Judge Thomas did a masterful job of keeping it all orderly.

A key point of the defense was proving that the men were in Sulphur Springs that morning and couldn't have been at the murder site when the shooting was done. They went to great lengths to place the men in town at three times: before 7:00, midmorning, and around noon. They stressed that it was eight or nine miles to Frisco Hill, where Mack and Allen were gunned down. Since normal walking pace for most people is three or four miles per hour, the defense was able to contend that it was easily a two-hour hike each way, and closer to three hours, so the defendants couldn't possibly have been there when the crimes took place.

Next-door neighbor James Adrin Williams was married to Allen's and John's cousin Mary Elizabeth Moss. He and his wife, as well as Allen Marsden's wife, all testified that Allen and Tommy left on their hunt before 7:00 that morning. Williams further testified that he saw the three near Sulphur Springs again between 9:00 and 10:00 that morning. Then he and two other men saw them back there before 1:00 p.m. From 9:00 to 1:00 is a window of almost four hours, the prosecution said. So if they hurried, the murderers might have made the hike in time to commit the crime.

Still, the defense argued, they might not have had almost four hours. What if James Williams saw them the second time closer to 10:00 than 9:00? And the time at which the shots were heard varied from 11:00 to 12:00. So if it was 11:00, the hunters would've had only two hours to get there, lay in wait, and fire their shots.

The prosecution pointed out that people who were on the streets of Antonia that day were sure Mack's horse and wagon came in at 12:15, and that was just over two miles from the murder site. The horse was moving quickly, which puts the time of the shooting very close to 12:00. But the defense used that to its advantage too. If it was 12:00, the killers couldn't possibly have had time to get back to Allen's house in Sulphur Springs before 1:00.

James Williams's testimony remained the most dubious element of the trial. He was the only one who reported seeing them at midmorning. Could he have been lying to help his neighbor Allen? He certainly could have been lying to protect his wife's Moss cousins. In fact, James and Mary were identified in court as Allen's neighbors, and it never came to light that she was kin to the Moss boys.

Williams's testimony cut the defendants' available time precisely in half. But if that "midmorning" testimony from Williams is eliminated, the hunters had from 7:00 until about 1:00 in the field, plenty of time to commit the murders and get back. If one were planning such a crime, that's exactly what they'd want to do, get there early and wait until the victims appeared.

Striding to the witness box, Samuel Marsden made quite an impression with his white hair and beard. He had the sloping but broad shoulders that were characteristic of the Marsden men. Though he moved slowly, he did it with grace, and when he spoke, it was with the authority of age.

It was common knowledge that he had spent a lot of time and effort becoming his own amateur investigator. With an engineer's analytical mind, trained to rely on measurement, he knew the travel time from

Sulphur Springs to the murder site was crucial to proving the prosecution's case. So back in August of 1884 he took his son-in-law Clay Moss and grandson Joseph King and actually walked the killers' route. Samuel was fifty-seven years old then, twice the age of the accused men, and he, Clay, and Joseph covered the distance in one hour and seven minutes. They were walking at a brisk pace. Younger men, running to escape a crime scene, could certainly have made the trip faster.

Still, all the varying times, 7:00, 9:00 or 10:00, 11:00 or 12:00, 12:00 or 1:00, made everything just loose enough to create a doubt in jurors' minds. And just in case that wasn't enough, the defense made Samuel Marsden admit that he, Clay, and Joseph carried no big, heavy rifles or shotguns on their hike. For men of such stature, that wouldn't have slowed them down enough to make any difference, but Samuel didn't have a chance to say that, and it was one more point for the defense.

One of the most critical pieces of the puzzle was the distance from Sulphur Springs to the murder site on Frisco Hill. The prosecution repeatedly referred to it as "eight or nine miles," which it was, if one took the road through Antonia. But by the most direct route, along Glaize Creek, then cutting off across country, or on Dry Fork Road, it's truly less than seven miles. The great failure for the prosecution was that they never clearly established that fact, and the difference of two miles was a difference of twenty minutes each way in the minds of the jury.

Another young man named Wittenberg, totally unrelated to any of the people in the case, said that he saw three men pass through his father's field, which is on the way from Sulphur Springs to Frisco Hill, about 7:00. They were carrying something, but it could have been guns or something else. He also had to admit he wasn't close enough to identify them, so his testimony proved meaningless.

Perhaps the most interesting witness at the trial was the one given the least credibility. Lettie Castile, the daughter of a family that lived on Glaize Creek, did housework for various families in the neighborhood.

If she worked late, or if she was needed for a few days, she spent the night in her employers' homes. Lettie had been working for the families of James Williams and Allen Marsden, she said. The night before the murders she was staying at the Marsdens' when, she said, "Mr. Marsden came in with Mr. Moss about 11 p.m." Mrs. Marsden fixed them dinner while they whispered at the kitchen table. Before going to sleep they set an alarm that roused them at 2:00 a.m. They got up and loaded their rifles while Mrs. Marsden fixed breakfast for them, and they left as the sun was on the horizon.

At midday, Lettie was cleaning up after the family's lunch, and saw the men return drenched in sweat. They took their shirts off and Mrs. Marsden put them to soak. She went to the neighboring farmhouse and borrowed a clean shirt for Tommy from Mrs. Williams, as Tommy was about Mr. Williams's size, very tall, and Allen's clothes wouldn't fit him.

It was a fascinating twist on the case that Lettie didn't know the men well, certainly not well enough to distinguish the difference between Allen and his brother John, who looked so much like him. She didn't realize that she had seen Tommy and John return to the house, not Tommy and Allen.

The defense quickly moved to counter her testimony by examining Allen and Williams, their wives, and Tommy, and they all contradicted everything Lettie said. The Williamses even said Lettie stayed at their home that night, not the Marsdens', so she couldn't have seen the men come in for a midnight kitchen conference. A couple of other Sulphur Springs men said they had seen Tommy and Allen that day around 1:00. Like Lettie, they had no idea they actually saw Tommy with John. The defense was able to use those men to confuse the times at which Lettie said the hunters returned and the family ate lunch.

Lettie's testimony had been key and damning, and she would have no reason to lie. But there was nobody else who supported her stories of the midnight conversation and the sweaty shirts. Besides, she was a young, common girl and easily discredited, and in the end she was dismissed as an untrustworthy witness.

Jimmy Moss played little part in the trial. The hunters picked him up, near his home, less than a mile outside of town, and in fact made it sound more like a chance meeting than a pre-arranged one, saying they "induced" Jimmy to go hunting with them. Of course, he was already out with his shotgun, so that coincidence was suspect. It was never revealed that John had spent the night at Jimmy's house. And in a key coincidence, after the shootings Jimmy went home to clean up, not to the Allen Marsden home with Tommy and John. That meant not one person could ever say they saw the three together that morning.

The prosecution complained to the judge that some key evidence was missing. After all, almost three years had gone by. Jimmy Moss's shotgun couldn't be produced. The judge called a recess and assembled the lawyers in his office. There the prosecutor complained, the defense complained, and the judge indulged them only so far. The defense objected to Delo Rogers as a witness and the judge agreed that his testimony was nothing but hearsay. Gillman had been summoned, but couldn't be found, so he couldn't confirm or deny Delo's testimony. In the end, the state wasn't allowed to introduce anything Gillman told Delo. As a result, John Marsden's false alibi and changing shirts in the DeSoto alley could never be presented in court. It was discussed in chambers, but the judge said the current testimony was all that mattered. What anybody said two years ago didn't matter. Two brothers trading shirts in DeSoto didn't matter. John Marsden was not on trial, he reminded them. The question was whether the three accused men, Allen, Tommy, and Jimmy, could be placed at the crime scene without a doubt.

With so much testimony eliminated by the judge, the pace at which the trial whizzed by was dizzying. It all took less than two days, starting Wednesday morning, with all the evidence presented by the middle of that afternoon. The lawyers' arguments started, but the judge had to call a halt to it at sundown.

Chapter Twenty-Eight
Another Getaway

Of course, the jurors weren't sequestered, so they were free to chat about the case with townspeople, and to make their decision over a beer Wednesday night. The gray stone tavern and hotel of Primis Fromhold, across the street east of the courthouse, was even more packed than election night when everyone met there to await the results. Beers were passed out to the crowd standing in the street, and it was a loud, memorable night, for sure. Of course John wasn't at the bar. While his brother and the others waited in jail to hear their fate, he was huddled in a chair at the Laffoons' house with a rifle in his lap. He drank coffee and didn't nod off to sleep until almost sunup.

The arguments wrapped up by noon on Thursday. After a break for lunch, the jury retired, and was out only a short time before returning a verdict of acquittal for all three men. Faces lit up, and faces dropped. Reactions were muted, as it seemed that both sides knew the outcome before it was announced. Later, more than one juror opined that there was little need for discussion, as their minds were all made up after hearing the evidence the previous afternoon, before the lawyers even spoke.

John Marsden may have been the most relieved of the bunch as he leaned over the railing to shake his brother's hand, then the others. Their acquittal meant that not only did his alibi work, but his plan, which once put his brother's neck in a noose, had finally been vindicated.

The stone tavern still stands across the street from the courthouse. In the 1880s it was the place to be on election nights while waiting for returns. It was just as crowded during the Marsden trials.

The crowd began to stir, talking, calling across the room, and gathering their coats and hats. The court clerk handed Judge Thomas a note about Tommy Moss's old indictment for stealing hogs. It had been a mere sidelight to all the excitement back in '83, but now it had to be addressed. Amid the excited voices and shuffling chairs, Judge Thomas called Tommy and his attorney to the bench. People were talking and beginning to leave, and the judge pounded his gavel. It was all he could do to hold them long enough to hurry through that bit of unfinished business. He quickly set bond at $300, and nearly every one of Tommy's relations in the courtroom chipped in, so he could walk out. Turning their pockets out to make up the bond were his much older half-brother Claeborne, cousin Richard, who gave expert testimony, and cousin James Thomas Moss, along with J. T's son-in-law R. G. Hoeken, son-in-law lawyer Sam Byrns, and a neighbor, Jonathan O'Fallon. Judge Thomas tried to keep them quiet as they counted their money and joked. Finally, the bond raised, the case was continued, and

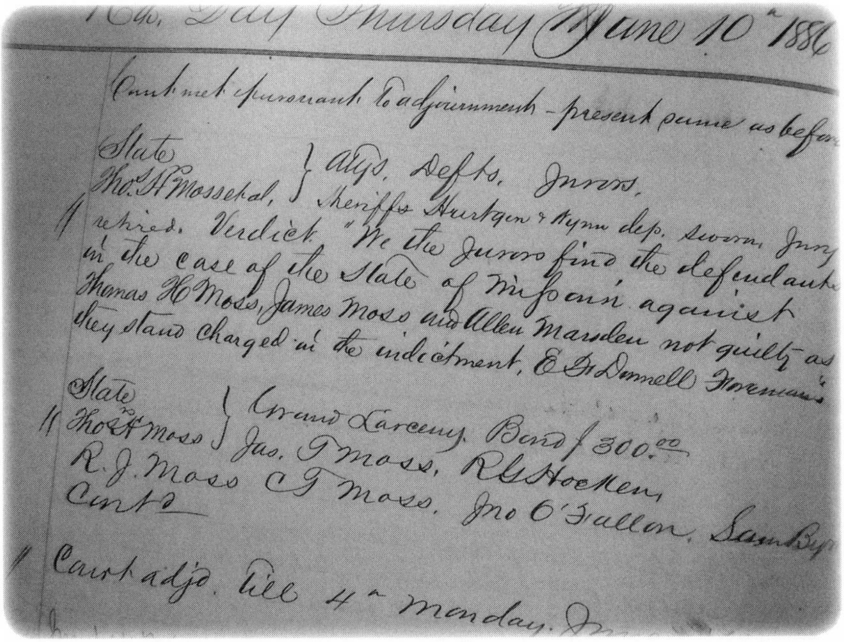

16th Day Thursday June 10th 1886

Court met pursuant to adjournment – present same as befor

State } Atty's, Defts, Jurors.
Tho. H. Moss et al, } Sheriffs Hurtgen & Wynn dep. sworn. Jury
retired. Verdict, "We the Jurors find the defendants
in the case of the State of Missouri against
Thomas H. Moss, James Moss and Allen Marsden not guilty as
they stand charged in the indictment. E. O'Donnell Foreman."

State } Grand Larceny. Bond $300.00
Thos H Moss } Jas. T Moss, R.G. Hocken,
R. J. Moss C. T. Moss. Jno O'Fallon, Sam By
Cont'd

Court adj'd. till 4th Monday.

The court record of the acquittal of John, Allen, and Tommy in the murder of Mack and Allie. Shown below is the record of Tommy Moss's bond for the hog stealing charges.

Tommy smiled, because they all knew he would soon be long gone. With Mack dead, there was nobody to testify against him, and the prosecutor would eventually drop the charges.

That was it, and the crowd was free to release its emotions. The defendants had entered the court confident, and they left jubilant, finally exonerated from the crime that had haunted them for three years. Samuel Marsden hung his head, unable to watch them walk out as free men.

There was someone else who couldn't stand watching them walk out, any more than he could stand to see his friend Samuel in such pain. Standing there in the emptying courtroom, he resolved that it wasn't over. Somebody had to take action.

The freed men and their families wanted to get back to Arkansas on the train as quickly as possible. Most people would have taken the hack from Hillsboro down to Victoria, but the hack was driven by Mack's cousin. Besides, at Pevely, where they caught the train two years before, there would just be fewer people. One of the Moss cousins took Jimmy, Tommy, and their families directly to the station to await the evening train. Laffoon took Louisa, John, Allen, Elizabeth, and their sons to the house for a short visit.

They couldn't know they were followed by a silent figure on horseback. He kept a good distance, dismounting in the woods near the Laffoon home. He had a pretty good idea where they'd go from there. Seeing them leave after their visit, he crushed his smoke between his calloused fingers, mounted his horse, and followed again, keeping to the edge of the trees where he could see them on the road. Then once they started east, across Sandy Creek Road, which led directly from the covered bridge to Pevely, he knew for sure they were boarding the train at Riverside. He left the road and trotted quickly off on a game trail through the woods.

With the sun gone behind their weary shoulders, the wagon was about to emerge from the trees and enter the grassy fields that led to the big spring on the western edge of Pevely. With Laffoon driving, John turned abruptly to speak to Allen, who was in the wagon bed with Elizabeth, Louisa, and the boys. At just that instant, a pistol shot cracked from up ahead, where a bold marksman had stepped into the left side of the road, a broad hat low across his face, left foot forward, both arms reaching to hold the revolver as he took careful aim at his target. Settled in his hand, still smoking, was the Colt 1860 Army, an old percussion cap model, long and heavy compared to the new cartridge-firing guns, but it was the one he knew and trusted. He expected the opportunity for only one shot, and that's all he would need.

John's right arm flew up to shoulder level and he wheeled to his right, away from Laffoon and off the wagon, the back of his head smacking hard against the wheel rim. Laffoon jerked the horse to a stop and, expecting more shots to follow, jumped down beside John. When no more shots came, he peeked over the horses and looked back up the road. The danger was long gone; the phantom vanished as if he'd never been there. In the trees he mounted the horse that brought him, his heart pounding, his shirt soaked with sweat, and he began a sweep to the north that would take him home, back to Sandy by a different way.

Laffoon checked John, and found he was unconscious, but not quite as dead as the marksman thought. Because of that sudden turn toward the wagon bed, the bullet intended for the heart had hit him in the right shoulder, passing clear through. No bones broken. It was a big slug, a .44, and tore up the flesh, but Allen refused Laffoon's plea to get John to a doctor. No time for that, he said. They all needed to get away. Finding a doctor could wait until they got down the line to Pocahontas. "The less attention we attract, the better. We've just got to get out of here as soon as possible," Allen commanded.

They got John into the wagon, and it wasn't far to the spring, where they soaked a cloth and bathed his face enough to revive him. At the Pevely station, the Marsden wagon was heard before it was seen, grinding along the gravel, pulling in about 8:05. At that sound, the Mosses felt safer, all of them together now, anticipating the welcome moment they'd step onto that train and be on their way to a new life. From the left there was a distant whistle, then the Mosses saw the headlight, bouncing against the trees a mile away, and heard the clacking of the train that would take them to freedom.

They turned back to see their fellow travelers pull in, and it wasn't until the wagon got close, in the light of the station lamps, that they could see John lying motionless in the back. The men cursed and all talked at once. By then the train was in the station, louder than anything else on earth, steam pouring from beneath its pulsing belly.

"Don't attract any attention," Allen commanded the little circle. They had to remember this was no pleasure trip. It was their second getaway. Everyone collected themselves, looking back up the road, their eyes sweeping the gathering darkness to make sure the man who shot John wasn't still coming.

"Allen's right," Tommy insisted. "We just need to get on the train."

They slipped John's coat around his shoulders, which concealed the wound. He still wasn't quite awake, but they held him between them and the women distracted the conductor enough that he didn't notice the slumping figure. They got John, the women, and the children on the train first, then Allen and the Mosses picked up the bags and boarded, quietly greeting the conductor. The men tried to look relaxed, but wished they had their trusted long guns with them.

The train wasn't crowded, so they were able to sit together in an area away from the other passengers. Tommy settled the children. The others laid John back on the burgundy leather seat, and he grimaced as Jimmy pressed a towel into the wound in the front of his shoulder, and Allen pressed one on the back. Tommy pulled a bottle from his pocket and gave him a drink of the warm, clear liquor. They all needed a shot, so the bottle was passed around.

Down the track, leaving the danger behind them, Allen finally relaxed enough to describe what happened. Tommy and Jimmy looked at each other. It was a heck of a shot, they agreed, with a pistol at about seventy-five feet in the half light of sundown, and looking into the dying sun. Whoever he was, they knew he was a cool customer, a man who'd peered down those Colt sights at a man before, an ambusher of ambushers.

They were still on their guard at the Victoria stop. A couple of people boarded the other car, then at last they were able to relax a bit as the train rolled into the black woodlands. The little group surrounding the wounded John looked at each other and knew without a doubt, they were smart to get out of Jefferson County that very night. They made their second getaway in the nick of time.

When dawn broke over Sandy Creek the dust was settled. Cicadas again raised their clatter. Farmers, miners, shopkeepers, and homemakers went back to work. Justice was undone, and yet Jefferson County had won the peace the people so deeply desired. An end, in spite of the means.

Epilogue

After that, life around the sheriff's office was uncommonly quiet. Leaning his chair against the wall out in front of the jail, Hurtgen watched his town and pulled on his pipe. "You know what bothers me?" Hurtgen mused to Deputy Tom Frazier beside him. "The shotgun."

"The shotgun?"

"Yeah. It was a shotgun killed Mack and Big Allie. Yerger too."

"Yessir."

"Suppose it was the same shotgun?"

Hurtgen would never be able to answer his own question, but he was already a local hero, the right man in the right job at the right time. He could have easily won re-election but chose to run for county administrator instead, and served a term in that office. When his civic duty was done, he returned to his blacksmithing.

Of all the crimes described in this tale, and many more attributed to the gang, only one was solved. Only one culprit paid his debt. That was John, who pleaded guilty to stealing pigs. John was never tried for the murders of Mack and Allie.

But life doesn't wait for mysteries to be solved. It goes on, always making new stories. July and August are still dreadfully hot and humid months in Jefferson County. The Meramec and Mississippi still roll, and Sandy Creek still sings. Folks still go to services and get buried at the same Sandy Baptist Church. Lemay Ferry Road has been paved and striped for a hundred years, and its two narrow lanes still follow almost exactly the same route to the stately red covered bridge, which is now the centerpiece of a beautiful little state park. A store was built nearby, which had various owners through the years. One of them was named Goldman, and his name stuck, so the community is no longer Sandy, but Goldman.

Did Mack fail the family? Or did the family fail Mack? Blame is a waste, reserved for those who are desperate to save themselves. It's far more beneficial to simply know that we can almost always do a little better. There's always more love to give, another encouraging word, one more helping hand. Mack was a man who took one step over the line, and couldn't get back. And that kept him from being the man he was born to be.

In this story there's no bad family. There's no lingering Civil War animosity, no epic family feud, no highly organized crime ring. There are only some young people who went wrong, which happens even in the best of families. As for John, Allen, Tommy, and Jimmy, maybe someone could have made a difference in the lives of the young stallions who terrorized Sandy Valley. Maybe not. By the time anyone knew there was trouble, those men were living by the rifle and the rope on a road that has no good end.

We spend our time on this earth making choices. Our parents do the best they can with what they have. Then it's up to each of us to learn from them and decide how we'll walk through this world. If there's a lesson in Mack's legacy, it's that the kids are all right when they choose to be all right. The eyes in old photographs are windows, and through them we can see the stories. The pain and joy. The devotion. We can see that each of us is given a piece of time that's long enough to be vastly important, and yet will seem to be over before it's begun. Preceding us and after us, the tide of family rolls on, regardless of the choices any of us make. Love and life will prevail.

Sometimes a person comes along who takes a stand and decides to be faithful to this direction, not that one, changing the path for all those who come after. Little Sammy Marsden was such a person. He was four when his father was murdered, certainly old enough to miss him. As he grew up, he must have heard the accusations against Mack, and he might have believed them. He could have been angry. He could have chosen a dark road. Fortunately, his devoted grandfather Samuel gave him a lot of attention, teaching him what it means to be a real man, at once both gentle and solid.

Samuel Marsden was a defeated warrior who never stopped believing in his son's innocence. He sold off most of the farm, keeping fifty acres and a house big enough for him, Emma Jean, and Sammy. After 1883 his only joy was in the gift of time he spent with Sammy. Those hours of bliss, however, couldn't save him from grieving himself to death six years after the trial. To the end he was a relentless romantic, and his family would follow his starry-eyed plea, "Bury me at the entrance to the mine." Well, it wasn't exactly "at" the mine, but close enough for a hillbilly philosopher. The Marsden family burying ground holds him, and probably Mary, Mack, Priscilla, and maybe others. But the stones are gone, and the cemetery lost to the ages.

For Emma Jean, as a divorced, then widowed mother in her thirties, distanced from her parents, life only seemed to get harder. She said when Mack was killed he left her with 90 cents and a milk cow. She was also pregnant with a baby girl who wouldn't live long enough to be named.

Emma Jean cried, but would not cower. To make money, she collected rags and learned to weave them into rugs. As Samuel lay dying in December 1888 he said to her, "Emma Jean, you must get the boy back in church." She honored his request, and it felt good to be once more among the faithful, fortified every Sunday at Sandy Baptist.

Though Samuel died intestate, his faithful friend and pastor Sull Frazier was appointed his administrator, and he parceled out Samuel's last few dollars to Emma Jean. Her father, Leander, also passed, leaving her a little piece of land, which she had to sell to buy food.

Top: Cornelius Marsden got along with everybody. Here he is, third from the right, fifteen years after Mack's murder, on a hunting outing with James Green, who prosecuted Mack, far right, and nephew Edgar Marsden, petting the dog. The bearded man is Dr. Mockbee, whose kindness made it possible for Emma Jean to own a home. Bottom: Emma Jean's two acres. The house and well were at center, on the knoll, near where the farthest cow stands in this photo.

In a show of chivalrous compassion, the men who won the battle against Mack felt it their responsibility to help his widow and child. Prosecutor Green's sister was married to George Mockbee, the new favorite doctor in the valley, and the coroner, following Brewster. He was also kin to the Moss and Williams families. With Emma Jean unable to afford a place to live, Green and his confidants agreed that it was never their intention for her and the boy to suffer so, and they had a responsibility to help. Mockbee sold her two acres with a little cabin and a good well on it near the corner of Sandy Mines Road and Sandy Church Road, at a small fraction of its market value. It was a good place for a boy to grow up, a stone's throw from the old mine, and next door to Sammy's Uncle Gabe Johnston, who had been such a close friend to Mack.

Gabe's sister Lizzie was married to Jasper Hamrick. People said, "He was a huge man and she was about as big as a minute." Jasper was a teacher and farmer who, at the age of thirty-three, had a revelation and became a circuit preacher who "could quote the Good Book from kiver to kiver [cover to cover]." Their daughter Stella grew up with Sammy, similar to the way Emma Jean and Mack grew up together. They found themselves

Jasper and Lizzie Hamrick, parents of Stella Marsden, who married Sammy.

at one Baptist church, then another, revivals, tent meetings, and church socials, and it just seemed that their romance was divinely ordained.

Two of Emma Jean's brothers became evangelists, but Sammy was closest to Clarence, the wild one. He felt sorry for Clarence because he had no livestock of his own, and he gave him a pig. Jasper didn't approve of that, and by the way he didn't want Sammy marrying his daughter either. He made Clarence sell the pig, but he couldn't convince Stella not to marry the boy. Sammy and Stella wed and raised five children in a two-story log house on Jarvis Lane. It was an amazing structure, a monument to a caring frontier craftsman who's lost to history. The twelve-foot-square cabin was simply two log squares, one on top of the other, but it was uncommonly solid, built of massive walnut logs, fitted as if by machine. His Uncle Richard let them live there until they could buy it.

Like John and Allen Marsden, and Tommy and Jimmy Moss, Sammy grew up without a father. But he was living proof that it's not the circumstances or the turns of fate that make a person. Rather, it's what the person makes of the circumstances. He was a slight, but strong and energetic, man with a ready smile, an infectious laugh, and a kind word for everyone.

He was a good hand with livestock, and made most of his money milking ten cows and delivering a dairy route. He was one of the first in Sandy to own an automobile. With no instruction on how to handle it, he somehow got it home safely, then practiced all night long, driving it around the pasture until he mastered the contrary machine. Sammy and Stella's children all learned to play basketball on the front yard dirt and became high school athletes. Sammy needed them to work the farm, but Stella was determined that they should go to college. She told Sammy she'd do a man's work in the fields if he'd send them to college, so off they went, and all but one became educators. When the children were grown, Sammy and Stella sold the home place and moved to a tiny farm inside the Hillsboro city limits in 1935. There,

Sammy and Stella with their children in the late 1920s.

they raised a few hogs, calves, and chickens, and he became Hillsboro's popular postmaster, greeting postal customers with his familiar smile and handshake for many years. All his life Sammy was fond of quoting Proverbs 22, "Train up a child in the way he should go, and when he is old, he'll not depart from it."

When Sammy and Stella married, he built a kitchen onto the square log house, with a room above it for Emma Jean. Almost every day she would walk a half mile down a trail through the woods to help Mack's brother Buzz and his wife, Maria, who was sick and bedridden. Although four of their babies died, Buzz and Maria raised a fine crop of twelve children. Emma Jean's help around the home was welcome, as Buzz had a farm to work, and they still had a teenage son at home. He was Matthew, and they called him Mack, a living tribute to his uncle.

Maria died in 1903. A year later, Buzz and Emma Jean married and moved in with Sammy and Stella. But both were in their sixties, set in their ways, and they squabbled constantly, so that was miserable for all concerned. Buzz soon moved on to live with his children.

Emma Jean, Matthew (Mac), and Buzz, at work in the garden at Buzz and Maria's home, 1901. Courtesy of Paula London Glanzner.

The daughter that George Marsden left behind in Franklin County, Esther, got married, had five sons, became a teacher, and lived in South Dakota until 1910. When George's Franklin County–born sons were grown, about 1873, they all moved to Texas, and though two later moved back to Franklin County, none of them had any further contact with the Jefferson County Marsdens.

Every one of the people in Mack's story has his or her own story. Even the houses have stories. Samuel and Mary's original log house became the home of Virginia Lillie Moss and her husband, Alexander Benjamin Hensley. Virginia was a woman ahead of her time, a no-nonsense sort who opened a store in their home and took over as postmistress after Zimpfer closed the Yerger store in Sandy. Then in 1893 the building became the object of one of the great engineering feats in Jefferson County history. One evening Alexander and Virginia strolled along the little cedar-dotted ridge near the house. As she smoked her corncob pipe they talked about how nice it would be to have their back porch in that spot. Besides, the ground around the house stayed so damp in the springtime.

So Alexander put log rollers under the house, hitched it to a team of oxen, and moved it. Men, women, and children came to watch and help. Excitement was high, and the chaos was ordered by men who knew their jobs and buckled down to them. They snapped the lead reins and yelled, "Getup!" at the oxen, straining at their traces. Others grasped halters on the oxen, pulling them along and keeping their path straight as a plum line. As the building rolled off of each log in the back, sweat-soaked men pulled it out and reset it in front, and so on, over and over for a hundred yards up a rise to the northeast. When it was set, everyone agreed it was an even prettier spot than before.

Virginia moved her business into the old Yerger-Zimpfer store across the road, and Alexander added onto the log house. Then their daughter Lillie Virginia moved in with her husband, Samuel J. Marsden, Mack's little brother. It would be the home of them and their children for another seven decades.

After the murders in 1883, Jesse Johnston left the county. He was back in late 1885, and following the trial in '86 he and his children, except for the married daughter, Julia, moved to good jobs and a taste of the city life in St. Louis. Richard and Elizabeth Marsden raised a house full of five kids. His love for horses grew throughout his life, and his great joy was taking his grandchildren riding. Mack's little brother Clarence married Constable Tom Frazier's little sister Jennie. Clay Moss and Priscilla, Mack's sister, named one of their children Clardy, in honor of the revered major, Mack's lawyer. After Priscilla died, Clay married again, fathered a total of twenty-one children, and lived until 1930.

Judge Thomas, who presided at both murder trials, became a Missouri Supreme Court justice. Judge Emerson, who presided in the hog stealing case that never got to trial, would go on to a singularly successful career as a businessman. Certainly a man who spanned the ages, he

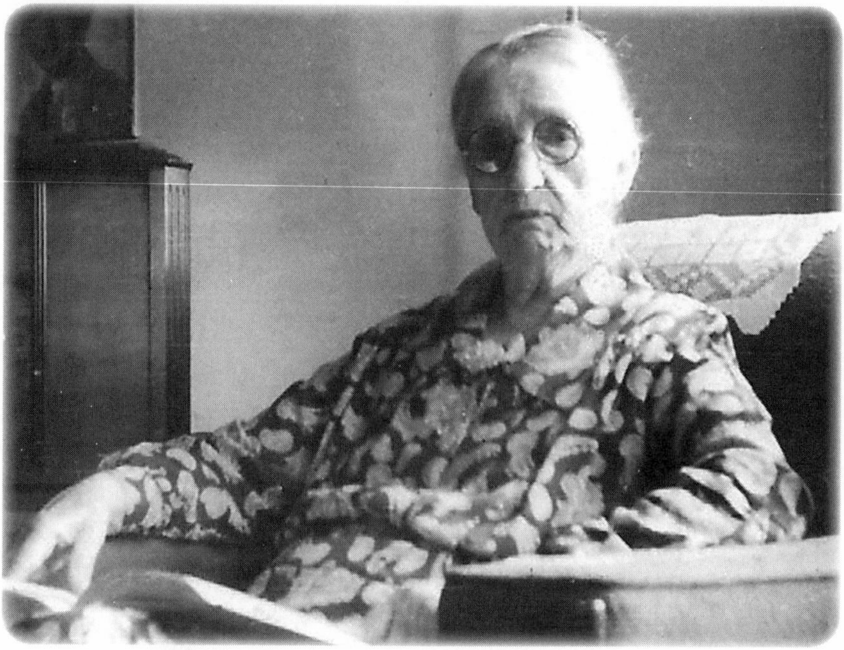

Lillie Virginia Hensley Marsden.

founded the industrial giant Emerson Electric Company, which prospered into the twenty-first century.

Prosecutor James Green and his wife raised their children with the help of household servants, and life was good. The Marsden case established his name, and his continued success as a prosecutor kept him in that position until 1890, when he was rewarded with the county judgeship. After the children were grown, the couple moved to St. Louis, and he spent the rest of his career as an attorney for the Missouri Pacific Railroad.

Fidelo Rogers's claim to fame for many years was the ownership of a stately bay Percheron stallion, which was in demand for breeding magnificent draft horses. It was so special that it made the papers years later when he sold it. He and his wife moved to Alaska in 1898, eventually returning to live their final years in Jefferson County. They're buried in the Rogers family cemetery, which is full of beautifully carved stones.

The DeSoto home of Prosecutor James F. Green, far right, with his wife and children.

Nearby lies Delo's sister Elizabeth, who stuck by her husband, John Gillman. He's buried there too, but they never gave him a marker.

Louisa, the widow Yerger, was happy to have Martin Zimpfer's able business skills, not to mention his attentions. They married in September of 1884 and soon had two children. Unfortunately, Louisa died January 7, 1887, three days after delivering her seventh baby, a stillborn son.

When Doc Adams felt he was getting near the end of his time on earth, around 1930, he summoned Leander Hensley's great-grandson Joe Wibble and asked him to bring his son Roy with him. Doc told them he had been carrying a secret for near thirty-five years and didn't want it to go to the grave with him. He said after the gang was acquitted at the trial, he just couldn't stand seeing Samuel Marsden's heart broken that way. So he followed the murderers, and before they could board the train at Pevely, well, they didn't all get away. It wasn't the Moss boys, he said. He didn't want to gun down his own cousins, even if they were skunks. And in all those years he never told, because the killing had to stop someplace. If he'd told, it might have kindled a family feud with no end. But now that the years had passed, and before he passed on, he just wanted someone in the family to know he shot and killed one of them.

Doc was almost right. He did shoot one. And because the ones making the getaway avoided the people of Jefferson County from that time on, Doc had no way of knowing John Marsden survived his pistol attack.

John and Allen Marsden, along with Tommy and Jimmy Moss, and their wives and children, did a good job of disappearing from Jefferson County, but even after being acquitted of the Frisco Hill murders, they still felt like fugitives. Since John had been ambushed, and since everybody back in Jefferson County knew they lived in Pocahontas, they figured it was only a matter of time until another vigilante tracked them down there. So they faded into the nearby Arkansas hills. And yet their lives were never without fear, because there was no way to know how long the desire for revenge might live in the heart of some relative or friend of Mack Marsden. Although Sam Byrns bought the three pieces of land abandoned by Louisa, John, and Tommy, intending to hold the property until they returned, they never came back.

Not long after the trial, Allen's wife, Elizabeth, insisted that they get away from John, and Allen didn't disagree. He was finished with John and had a wife and sons to care for. So they said goodbye, Allen took his family back to Missouri—but not to Jefferson County—and he never saw his brother again. Elizabeth soon passed away, and Allen was left to live in one town, then another, always looking over his shoulder while raising the boys. He was staying with their son Walter when he died in Doniphan in southeast Missouri in 1916.

As expected, Thomas Henon Moss's hog stealing charges were dismissed when James Green said there was not enough evidence to prosecute. Tommy and Bessie stayed together, and their first baby was born

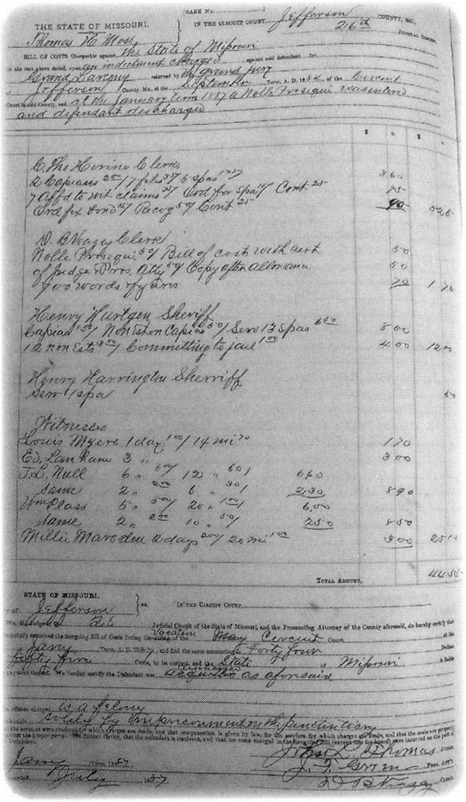
THE STATE OF MISSOURI. IN THE CIRCUIT COURT Jefferson COUNTY, MO. 26th Judicial Circuit

Thomas H. Moss

BILL OF COSTS Chargeable against the State of Missouri against said defendant for
in the case above stated, upon an indictment charged
Grand Larceny returned by the grand jury
Jefferson County, Mo., at the September Term, A. D. 1884, of the Circuit
Court in said County, and at the January term 1887 a Nolle Prosequi was entered
and defendant discharged

C. The Herine Clerk
2 Capiases 2.00 / 7 files 35 / 5 spas 1.25 — 3.60
7 Affd to wit claims 35 / Ord for spa 15 / Cont 25 — 75
Ord fix bond 15 / Recog 5 / Cont 25 — 90 — 5.25

D. Blazey Clerk
Nolle Prosequi 50 / Bill of costs with cert — 50
of Judge & Pros. Atty 50 / Copy after allowance — 50
900 words 70 — 70 — 1.70

Henry Hurtgen Sheriff
Capias 1.50 / Non Est on Capias 50 / Serv 13 spas 6.50 — 8.00
12 non Ests 3.00 / Committing to jail 1.00 — 4.00 — 12.00

Henry Harrington Sherriff
Serv 1 spa — 50

Witnesses
Louis Myers 1 day 1.00 / 14 mi 70 — 1.70
Ed. Lanham 3 " — 3.00
T. L. Null 6 " 6.00 / 12 " 60 — 6.60
same 2 " 2.00 / 6 " 30 — 2.30 — 8.90
Wm Plass 5 " 5.00 / 20 " 1.00 — 6.00
same 2 " 2.00 / 10 " 50 — 2.50 — 8.50
Millie Marsden 2 days 2.00 / 20 mi 1.00 — 3.00 — 25.10

TOTAL AMOUNT, 44.55

STATE OF MISSOURI. County of Jefferson } ss. In the Circuit Court,
We, the Judge of the 26 Judicial Circuit of the State of Missouri, and the Prosecuting Attorney of the County aforesaid, do hereby certify that we have carefully examined the foregoing Bill of Costs during the Vacation of the May Circuit Court, at the Jany Term, A. D. 1887, and find the same amounting to Forty four Dollars fifty five Cents, to be correct, and the State of Missouri is liable for the payment thereof. We further certify the Defendant was discharged as aforesaid

the offense charged is a felony
punishable solely by imprisonment in the penitentiary
the services were rendered for which charges are made, and that compensation is given by law, for the services for which charges are made, and that the costs are properly against the proper party. We further certify, that the defendant is insolvent, and that no costs charged in the foregoing Bill (except fees for board) were incurred on the part of Defendant.

Jany Term, 1887 — Thos L. Thomas, Judge
July 1887 — J. T. Green, Pros. Att'y
D. D. Blazey, Clerk

The court record showing that the hog stealing charges against Thomas H. Moss were dropped.

in 1885. Emily Moss, the boys' long-suffering mother, came to live with them until her death in 1891. Then Tommy, Bessie, and her brother John slipped quietly back into Missouri, leaving Jimmy and Jane Moss somewhere in Arkansas, never to see them again.

John's wife, Millie, stayed with her parents in Jefferson County and divorced him in 1887. About the same time, his steadily worsening vision left him blind, a lingering effect of the severe blow to his head when he was shot from the wagon. Unable to live independently, he stayed with Bessie and Tom.

Being fairly young, only in his thirties, John did all right. He developed a game of chance, along with a knack for knowing what kind of money people were laying down. People couldn't believe a blind man could tell the difference between a one dollar bill and a five, or if they shorted him in a handful of change. So he made his living that way in bars and at carnivals.

Things went so well for him that six years later he met and married Elizabeth Young, and they had a son. But as John got older, his ability to amaze his audiences faded. Then Elizabeth died, leaving the grown son to care for his sightless father, who lived miserably into his eighties. They were living with Tommy and Bessie in Neelyville when the son died, and a year later, in 1933, John passed away. Filling out the death certificate, his best old friend Tommy told the coroner he didn't know who John's father was, a strong indication that John didn't know either.

Tommy and Bessie, with their three daughters, stayed on the move for many years, their life continually characterized by the blind John tagging along, even while he was married to Elizabeth. Somehow Tommy maintained his reputation as a snappy dresser, though he never learned to make money. It was said that he could walk five miles on a muddy street and never get his shoes dirty. He played the gentleman, and even after his hair turned snow white, he was constantly grooming his mustache and a thick lock of curly hair that swept across his forehead. He and Bessie ran a rooming house in St. Louis for a few years, although everyone said she did all the work. Then they settled in Shannon County, where they lived into the twentieth century.

After the trial of 1886, John, Allen, Tommy, and Jimmy never set foot in Jefferson County again.

Sources

Elsea, Albert Felix, and Neil Moss. *Our Missouri*. New York: Macmillan, 1939.

Eschbach, Walter L., and Malcolm C. Drummond. *Historic Sites of Jefferson County, Missouri*. [St. Louis]: H. Bartholomew, 1968.

Family interviews/oral histories.

Goodspeed's History of Franklin, Jefferson, Washington, Crawford, & Gasconade Counties, Missouri. Chicago: Goodspeed, 1888.

Halleman, Dave. *Hallemann's Interpretation of the 1876 Historic Atlas*. N.p.: Author, 1996.

Hillsboro 1839–1989. Hillsboro: City of Hillsboro, 1989.

Jefferson County, Missouri, Atlas. Philadelphia: Brink, McDonough & Company, 1876.

Rader, Perry S. *Civil Government and History of Missouri*. Columbia, MO: E. M. Stephens, [18--]; New York: Macmillan, 1933.

Rutledge, Zoe Booth. *Our Jefferson County Heritage: Reminiscences of Early Missouri*. Cape Girardeau, MO: Ramfire Press, 1970.

Newspapers:

Jefferson County *Democrat*, transcribed by Lisa K. Gendron

The New York Times

The St. Louis Globe-Democrat

The St. Louis Post-Dispatch

Firearms research:
Roy G. Jinks, historian, Smith & Wesson
www.joesalter.com

Fox Trotter horse research:
Donna Watson, events and facilities manager, Missouri Fox Trotting Horse Breed Association, www.mfthba.com
Dyan Westvang, managing director of the Foundation Foxtrotter Heritage Association, www.missourifoxtrottersatoz.com

Jesse James research:
The Old West. Alexandria, VA: Time-Life Books, 1980.
The Gunfighters. Alexandria, VA: Time-Life Books, 1974.
Wild West Magazine 19, no. 4 (December 2006)

Railroad and depot history:
Tim Jones and Jacob C. Jones, Missouri Illinois Railfan Site. http://moshortline.com.

Public institutions:
DeSoto Public Library
Festus Public Library
Jefferson County Historical Society, rootsweb.ancestry.com/~mojchs/index.html
Jefferson County History Center, Jefferson College Library, Hillsboro, MO
Library of Congress, loc.gov/index.html
Missouri Birth and Death Indexes. deathindexes.com/missouri/index.html
Missouri History Museum, mohistory.org
Missouri Secretary of State Archives, sos.mo.gov/mdh
Office of the County Clerk, Jefferson County, MO

Index